WILLIAM KNOX YEWANDE
ESSICA MONCADA KONTE K
RIANA KOREN NAA OYO A.
EWIS ADRIAN LIPSCOMBE MALCOLM
IVINGSTON II GLENN LUTZ LAZARUS
YNCH KRYSTAL MACK SARINA MANTLE
ARAH LADIPO MANYIKA KALISA MARIE
ARTIN ISAIAH MARTINEZ RAHANNA
ISSERET MARTINEZ GEORGE MCCALMAN
ENISE MCKENZIE-LEE TRACYE MCQUIRTER
DRIAN MILLER KLANCY MILLER DANIEL
INTER MICHAEL OTIENO MOLINA SHANNON
USTIPHER FREDA MUYAMBO GAIL
ATRICIA MYERS THÉRÈSE NELSON DADISI
LUTOSIN FREDERICK DOUGLASS OPIE
HRISTOPHER PEARSON LEAH PENNIMAN
HOTOGENIC SALON ASHANTÉ REESE
ARINA RIVERA FRESH ROBERSON DEBORAH
OBERTS STEPHEN SATTERFIELD DAVID
CHMITZ ELLE SIMONE SCOTT SUMMER
EWELL SAVANNAH SHANGE ALEXANDER
MALLS OMAR TATE NICOLE TAYLOR PIERRE
HIAM LATHAM THOMAS DUVAL TIMOTHY
ONI TIPTON-MARTIN JACOB FODIO TODD
ICHAEL W. TWITTY BETTY VANDY PAOLA
ELEZ MARVIN K. WHITE MONICA M.
HITE PSYCHE WILLIAMS-FORSON RENÉE
ILSON AMANDA YEE SITHANDIWE YENI

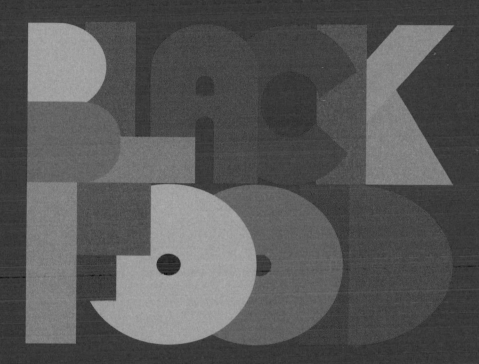

# BLACK FOOD

## STORIES, ART & RECIPES FROM ACROSS THE AFRICAN DIASPORA

### EDITED & CURATED BY BRYANT TERRY

4c

**4 COLOR BOOKS**

An imprint of TEN SPEED PRESS

California | New York

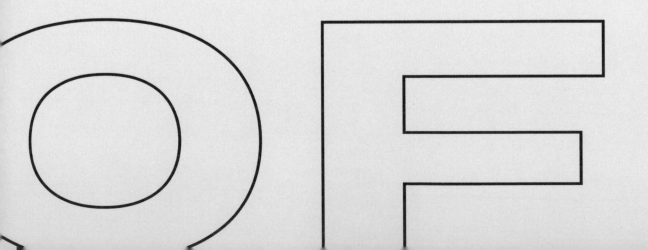

= Vegetarian    = Vegan

# INTRODUCTION

*"Sometimes we are blessed with being able to choose the time, and the arena, and the manner of our revolution, but more usually we must do battle where we are standing."*
—Audre Lorde

*Black Food* is a communal shrine to the shared culinary histories of the African diaspora. These pages offer up gratitude to the great chain of Black lives, and to all the sustaining ingredients and nourishing traditions they carried and remembered, through time and space, to deliver their kin into the future. Every one of us who came together to make this book invoked sacred energies to support the creation of a beautiful, delicious, and thought-provoking compendium. We pray that this collection facilitates reflection on and veneration of our sacred foodways.

Recipes are the through line of *Black Food*. Without being overly prescriptive, I asked brilliant colleagues to offer dishes that embody their approach to cooking and draw on history and memory while looking forward. I encourage you to make many recipes in this book and create space for meaningful, visceral experiences. Trust me, the food will provide more sustenance, more nourishment, more health, more pleasure, and more life. But that's not all. *Black Food* also includes moving visual art, thought-provoking essays, and imaginative poetry that will encourage spiritual and intellectual exploration, renewal, and growth.

We seek, in these pages, to promote a concept of food that embraces courage, commitment, and self-discovery, and ultimately moves each and all of us to a better place. In my graduate school advisor Robin D.G. Kelley's 1994 essay collection *Imagining Home: Class, Culture, and Nationalism in the African Diaspora*, I discovered a profound rumination by the late South African scholar-activist Bernard Magubane. Diasporic consciousness arose from "a determined effort on the part of Black people to rediscover their shrines from the wreckage of history." In this book—this altar—we lay out, and lay on it, the collective weight, the push of experiences and traditions of the African diaspora, the movement of Black bodies and Black food far and wide, from pre-Columbian voyages out of Africa to the violent dislocations of the trans-Atlantic slave trade and colonialism.

This collection also urges us to *stop* and dive deeply into the politics of pleasure, of rest—as in Tricia Hersey's concept of the Nap Ministry and R&R as resistance—and of Black leisure, whether stretching out to chill and sip "beautiful" drinks in the afternoon at Oakland's Red Bay Coffee or strolling through Paris all evening with nowhere specific to be, brushing dirt off one's shoulder like the flyest flâneur. We subscribe to the philosophies of Toni Morrison, a joyful warrior wielding her quill and freedom dreaming, insisting we shut out the nightmarish distractions of racism. We let Morrison show us how, with a fresh pair of eyes, we can perceive a world full of love, light, peace, pleasure, and rewards previously denied. We are grateful for Sarah Ladipo Manyika's remembrance, "Jollofing with Toni Morrison," and for Penguin Random House editor Porscha Burke's wealth of wisdom and experience, whether in guiding the 35th anniversary reissue of Morrison's groundbreaking *Black Book* (a major inspiration for the volume before you) or the reissue of *The Autobiography of Malcolm X.*

In our "Black, Queer, Food" chapter, we are fortunate to witness the most profound dialogue by and about our diaspora's most marginalized, and most resilient and brilliant, community: Ebony Derr, Lazarus Lynch, Zoe Adjonyoh, and Leigh Gaymon-Jones lead us in a timely conversation about how LGBTQ activism is the vanguard of creating vibrant culture, love, and kinship out of disruption and rejection. Crucial to us thriving is creating the broadest table, with seats reserved for *all* of our people throughout the diaspora. Like the Black men depicted in Kerry James Marshall's *Garden Project*—a series of large-scale paintings set in Chicago's South Side—we should all weed, rake, and dig deeply to uproot attitudes and habits that marginalize, reject, or erase any of us.

The many mansions of Black food have always had—and will always have—room for everyone. As our clear-sighted Black liberation activist Anna Julia Cooper insisted, each soul can and should decide when and where they enter into this rich tradition. Our aim in *Black Food* is to maintain this practice of openness, to encourage the sharing of these journeys and discoveries across the diaspora at large. *Black Food* is rich with points of connection, in which the reader can engage with and perhaps more deeply appreciate the many-colored threads in this diasporic epic of Black exodus and redemption.

Each chapter and verse, each poem, photograph, painting, think-piece, and recipe is a portal to beloved communities of plants and animals, food and pleasures, leisures, tastes, and cultures across many eras. Learn how to make sacred spaces suited to your own home and kitchen, at your own pace of growth. Perhaps you will begin with something simple and soothing like Krystal Mack's update on traditional Yoruba okra baths. Or you may be drawn to more elaborate practices, as with Latham Thomas's and Jocelyn Jackson's guidelines for intentional ritual creation, altar making, and seed weaving.

*Black Food* is an offering in which the contributors, whether chefs, artists, activists, scholars, journalists, or poets, seek to honor a pantheon of revered ancestors: we deify Octavia Butler in "Caring for the Whole Through This Black Body," adrienne maree brown's introduction to our chapter on Radical Self-Care. Audre Lorde's life and legacy are writ large across that chapter's focus on defining, nurturing, and defending one's self, as are other spiritual forebears like bell hooks and Cedric Robinson. We stand on iconic shoulders, like those of Black liberation theologians Reverends James H. Cone and Albert Cleage, in our chapter on Spirituality. Intellectual titans like W.E.B. Du Bois inform deeply personal reflections like "Beyond the Tree Line," Rashad Frazier's return to his native North Carolina's rural spaces, disrupting the racist histories of color-lines.

With Thérèse Nelson and Rahanna Bisseret Martinez, we give thanks to visionaries like Lena Richard and Vertamae Smart-Grosvenor, whose prescient critiques of the US evolution from domestic food work to professional kitchens help us find footing for Black creativity and entrepreneurship in a booming food media landscape. With Tracye McQuirter and Fred Opie, we cherish Dick Gregory, who, in the tradition of prophetic truth-tellers like Elijah Muhammad, Peter Tosh, Coretta Scott King, and KRS-One, aggressively rejected the toxic food traditions of slavery, colonialism, and industrialized food systems.

In "Land, Liberation & Food Justice" and "Black Women, Food & Power," inspired by the ingenuity of celebrated grassroots organizers like Fannie Lou Hamer and Georgia Gilmore, our contributors Monica White, Charlene Carruthers, and Psyche Williams-Forson explore how Black folk fought for life and liberty by leveraging fecund land and delicious food. In the names of these ancestors we claim and reclaim radical models of food, health, and wellness for Black communities, revolutionary not only in their newness, but also in their rootedness in ancient African traditions.

This book is a Sankofa bird, standing astride the crossroads of past and present, with a neck craning back to what came before, measuring our progress. Its feet point toward what is to come, with an egg signifying the future held protectively in her beak. To paraphrase Zora Neale Hurston, the present is an egg laid by the past that has the future inside of its shell. *Black Food* represents a bridge from our ties to traditions in the Motherland to our wildest dreams that will manifest in the future.

*Black Food* is meant to live alongside you not only on coffee tables, credenzas, and night stands. Toss it in your bag, satchel, purse, or on the passenger seat, and ride out to your local farmers' market and grocery store. Level-up your skills with practical cooking know-how shared by our brilliant chefs. Expand your African diasporic cooking repertoire and impress your family and friends. Pass it around at cookouts, barbecues, and family reunions. Like Black people, this book contains multitudes.

# SPIRIT

"Mother Earth" by Cindy Blackman Santana from *Give the Drummer Some*

"Black Voices" by Tony Allen from *Black Voices*

"Talking Drums" by Guy Warren from *kpm 1000 Series: Native Africa 1*

"Garvey's Ghost" by Max Roach from *Percussion Bitter Sweet*

# MOTHERLAND

"Blue Nile" by Alice Coltrane from *Ptah, the El Daoud*

"Petit pays" by Cesária Évora from *Cesária*

"Yègellé Tezeta (My Own Memory)" by Mulatu Astatke from *Éthiopiques 4: Ethio Jazz & Musique Instrumentale, 1969–1974*

"Ndiri Ndanogio Niwe" by Mibiri Young Stars from *Kenya Special: Selected East African Recordings from The 1970s & '80s*

"I.T.T. (International Thief Thief)—Edit" by Fela Anikulapo Kuti & Afrika 70

"Last Revolutionary" by Seun Kuti and Egypt 80 from *Black Times*

"Hello Africa" by Blitz the Ambassador from *Diasporadical*

# MIGRATIONS

"Butterfly" by Kimiko Kasai from *Butterfly*

"All Blues" by Miles Davis from *My Funny Valentine: Miles Davis in Concert*

"Slave Driver—Jamaican Version" by Bob Marley & The Wailers from *Catch A Fire*

"Follow the Drinking Gourd" by Alex Foster, Michel LaRue, and The Drinking Gourds from *Follow the Drinking Gourd*

"Gone" by Alex Isley & Jack Dine from *Gone*

"Big Lost" by Diplo from *Florida*

"85 to Africa" by Jidenna from *85 to Africa*

"La Bamba" by La Negra Graciana from *La Negra Graciana Sones Jarochos with the Trío Silva*

# SPIRITUALITY

"Allah" by Youssou N'Dour from *Egypt*

"Triptych: Prayer/Protest/Peace" by Abbey Lincoln & Max Roach from *We Insist! Max Roach's Freedom Now Suite*

"Part IV (with Mahalia Jackson)—aka Come Sunday" by Duke Ellington and His Orchestra Featuring Mahalia Jackson from *Black, Brown and Beige*

"Satta Massagana" by The Abyssinians from *Satta Massagana*

"Voodoo" by The Dirty Dozen Brass Band from *Voodoo*

"Jew Tang Forever" by Your Old Droog from *Jewelry*

"No Church in the Wild" (feat. Frank Ocean and The-Dream)" by Jay-Z and Kanye West from *Watch the Throne*

# LEISURE & LIFESTYLE

"Postpartum" by Taylor McFerrin from *Early Riser*

"Glowed Up (feat. Anderson .Paak)" by Kaytranada from *99.9%*

"Laputa" by Hiatus Kaiyote from *Choose Your Weapon*

"Merlot" by Smino from *Noir*

"Slow It Down (feat. Emmavie, ScienZe)" by Àbáse from *Slow It Down*

"Binz" by Solange from *When I Get Home*

"Funny Thing" by Thundercat from *It Is What It Is*

## LAND, LIBERATION & FOOD JUSTICE

"Beans and Cornbread" by Louis Jordan & His Tympany Five from *At the Swing Cat's Ball*

"Salt Peanuts" by Miles Davis Quintet from *Steamin' with the Miles Davis Quintet*

"Succotash" by Herbie Hancock from *Inventions & Dimensions*

"Watermelon Man" by Herbie Hancock from *Head Hunters*

"Cola" by Arlo Parks from *Cola*

"New World Water" by Mos Def from *Black on Both Sides*

"Beef Rap" by MF DOOM from *Mm..Food*

## BLACK WOMEN, FOOD & POWER

"Les Fleur" by 4hero from *Creating Patterns*

"Don't Touch My Hair" by Solange from *A Seat at the Table*

"20 Feet Tall" by Erykah Badu from *New Amerykah Part Two (Return of the Ankh)*

"In My PJ's" by Zilo from *In My PJ's*

"Little Man" by Little Dragon from *Ritual Union*

"Bemoanable Lady Geemix" by Jyoti from *Mama, You Can Bet.*

"Creator (vs. Switch and FreQ Nasty)" by Santigold from *Santigold*

## BLACK, QUEER, FOOD

"Family (feat. Janet Mock)" by Blood Orange from *Negro Swan*

"Pink Matter" by Frank Ocean from *Channel Orange*

"Love Song #1" by Meshell Ndegeocello from *Comfort Woman*

"Like Me" by Steve Lacy from *Apollo XXI*

"Kitchen, Barber, Beauty Shop" by Roy Kinsey from *Roy Kinsey*

"Miss Me" by Leikeli47 from *Wash & Set*

"DO IT" by Kaytranada from *BUBBA*

## RADICAL SELF-CARE

"Sun Is Shining" by Bob Marley & The Wailers from *Reggae Anthology*

"Declaration of Rights" by Johnny Clarke from *Rockers Time Now*

"Beat Down Babylon" by Junior Byles from *Beat Down Babylon*

"Revolution" by Dennis Brown from *Sly & Robbie Presents Taxi Trio (Dennis Brown, Sugar Minott, Gregory Issacs)*

"Small Axe" by Bob Marley & The Wailers from *Countryman*

## BLACK FUTURE

"No More Walking Alone" by Spoek Mathambo from *Hikikomori Blue*

"Best Part (feat. H.E.R.)" by Daniel Caesar from *Freudian*

"Good Days" by SZA from *Good Days*

"Yah / Element—Medley" by Joy Crookes from *Yah / Element—Medley*

"Sweet Love" by Moonchild from *Little Ghost*

"Floor Seats" by A$AP Ferg from *Floor Seats*

"Juice" by Tobe Nwigwe from *Juice*

PART 1

PROLOGUE

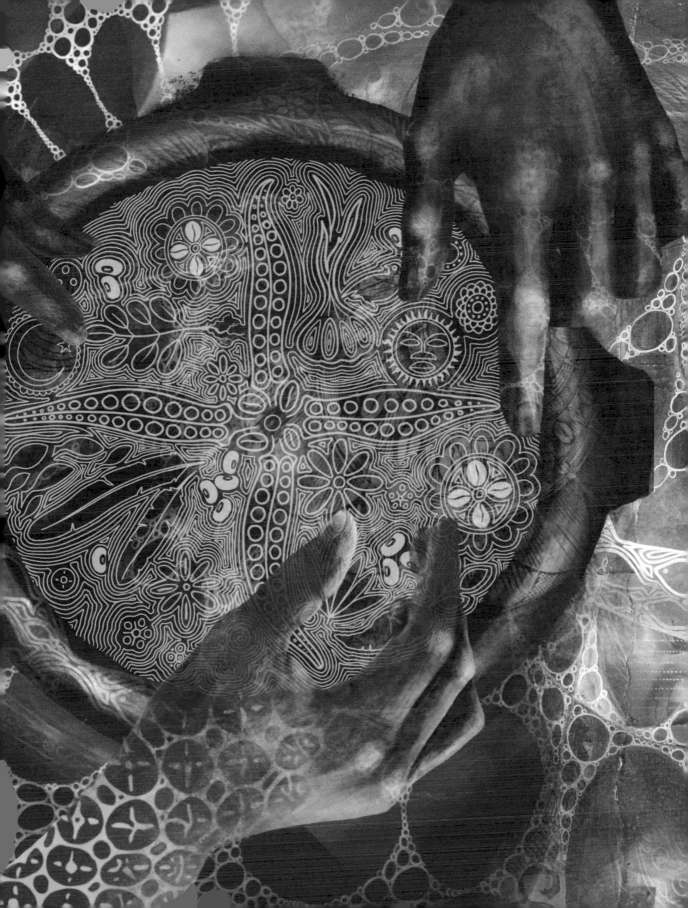

# FROM SCRATCH

## by Rev. Marvin K. White

On the first day, God made a meal plan. Finally had it all figured out. Finally had a taste for something. On the second day, God made a grocery list. "One of everything," God thought. On the third day, God planted a garden—God's own farmers' market. On the fourth day, God sharpened God's knives. God created iron and cast it into skillets. God pre-heated the oven and forgot about it. We will talk about this hell another time. On the fifth day, God chopped, and God baked, and God boiled, and God braised, and God broiled, and God fried, and God grilled, and God roasted, and God poached, and God steamed, and God stewed. For hours, God stewed. On the sixth day, God opened all the pots and a mist went up from the pots and watered the whole face of God. And God sweat the vegetables. On the seventh day, God created Company and they came over and they ate with God. And God looked around at God's kitchen and ended Their work which They had done, and They rested. On the eighth day, itis.

This is the history of cooking by sight and by smell. This is the history of creation of the heavens and the Earth and Soul Food. Before any Tupperware, before any tinfoil, before anybody said how they woulda made it, God created satisfaction.

Let us pray. Yes, God. The Perfect Planter. Okro, Okwuru, Kingombo. The Perfect Picker. Quiabo, Quimbombó, Gombo. And the Perfect Pickler. Bhinda, Dherosh, Vendai Kai. You who let creation stew on Sunday morning and ate gumbo and tomatoes, corn and lima beans that afternoon. Bende Kayi, Qiu Kui.

Let us pray for First and Last Suppers and knowing that we can trace our divinity by the meals that were served as our sacred text. Yes, for this new Theology of Gastronomy, thank God.

This prayer whispered over everything and everyone. This blessing breathed over everything and everyone. This libation poured over everything and everyone. And this knowing that everyone gets fed.

Bamia, Bamyeh, Bamija, Molondron. Thank you. My true vine. Abelmoschus Esculentus, the Mucilaginous One. Remind us you are in this slime with us. Thank you. Glory. We thank you. For every plant we bent down to pick and for every muscle memory bending into this feast, thank you. For this meal for three, stretched to serve all of humanity. Thank you for this spread and for multiplying our love budget enough to send a plate to our neighbors and for making our eyes bigger than our stomachs.

Rise and Flour, Hercules Posey.
Rise and Flour, James Hemings.
Rise and Flour, Edna Lewis.
Rise and Flour, Lena Richard.
Rise and Flour, *Lucille Elizabeth Bishop Smith, Rise and Flour.*

# THURSDAYS OFF

## by Thérèse Nelson

Fifty years ago, food media was not the juggernaut industry it is today. People mostly cooked at home, and when they did dine out, the chef was certainly not the hero of the experience. Until 1977, a professional cook—no matter where in the hierarchy of the professional kitchen they stood—was classified by the US government as a domestic worker. This makes a certain sense, given that most people who cooked in restaurants were Black and brown. But a shift in the 1970s brought a renewed deference to European aesthetics, an investment in European-focused culinary schools and the mass import of European talent. The most notable import was the French culinary legend Jacques Pépin, who incidentally credits the Black cooks he encountered in kitchens all over New York City with teaching him about American culinary techniques.

At the precise moment America was learning how to dine like the French and getting serious about building a more robust culinary industry, hard-won civil rights were finally being afforded to Black cooks, giving them access to new professional opportunities outside of kitchens. This created a culinary generation gap that made the subsequent whitewashing of food an easier task to accomplish. This fact becomes powerful commentary on the struggle modern Black food creatives have had in making headway in an industry that seems to have a curiously short historical memory. What ensues is the creation of a multi-trillion-dollar culinary industry that disempowered Blacks,

stripping them of their historic birthright, and then asks why they don't have more visibility and authority in the marketplace.

The clearest rebuttal to this historical amnesia is Dr. Vertamae Smart-Grosvenor's lesser-referenced 1972 work *Thursdays and Every Other Sunday Off*. She called the book "a domestic rap" in the days when she was in community with the Last Poets, as they were birthing the vocabulary of hip-hop. In this stunning follow-up to her watershed cookbook *Vibration Cooking: or The Travel Notes of a Geechee Girl*, Dr. Grosvenor invited her readers to think about how language defined perspective. She understood that American culture needed to have critical conversation about the values being placed on domestic labor. She challenged readers to consider the domestic as the hero. As she made clear in her book, there needed to be deference paid to the legacy of Black people as standard-bearers of the craft of food. She asked them to consider why society was comfortable disregarding the enormous wealth of heritage these domestics carried with them. Reviewing the nearly fifty years of American gastronomy that followed, her words were prophetic.

While *Thursdays* was written for a general audience, I believe Dr. Grosvenor was also having a parallel conversation with Black folks. Dr. Grosvenor knew that she had to give us culturally specific wisdom that would be important long after the book was published. The fact that we sit in a modern moment where we Black folks working in food still find ourselves amid a cultural identity crisis is why her work and *Black Food* are so important.

When I first came to food, I didn't see the correlation between my Blackness and the professional food world. It's more accurate to say that the food world didn't see a correlation, and I didn't challenge the notion that there was a distinction to be made. I hadn't found the truth yet. In the early 2000s there was an emerging food media landscape that didn't quite have room for expansive Black stories. That lack of imagination left a void, which signaled to me that Black foodways weren't valuable, and in the absence of representation, I felt unseen.

The world wasn't quite ready to listen to Dr. Grosvenor in 1972 either. Her wisdom was just waiting for us to be brave enough to receive it. I read her work today and see it as precisely the balm we need as we enter a new decade, battling a pandemic that has rocked our industry and has everyone, regardless of station, reevaluating their work. We are finally asking harder, more substantive questions about priorities and parity, not just about representation but also about whether the systems we participate in actually serve us. That said, we have some serious work ahead of us to ensure that we never again experience a generational gap that erases our story from the narrative. Now it's more important than ever for Black food creatives to remember that we define the times in which we live with our voices and craft. It is time to require the food world to contend with our culture. After all, history as a barometer is only as valuable as how we apply its lessons.

I believe that one of the most important questions Black food folks must be asking in this moment is clear.

Why do we do this work?

If we don't know why we do this work, then how can we expect to tackle the harder issues we must face? How do we define our cultural cuisine? How can we operate more effective and viable businesses? How can we create and support a more fair and equitable food system? How do we tackle food security? Land sovereignty? Pay equity?

To be a Black food creative in this modern moment is to be one part artist, in search of perfection, one part steward of a craft that is in constant flux and beholden to capitalism, and one part storyteller, charged with defining a collective culinary identity that requires far more rigor and care than our industry typically has given its attention.

We suit up as chefs, food writers, winemakers, farmers, historians, and all manner of practitioners to offer something delicious and essential to the world. That complicated work is hard. Doing this work requires bearing the responsibility of history and legacy. It's a lot to carry, but we have all the tools and lessons we need to make this next era in food impactful.

We also have the benefit of a curious and engaged zeitgeist. The fact that this book exists and that many of its readers will have no professional connection to food is amazing. That you've invested in learning more about Black food enough to buy this book highlights the fact that our voices have value in the marketplace. By buying this book and honoring the vulnerability and saliency of these amazing creatives, you not only give life to their thoughts but you also hopefully encourage publishers to be braver and more open to supporting our stories.

The work and love that have gone into this book is testament not only to Bryant Terry and his vision but also to the embarrassment of artistic riches we have in Black culture. I hope that you sit deeply with this collection, that you are inspired by the brilliant artists you meet, especially the new voices you aren't familiar with, and come away thinking more broadly about who and what makes up *Black Food*.

# BUTTERMILK BISCUITS

## by Erika Council

**MAKES 12 TO 15 2-INCH BISCUITS**

*This buttermilk biscuit recipe is adapted from the recipe of my great-grandmother Sara, affectionately known as Big Mama. During tobacco season in North Carolina, she'd bake them outside over the fire, serving them to the laborers, mostly African Americans, who were working in the fields that day. Baking up biscuits that were sturdy and crisp, using leaf lard she'd rendered herself, she created pockets of steam that would fill you with warmth as you consumed them. From the stories I've been told of her, she exuded this same warmth herself.*

*Her daughter, my grandmother, adapted her recipe using butter instead of lard. These were her go-to biscuits used for the plate sales at the church during the civil rights movement of the 1950s and '60s. The funds raised helped both the movement and the community at large. The art of biscuit making was passed down to me along with these stories of the Black women who baked them to sustain us. My grandmother insisted the biscuits should always stand tall, be sturdy, and have an exterior crisp enough to withstand a ladle of hot gravy.*

**2½ cups all-purpose flour**

**1 tablespoon baking powder**

**½ teaspoon baking soda**

**1 teaspoon salt**

**2 tablespoons vegetable shortening, chilled and cut into ½-inch chunks**

**8 tablespoons (1 stick) unsalted butter, chilled and cut into thin slices, about ⅛ inch, plus more for brushing**

**1¾ cups chilled buttermilk**

Adjust the oven rack to the middle position and heat to 450°F.

In a large bowl, whisk together the flour, baking powder, baking soda, and salt.

Add the shortening to the flour mix and using your fingertips, break up the chunks, until only pea-sized pieces remain. Work in the butter slices in the same way, until the butter is incorporated. Place the mixture in the freezer for about 15 minutes.

Add the buttermilk to the chilled flour mixture. Stir with a fork, until the dough forms a ball and no dry bits of flour are visible. (The dough will be shaggy and sticky.)

Turn the dough out onto a floured surface and dust the dough lightly with more flour. With floured hands, pat the dough into about a ¼-inch-thick rectangle. Fold the dough into thirds, dusting each layer lightly with flour as needed. Lift the short end of the folded dough and fold into thirds again, forming a rectangle. Repeat this process, folding and patting the dough, until it is about ½ inch thick. Cut the dough into rounds using a 2-inch biscuit cutter. Be sure to press the cutter down into the dough firmly; do not twist the biscuit cutter. This is important: twisting it will seal off the biscuit edges, preventing the biscuits from rising. You should have 12 to 15 rounds out of this batch.

Place the biscuit rounds 1 inch apart on a baking sheet. Brush the tops with melted butter (optional). Bake for 15 minutes or until the tops are golden brown. Remove the biscuits from the oven and allow to cool slightly before serving.

# VEGAN SWEET POTATO COCONUT BISCUITS

## by Erika Council

MAKES 8 TO 10 BISCUITS

*"In late summer our work might be thinning the long vines off the sweet potatoes because my father would say we'd only have little stringy potatoes if we didn't." —From* Mama Dip's Kitchen *by Mildred Council*

*Mildred Edna Cotton Council founded Mama Dip's Restaurant in 1977. She was the daughter of a sharecropper, the granddaughter of a slave, and the founder of a culinary empire. She was also my grandmother. One of her most popular dishes was her sweet potato biscuits. I've adapted her recipe to make it vegan. Coconut milk adds a delicate richness, with cinnamon and brown sugar providing an extra hint of spice that elevates these biscuits to another level.*

2 cups all-purpose flour

1 tablespoon baking powder

2 tablespoons brown sugar

½ teaspoon kosher salt

¼ teaspoon ground nutmeg

½ teaspoon cinnamon

1 cup mashed sweet potato, chilled (from about 1 large sweet potato)

¼ cup chilled coconut milk, plus more as needed

Preheat the oven to 400°F. Line a large baking sheet with parchment paper and set aside.

In a large bowl, whisk together the flour, baking powder, brown sugar, salt, nutmeg, and cinnamon.

In a small bowl, whisk together the chilled sweet potato and coconut milk. Add this mixture to the large bowl and mix just until the dough comes together. Turn out the dough onto a floured surface and press together with the heel of your hands. If the dough is not holding together, add in additional coconut milk one tablespoon at a time—I usually need to add about 2 tablespoons.

Turn the dough out onto a well-floured surface. With floured hands, bring the dough together, then pat into a rectangle that is about 1 inch thick.

Cut the dough into rounds, using a 2-inch biscuit cutter. Place the biscuit rounds about 1 inch apart on the prepared baking sheet. Brush the tops of the biscuits with coconut milk.

Bake the biscuits for 12 to 15 minutes, until they are puffed and just barely golden.

CHAPTER 1

ART BY KEBA KONTE
PHOTOGRAPHED BY DAVID SCHMITZ

# MOTHERLAND

## by Freda Muyambo

I was born and raised in Botswana, a land beaming in the southern African sun. My parents come from Ghana, a country in West Africa. My ancestors? From elsewhere, and they carried with them a rich history, some of which I may never know. I love to imagine what that history could have been. For this, I rely on the memories that our culture still holds: our languages, our food, our poetry. But is that all it takes to make us recognize who we are as a people?

I was born a Botswana citizen. But, having parents originating from another country, my citizenship was something I had to claim again when I was older. I experienced one of the most profound moments in my life when I first applied for my national identity card. The card is called an *Omang*. "O-mang," Setswana for "who are you?"

The answer often begins with where your home is, as was my case. I had forms to fill out, and my first answer was rejected. "Where are you from?" asked the clerk. "Francistown" was my response. "But nobody comes from the towns or cities in Africa. Those are just establishments." I grew bewildered. I knew no other place. What I knew as home, in Botswana, was where I was born and where I had lived. I did not consider that any other place would be relevant in that moment. "If you want to know where you are from, then tell me, where is your chief?" the clerk asked. I took in a sudden breath as those words met my ears. I have been pondering that question ever since. I wrote down Osu, where my father's people call home, and that answer

was accepted without question. Oddly enough, Osu is a largely commercial neighborhood in Accra.

A few years later, I was preparing to marry the love of my life, a Shona man from Zimbabwe, whose ancestry traced to Mozambique. We had met in Melbourne, Australia, where I was studying at the university, and he was working. We abandoned the idea of having a fairy tale wedding abroad because my mother declared that the wedding had to happen where the bride came from. So, there we were, flying from Melbourne, Australia, to Francistown, Botswana, in a frenzy of pre-matrimonial activities. As a couple from enlightened Christian families, I expected to breeze my way through to "I do" without the roadblocks from earlier times. I was wrong. The customary laws of the land dictated I could not get married until his chief, who was located somewhere in Zimbabwe, issued a declaration. This was yet another frustration adding to a long list that would eventually form a rite of passage of sorts. We needed to know that this man was not already married. And his chief had all the answers. Gladly, we got a letter from his chief in Mutare, hand-delivered by my father-in-law. We could now get our marriage license and proceed with the wedding plans.

The next step was the lobola ceremony. Lobola refers to the dowry, or bride price, that the bridegroom pays to the head of the family of his potential wife. I was to be marked with a price and paid for in cash or in kind. Intrinsic to this process for my husband and me were our uncles. As such, we could have married without even being physically present. As long as our chiefs and our ward, our families, were present, we were good to go. Once again, I realized how much my existence and destiny were guided by forces I was not familiar with; no one cared that I was a modern city girl, not even the laws of the land. Despite living far away from my motherland, where I was carving out my own life and personal culture, in this moment, I had no authority over my identity, my worldview, or my future. As an individual, I did not matter. *Motho ke motho ka batho babangwe:* I am because we are.

This infuriated me. Because at the shy age of twenty-three, I knew everything. What good was that culture to me, when I felt so far removed from it? I felt misunderstood every time I tried to chime in with my intelligence and rationale. And I resented the sudden enforcers of these traditions: my mother, my aunties, family friends, and even pastors. "Have you seen her nakedness?" was a question posed by my Ghanaian pastor during premarital counseling. I thought my personal culture was a unification of my lived experiences, but I did not grow up in the culture that was now being presented to me. So why did it have to matter now? Whom would I offend if I rejected it? And if it was my chief, I did not even know his name. My justifications and protests fell on deaf ears, and I was pushed aside and marked as disrespectful and full of myself to anyone with no time to reason. In spite of this, I complied with every cultural request and even agreed to wear red lipstick, as specified by my mother. The wedding day finally arrived.

"I do." Chin chin and togbei were prepared for the masses. The select few, three hundred to be exact, could follow to the grand reception at the hotel where we were served rotisserie chicken, pilau rice with curry, and some dessert. No alcohol was served. As a young couple, our budget was slim. No traditional speeches or libations were made, and no schnapps was dedicated to the ancestors and thrown to the ground. There was only a reference to my father, who was probably rolling over in his grave at my getting married to a man I had chosen. "Why don't you marry a Ghanaian?" was a question posed by my Auntie Edna just days before the nuptials.

After the wedding, we flew back Down Under. I put as much distance as I could between me and those who had imposed their irrelevant ideals. I rejected all things traditional and customary because I thought they added no value to my life and attitudes. We went to church for the first time as a married couple. I chose the matching lace wrapper set and agbada my auntie had sewn for us in Ghana. Interestingly, agbadas are traditional Nigerian attire but loved by Ghanaians. They are not tailored to fit; traditional attire such as this never is. It was amazing to me that Auntie Peace got the sizing just right for us. I wore my white lace wrapper and top, with a wide neckline that sat delicately off the shoulder. The lace had baby blue accents and embroidery all over, both as a pattern and sewn in. My husband wore his three-piece agbada and completed the look with its matching cap. Off we went to announce our new status as newlyweds to our dear friends at church.

We were met with stares and questions. It hadn't dawned on us that we would look strange in a contemporary church community filled with Australians and several other nationalities. "Why are you wearing matching outfits?" "Does it have a meaning?" "Why do African couples match their outfits?" I gave up. "We wear it as a symbol of blessings and fertility." I lied. My explanation was accepted without question. To this day, I am not entirely sure why couples wear matching outfits or whether it is tradition or fashion or both. There I was, less than seven days after disavowing a culture I was adamant was not serving me, clinging to its literal threads.

Being far away from home made me miss my culture. I realize now that I desired some form of autonomy in my cultural expression. Beyond everything, it had made me who I am. When I could not express myself, I grew frustrated with my culture, especially when I didn't know what was expected of me.

Over the years, I began to realize that I needed to hold onto my culture a lot tighter than I thought. After all, with a change in my name, a couple of moves across several continents, and a perpetual reminder that, beyond the children I have helped to gift to my new family, I was disappearing. And if all did not go well in my marriage, what would be left of me? I felt alone. Who was Freda Palm?

And so it was I turned to food. Not in the form of comfort eating but in the way that expressed how, despite having little knowledge of my mother tongue or my grandmothers' mothers' real names, I could cook the foods they had eaten and name the dishes. My nomadic journey has helped me relate to what my ancestors might have gone through. They moved from place to place, as I have. They started somewhere near the Nile, passed through Central Africa and Nigeria, and finally settled in Ghana some five hundred odd years ago. Perhaps all they had was the food and customs they carried with them. And maybe their chief.

I now live in Nigeria with my family. We are a unit in the motherland but strangers to the establishment that is Nigeria today. In these modern times, I have no concept of living in a community guided by a chieftainship. But I can see that my husband's community is still strongly affiliated with theirs, no matter where they are in the world. Perhaps my people lost a part of who they were in their journey or maybe they adopted parts of a new culture as their own. Just as I have. Perhaps our experiences are nothing alike at all. Maybe the answer lies in the stories that our own journeys tell, and as a collective, we can address the things we do not fully understand as individuals. Our food, our clothes, our music: perhaps they offer an explanation of the things we don't always understand. But if there is one thing that is very clear to me, it is the sense of longing that comes from the distance between me and the motherland. The culture. And so, I tell stories, I ask questions, and I cook food, and these all form a part of the journey of looking for something bigger than individual experiences.

# HOUSEHOLD SEED BANKS

## by Sithandiwe Yeni

One of the global challenges facing us today is a food crisis rooted in a vulnerable global food system that has become socially, environmentally, and financially dysfunctional. An industrial model of food production now dominates the food system the world over. This system is characterized by produce standardized in size and shape, the displacement of small-scale farmers, centralized markets dominated by a few retail companies, the loss of biodiversity and indigenous food varieties, an increased use of synthetic fertilizers, and genetically modified seeds and chemical pesticides, all of which contribute to ecological degradation. And as a consequence of this now dominant food system, we are seeing an increase in the number of hungry people, especially in poor societies. This food insecurity was evident in the 2008 food riots that took place in countries such as Cameroon, Egypt, Senegal, Ivory Coast, Burkina Faso, and others, while the corporations dominating the food system continued to score large profits. Scholars like Eric Holt-Giménez and Raj Patel have argued in their book *Food Rebellions* that to overcome the food crisis, we need to transform the food system. But what does that mean? Here I share some of the strategies employed by the women food producers of Ingwavuma village in KwaZulu-Natal province of South Africa, who have been pushing back against the industrial farming methods. These farmers practice agroecology, a farming system that is premised on preserving the ecosystem, a bottom-up approach that builds on local cultures and indigenous knowledge that has been passed down through generations of farmers.

In Ingwavuma, women food producers grow indigenous crops and preserve their own seeds by creating household seed banks. In 2017, I had the privilege of visiting three of these women, who were in their sixties, to learn more about the types of seeds they grow, their uses, how they preserve them, their nutritional value, and their importance for household food security.

Household seed banks ensure that there are seeds available for every planting season every year. The seeds referred to here are indigenous seeds, which the women described as seeds that have been around for many generations, have never been genetically modified, and were not purchased from the shops. While the seed varieties are kept and reproduced at a household level, other members of the village who wish to start their own seed collection are able to borrow seeds from those who have a surplus and return them after harvesting. Farmers also exchange seeds with their neighbors in order to expand their collection of varieties. The types of indigenous seeds in the KwaZulu-Natal province include sugar bean; maize; peanut; pumpkin; sorghum; sesame; sunflower; imbumba, a kind of bean; and amatabhane, a type of tuber. All of the three households I visited had these seeds in their seed banks.

In the current context of climate change, women food producers of Ingwavuma have observed a decrease in rain and more experiences of drought that pose a threat to their seeds, particularly with maize. While they believe that indigenous seeds have "natural powers" to withstand hot and dry conditions for a longer time than genetically modified ones, they have also started to soak the seeds in seawater for a few hours before planting. Seawater, they believe, helps to strengthen the seeds, enabling them to grow under harsh weather conditions, because the sea does not run dry during a drought and seeds soaked in seawater become drought resistant. Fascinating! Apart from the climate change-related threats, seeds also need to be protected from pests and bugs. The most common methods the women use to protect the seeds include keeping them in the kitchen, where the cooking is done over a wood fire. These kitchens do not have chimneys and therefore get very smoky. The smoke helps to preserve the seeds from being destroyed by insects and pests and prolongs their shelf life. To catch the smoke, the women hang the seeds from the ceiling

For those seeds such as beans and pumpkins that cannot be hung from the ceiling, they are kept in bags or plastic containers with ash added. In some cases, where there might be lots of bugs in the house, a few drops of paraffin are thrown in with the ash. Once the seeds have been planted and start to grow in the ground, the farmers pour certain types of tree extracts over the plants to prevent pests from eating the plants.

Once the seeds have sprouted into plants, the seeds are harvested and kept either on top of the roof (especially pumpkins) or in a traditional storage facility called an inqolobane, which keeps surplus food. During the years in which the harvest had been good, most households would store food in an inqolobane; otherwise, households would have only enough to eat and enough to keep as seeds for the next season. In other words, not all households have a full inqolobane every year.

The three women producers I spoke with told me that their harvest would usually last for up to ten months.

Below, I have provided examples of some of the crops grown and eaten in the three households I visited.

*Sorghum.* This grain is eaten raw, and the children like it a lot. It is usually planted in the maize fields, and during harvesttime, children eat it while they are harvesting. This not only keeps them from starving but also makes the work a little more enjoyable. Sorghum is eaten the same way as sugarcane. This type of seed expands, so it needs to be scattered so that it spreads widely across the maize fields.

*Beans.* The bean seeds these women plant yield different colors of beans, even though the seeds are from a single species. They are a good source of protein and quite filling.

*Imbumba.* Another filling crop, imbumba looks like a bean but tastes even better, according to the three women food producers. It can be cooked by mixing with beans, samp, and izinkobe, or eaten alone. It is a high source of protein.

*Amatabhane.* These are said to be quite filling and typically eaten on their own. They look similar to sweet potatoes but are quite tiny in size.

*Izindlubu.* A good source of energy, izindlubu beans are often boiled and eaten as a snack (similar to the way we eat nuts).

The women food producers of Ingwavuma are demonstrating the importance of indigenous knowledge in challenging the industrial model of farming. With their techniques for preserving seeds, these women food producers have been able to produce nutritious food for many years. They are a walking indigenous food library to be preserved.

# OUT OF AFRICA

## Musings on Culinary Connections to the Motherland

### by Jessica B. Harris, PhD

There are many different and differing views of the African continent. For some, it represents problematic politics and poverty; for others, it's empires and elegance. Our contradictory images include the mythical land of Wakanda, home of the Black Panther superhero, and the horrific reality of the brutal dictator, Idi Amin. We know the continent is vast, one into which the United States could fit comfortably three times. But, in fact, we know very little about this continent that is ringed in legends and even less about its foodways. Yet, the profound influence of those foodways can be felt a hemisphere away through the vicissitudes of the trans-Atlantic slave trade and the diaspora that it unleashed. Taste the food of São Salvador da Bahia de Todos os Santos in Brazil, and you have tasted Africa. Taste the rich brown stews of Jamaica, and you taste Africa's hand in the pot. Taste the food of Guadeloupe, Guyana, and Georgia's Low Country, and Africa's culinary influence, whether in technique, ingredients, or recipes is palpable. Africa's agricultural know-how rendered the fields of the New World more productive, while Africa's recipes morphed, took on New World inflections, and transformed the tastes of a hemisphere.

In my 2012 cookbook *Beyond Gumbo: Creole Fusion Food from the Atlantic Rim,* I categorized several tendencies that distinguished the foods of the creole world. The rich callaloos of the Caribbean, the collard and turnip greens of the southern United States, the use of leafy greens along with the consumption of their liquid called pot likker—these are culinary connectors. The abundant use of okra in gumbos or soupy stews or simply eaten alone is another; just think of a sopa de quimbombó in Puerto Rico or Cuba. There is also a marked preference for rice as a starch, an ability to cultivate it, and an extensive rice kitchen. The immense wealth of eighteenth- and early nineteenth-century South Carolina was based in the rice-growing know-how of the enslaved Africans from Sierra Leone, Liberia, and southern Senegal. The taste of those regions turns up on the plate in the form of rice breads, composed rice dishes, and a taste for cracked rice known as middlings. (In Senegal, *riz cassé,* or broken rice, is reputed to hold a sauce better than the whole grain.)

A mastery of frying in deep oil and a repertoire of fritters like the codfish fritters of the Caribbean such as "stamp and go" in Jamaica, bacalaitos in Puerto Rico, and acrats de morue in Guadeloupe and Martinique are two other culinary touchstones. Nuts are used as thickeners in the cuisine of Bahia and in the cuisine du Nord in Haiti. Seasoning pastes are also widely found. The Hispanic world uses sofritos, while in Barbados, there is Bajan seasoning, a verdant mix of herbs and hot chile that is placed into slits scored in fried chicken or fish.

Hot sauces as condiments are culinary touchstones of the African Atlantic world. One has only to look at the number of chiles in the marketplaces of western and southwestern Africa and their culinary counterparts in the Caribbean and Brazil or at the shelves in bodegas and the supermarkets throughout the Western Hemisphere. A taste for the spicy bite is a connector of people throughout the African Atlantic world so prevalent as to have been remarked upon by slave traders. The use of dried and/or smoked ingredients as seasonings is another marker. The dried smoked shrimp and mollusks of West Africa morph into the codfish used throughout the Caribbean, smoked pork in the United States, and the closely derivative dried shrimp in Brazil.

The almighty pig has ruled supreme over New World meats for centuries, whether served up barbecued, roasted, or fried. And the animal is eaten in its entirety, from the lechon of the Hispanic world, to the cochon de lait served at Christmas season in the French-speaking Caribbean, to the holiday ham in the United States. And then there are chitterlings, feet, and lips, as everything is consumed "from the rooter to the tooter" as the old saying goes. Increasingly the pig's primacy is being challenged by vegetarianism and veganism, but it remains a touchstone for many.

Confections using nuts, including coconuts, pecans, peanuts, and Brazil nuts, are another hallmark of African culinary lineage. Sugar cultivation brought millions of enslaved Africans to the Western Hemisphere, and it is not surprising to note that sweets of all sorts using local nuts and fruit pastes are found from south to north. Charleston's monkey meat, New Orleans pralines, and the pinda cakes of Jamaica are only some of the items that are often sold by street vendors.

A preponderance of professional women cooks throughout the African culinary diaspora is of particular importance, as are street vendors, both male and female. The development and continuation of the food of the African continent and its diaspora have often been the work of women under whose stewardship it has been maintained.

While the African roots of dishes in some parts of the Western Hemisphere are easy to document (Afro-Bahian dishes of Brazil and the Caribbean, like acarajé and dukanoo, even retain variants of their African names), the African culinary influences on the food of the United States can be more ephemeral and difficult to pin down. Nonetheless, these influences have long been the back story of American food, though hidden by oral transmission and the difficult-to-trace "taste" of the cook's hand in the finished dish. Recipes occasionally do reveal the African influence in the pot in some of the earliest cookbooks. Okra appears in *The Virginia Housewife,* the 1824 cookbook penned by Mary Randolph, in a recipe for a dish of stewed okra called "Gumbs: A West India Dish."

Twenty-first century African American chefs like Mashama Bailey in Savannah, Nyesha Joyce Arrington in Los Angeles, Syrena Johnson in New Orleans, Omar Tate in Philadelphia, and JJ Johnson in New York; culinary scholars like Thérèse Nelson and Michael Twitty; agricultural advocates like Matthew Raiford, Adrian Lipscombe, and Gabrielle Eitienne; writers and editors like Klancy Miller, Nicole Taylor, and Osayi Endolyn; and a growing number of others find inspiration in the culinary inheritance of the African Atlantic world. They are writing another chapter in the ongoing story of the food of Africa and its transformation into the food of the United States, the entire Western Hemisphere, and indeed the world.

# PILI PILI OIL

## by Bryant Terry

MAKES ABOUT 1 CUP

*Pili Pili (or Piri Piri) is the Swahili name for chiles. In many places throughout sub-Saharan Africa, bird's eye chiles are either blended with salt, fat, acid, and herbs, or oil is infused with bird's eye chiles and herbs and used for drizzling over vegetables, grains, and any other food to add some kick.*

| | |
|---|---|
| **2 teaspoons smoked paprika** | **2 (2-inch) rosemary sprigs** |
| **2 (2-inch) thyme sprigs** | **9 small bird's eye or Thai chiles** |
| | **1 cup olive oil** |

In a small saucepan, combine all the ingredients and heat over low heat, stirring occasionally, until the oil starts to sizzle and the paprika has completely dissolved. Immediately remove from the heat and set aside to cool.

Transfer the mixture to a small jar or bottle, seal, and refrigerate for a few days before using. Store in the refrigerator for up to 2 weeks.

# GREEN PLANTAIN CRISPS

## by Jacob Fodio Todd, Folayemi Brown & Duval Timothy, from *Food From Across Africa*

MAKES PLENTY

*For some reason, the making of plantain crisps always falls to me (Jacob)—I thought—because of my unrivalled chopping technique, and my beautiful knife. But a year, and thousands of crisps later, we purchased a mandoline. Yet, the task continues to burden me alone. Yemi and Duval's praise for my mandoline skills does not wash. The truth is, it is a job that has a few repetitive stages, so it requires patience.*

*On the upside we've learned a great deal about how to produce the very best plantain crisps. There is no need to make them fresh, as we misguidedly attempted to for our first few events because; if sealed properly, they keep well for up to two weeks. Use only the greenest green plantain to achieve a consistent outcome, which will be a crunchy, slightly sweet crisp. They are hard to stop eating once one has started, much like potato chips, for which they are substitutes in many areas of the world.*

**3 green plantains**

**8 cups cold water to use as a bath**

**8 cups sunflower oil, plus more as needed**

Slice off the tops and tails of the plantains and slice down the spines.

Forcefully but carefully remove the skins, using the side of a small knife to lift each skin, and then use your thumb joint to coax off the skin. Keep an eye on your fingernail, as plantain skin under the nail can be painful.

Placing the plantains horizontally, finely slice (using a knife or mandoline) into ⅛-inch strips; try to ensure the strips do not get any more than ¼ inch wide. Fill a tub or bowl with the water and add the plantain strips.

In a large heavy-bottomed pot, heat the oil to 375°F.

Rinse and drain the sliced plantains in a colander, then pat dry with paper towels so they do not spit when they go into the hot oil.

Fry the plantains in batches for 3 to 5 minutes, until they begin to brown. Remove each batch using a slotted spoon and place on a plate lined with paper towels to drain. (The crisps will color further on removal, so remove just as they take on a brownish hint.)

Place on a serving dish lined with paper towels to remove excess oil and pat dry. Allow to cool, remove the paper towels, and season with salt. It is good to season the crisps with salt while they are still hot, so the salt sticks to the crisps.

To store, put in a bag or a sealed container. They will last up to two weeks, or at least that's the longest that we've managed to keep them uneaten.

# CRISPY CASSAVA SKILLET CAKES

## by Yewande Komolafe

### MAKES ABOUT 24 CAKES

*Cassava is a versatile starch used by folks across West Africa and in the diaspora, as well as in South America and the Caribbean. Fresh cassava can be fried, steamed, or used as a base for exciting flavor combinations. These skillet cakes are made from fresh cassava and are one of my favorite ways to use these tubers. I serve them as an appetizer or side dish, topped with a bright, colorful salad.*

2½ pounds cassava roots (about 2 whole)

2 limes

1 cup minced red onion

1 ripe but firm mango, peeled and diced small

Kosher salt to taste

2 tablespoons red palm oil

4 garlic cloves, minced

1 teaspoon ground cumin

1 red Scotch bonnet chile, stemmed, seeded, and minced

1 tender inner stalk lemongrass, finely minced

1-inch piece ginger, peeled and grated

¼ cup sliced scallions

1 egg white, whisked until foamy

Safflower or other vegetable oil for frying

¼ cup chopped cilantro leaves

Red or green amaranth leaves for garnish

Remove the cassava root skins with a paring knife or a vegetable peeler. Move the peeled roots to a bowl of water to keep them from turning brown. Use the large holes of a box grater or the grater attachment on a food processor to grate the cassava, placing in cold water until done. Drain and squeeze out any excess liquid. Spread out on a kitchen towel to dry completely (excess water will result in soggy cakes).

Zest and juice one of the limes. Cut the remaining lime into wedges and set aside. In a small bowl, combine ¼ cup of the onion, mango, and the lime zest and juice. Toss together and season with salt. Set aside.

In a large nonstick skillet, heat the palm oil over medium heat and add the remaining ¾ cup onion. Sauté, stirring frequently, until soft and just beginning to brown, about 4 minutes. Add the garlic, cumin, chile, lemongrass, and ginger, stir for an additional minute, season with salt, and remove from the heat. Allow to cool slightly.

In a large bowl, combine the cassava, cooked onion mix, and scallions. Season with salt. Add the egg white and gently toss, using your hands or a spatula to incorporate the ingredients. (The mixture will be damp but shouldn't be runny.) Cover the mix and refrigerate to chill slightly for at least 15 minutes before shaping and frying.

Wipe out the skillet and add ¼ cup of the oil over medium-high heat. Working in batches, use a table-spoon measure to scoop heaped portions of the mix into the oil. Press down each portion with the bottom of the spoon to shape into a round patty. Cook until the contact side is golden brown, 2 to 3 minutes. Turn, using a wide spatula, and brown the other side, about 2 minutes. Remove the cooked cakes from the oil and transfer to a plate lined with paper towels. Repeat the frying, until all of the mix is used up, adding more oil as necessary to keep the cakes from sticking.

Toss the cilantro in with the mango mixture. Serve the fritters topped with fresh amaranth leaves, the mango salad, and lime wedges for squeezing.

# SWEET POTATO LEAVES

## with Eggplant & Butter Beans

# by Betty Vandy

MAKES 4 SERVINGS

*I always see beauty in eating the traditional staples of my homeland, Sierra Leone. I know that every part of the meal is created to produce the most robust of flavors while limiting waste. Whether nourishing, healing, cleansing, or refreshing, my food legacy is one of complete sustenance. Sweet potato leaves are one of the many green leaves, known collectively as plasas, that are prepared and cooked in Sierra Leone as well as across West Africa. As African as you can get, sweet potato leaves signify the transformation of simple ingredients into a wholesome and delicious meal, reminding us as Africans that we shall never lack. In our Krio language it's known as* petehteh *leaf, not to be confused with other potato leaves, some of which are inedible and poisonous.*

*Growing up I assumed the potato leaves we ate came from the humble potato, so visiting my father's farmland and discovering that they were attached to a sweet potato came as a pleasant surprise. When eating good potato leaves we say in Krio, "di petehteh leaves e sweet." Omitting the very word that embraces the sentiment to this delicious dish always has me wondering why we don't start calling them sweet potato leaves. They are not as adored as our other staple tuber leaf and national dish, cassava leaves, but they are just as delicious.*

15-ounces dried white butter beans or red speckled butter beans, or 2 (15-ounce) cans, drained

1 tablespoon plus 2 teaspoons salt, plus more as needed

2 onions

2 habanero chiles, stemmed and seeded

1 teaspoon ogiri (a traditional West African stock seasoning similar to miso, made from fermented sesame seeds)

½ cup water

10 ounces sustainable West African palm oil or extra-virgin coconut oil

1 large bunch sweet potato leaves, washed and finely sliced, or 2 large bunches tender spinach

6 ounces fresh okra, finely sliced

4 eggplants, chopped into bite-size wedges

Pepper to taste

If using dried beans, soak them overnight in cold water. Add 1 tablespoon of the salt to the water. The next day, drain the water from the beans and rinse. Place the beans in a medium-size pot and add enough cold water to cover along with the remaining 2 teaspoons salt. Bring to a boil and cook at a vigorous simmer for 40 to 60 minutes or until the beans are soft. Drain and rinse with cold water and set aside.

Coarsely chop 1½ of the onions and add to a food processor along with the chiles and ogiri and process until the mixture has reached a medium-smooth consistency. Transfer to a medium-size pot along with the water and oil and bring to a boil on high heat for 6 to 7 minutes or until the onions become translucent. (The ogiri has quite a pungent smell as you cook it, but the smell will recede a bit.)

Lower the heat to medium and add the sweet potato leaves, okra, and eggplant. Stir well so all the leaves are submerged. Cover the pot and cook for 6 to 7 minutes more or until all the vegetables are tender.

Finely slice the remaining ½ onion and add it to the pot along with the beans, combining thoroughly, and cook for an additional 4 minutes. Add salt and pepper to taste. Serve immediately.

# SOMALI LAMB STEW

## by Hawa Hassan

MAKES 6 TO 8 SERVINGS

*Harissa, a spicy North African pepper paste, is often used to add warm heat to dishes in East Africa, too. You can find it in small jars, cans, or metal tubes. The spiciness varies quite a bit by brand, so start with a tablespoon and go from there, depending on your tolerance for heat.*

**XAWAASH SPICE MIX**

**One 3-inch cinnamon stick**

**¼ cup coriander seeds**

**¼ cup cumin seeds**

**1 tablespoon black peppercorns**

**2 teaspoons cardamom pods**

**½ teaspoon whole cloves**

**1 tablespoon ground turmeric**

**STEW**

**2 tablespoons extra-virgin olive oil**

**1 red onion, sliced**

**3 garlic cloves, finely chopped**

**1½ pounds boneless lamb shoulder, cut into ¾-inch pieces**

**1 tablespoon tomato paste**

**1 to 2 tablespoons harissa**

**3 cups water, plus more as needed**

**2 teaspoons kosher salt**

**2 russet potatoes, cut into 1-inch chunks**

**1 large carrot, cut into 1-inch chunks**

**1 red bell pepper, sliced into strips**

**Basmati rice, for serving (optional)**

**Green or red Somali hot sauce, such as *Basbaas*, for serving**

**Cilantro, lime wedges, and sliced banana, for serving**

**TO MAKE THE SPICE MIX:** Place the cinnamon stick in a small plastic bag and crush it into ½-inch pieces with the bottom of a skillet.

Place the cinnamon pieces, coriander, cumin, peppercorns, cardamom, and cloves in a small skillet over medium heat and cook, stirring constantly, until lightly browned and aromatic, 2 to 3 minutes. Let cool.

Transfer the mixture to a spice mill or mortar and pestle and grind into a fine powder. Sift through a fine-mesh sieve into a small bowl, then regrind any coarse spices. Stir in the turmeric and transfer to an airtight jar.

**TO MAKE THE STEW:** Heat the oil in a large Dutch oven or saucepan over medium heat. Add the onion and garlic and cook, stirring occasionally, until just beginning to soften, about 3 minutes. Add 1 tablespoon of the spice mix and cook until aromatic, about 1 minute. Add the lamb, tomato paste, and harissa and let sizzle for a minute or two. Stir to combine, then pour in the water and season with salt to taste. Reduce to a simmer and cover.

Cook until the lamb is almost tender, 40 to 45 minutes. Add the potatoes, carrot, and pepper and continue to cook, thinning with more water if needed, until the lamb is tender and the vegetables are cooked through, 20 to 25 minutes more.

Serve the stew over rice, if desired, then top with the hot sauce, cilantro, lime wedges for squeezing over, and bananas alongside.

**NOTE:** Xawaash spice mix can be made up to 2 months ahead. Store in an airtight container at room temperature or freeze for up to 6 months.

# MULLAH KARKADE

## with Millet Dumpling

ملاح كركديه مع عصيدة الدخن

## by Omer Eltigani

MAKES 4 SERVINGS

*A mullah is a stewlike gravy commonly made in Sudan as a main dish. Mullah karkade, or hibiscus stew, is a variation of another popular Sudanese stew called mullah tagalia, aka mullah ahmar, which translates as "red stew," owing to its main ingredient—tomatoes. Both stews are essentially identical, until the addition of red hibiscus, giving mullah karkade a slightly bitter edge that complements the sweet caramelized onion base.*

*Sharmoot, an air-dried ground meat, is traditionally used in these stews. Nomadic groups would grind the meat into a fine powder, allowing it to be kept for weeks or months, so it could be easily transported on long journeys over vast distances. This practice has continued, even as the general population has settled in urban areas.*

*Sudanese stews, or mullahat, are served with all types of Sudanese breads or dumplings such as kisra, goraasa, and asida. I particularly like to serve this stew with asidat dukhun, or a millet dumpling. Asida originated from western Sudan, where it's usually made with millet flour, while in central Sudan, it's made with fermented sorghum flour, as well as other flour varieties. Asida has a jellylike texture with a savory and sometimes sour taste of fermentation that complements rich Sudanese stews. This type of dumpling is common throughout the African continent and is known as fufu, garri, and ugali.*

**STEW**

¼ cup vegetable oil

5 tablespoons fried onions, or store-bought fried onions, finely ground

½ pound finely minced lean ground beef

Salt and pepper to taste

1 tablespoon ground coriander

2 tablespoons tomato paste

2 tablespoons peanut butter

4 cups tomato juice, or passata

2 tablespoons dried red hibiscus flowers, finely ground in a mortar and pestle

2 or 3 garlic cloves, crushed

2 tablespoons store-bought dried and ground okra

**ASIDA/MILLET DUMPLING**
عصيدة الدخن

4 cups millet flour

Salt to taste

2 cups water, plus more as needed

2 to 3 tablespoons coconut or olive oil

Vegetable oil for greasing the bowl

**TO MAKE THE STEW:** Pour the oil into a large pot over medium heat, gently stir in the onions, and cook for 1 to 2 minutes, until they gently sizzle. Gradually add the beef and cook until the meat releases its juices. Season with salt and pepper to taste, then add the coriander.

When the meat is no longer raw, add the tomato paste and peanut butter and mix together. Add the tomato juice and bring to a gentle boil. If you feel the mixture

CONTINUED

is too thick, add a little water to loosen it slightly. Use an immersion blender to blend all the ingredients in the pot into a smooth consistency.

Once the mixture is boiling, turn down the temperature to low or medium and cook, partially covered, for 20 minutes or until the oils rise to the surface and the stew thickens. (In Sudanese cooking, oils rising to the surface is known as *al wish* or "the face." The meaning is that at this stage, one can see the dish come to life, as the complete dish appears for the first time.)

Mix in the hibiscus flowers and garlic. Gradually add the okra and continue to stir. Allow the stew to thicken, until it can be easily scooped up with a wooden spoon.

**TO MAKE THE ASIDA/MILLET DUMPLING:** In a large bowl, mix the flour with an equal or slightly larger amount of water to create a runny batter. Add salt to taste and mix well.

In a large pot, bring the 2 cups water to a boil, then pour the millet batter into the boiling water and mix well, stirring constantly with a wooden spoon. Cook for 5 to 10 minutes, until the consistency is as thick as porridge. If it becomes any thicker than that, more like mashed potatoes, it needs more water; it should eventually pour easily from the pot into the bowls. Allow the batter to boil for another 2 to 3 minutes to ensure the flour is fully cooked. You can test for this by inserting a knife rinsed in water into the batter. If any batter sticks to the knife, then the flour needs to be cooked slightly longer; if the knife comes out clean, the flour is cooked. Mix the coconut oil into the asida before pouring into the bowl.

Grease a deep bowl with oil. Pour the cooked asida batter into the bowl and leave in a cool, well-ventilated area for 20 to 30 minutes to cool.

Once the asida has fully cooled, place a wider, shallower bowl on top and flip the asida into it. The asida should have a jellylike consistency.

To serve, pour the stew around the outer edge of the bowl to create an island of asida inside a moat of stew. Traditionally, diners use a spoon or clean hands to cut vertically into the outer edges of the asida and make contact with the stew, thus having a spoonful or handful of asida covered in stew.

### Variation—Kajeik

To make another popular dish from southwestern Sudan called kajeik, replace the ground beef with 7 ounces of dried fish.

To prepare the dried fish, rehydrate in steam or water until soft throughout, about 20 to 25 minutes, then carefully remove the larger bones. Using a food processor or by hand, break down the fish into small flakes, then remove the smaller bones. Soak in water for a short while to allow small bones to float to the surface, then drain.

**TIPS:** Adding ¼ teaspoon of sugar to the stew at the very end of cooking cancels out the acidity of the tomato juice.

Cereal bowls are a good size for setting the asida and provide the adequate dome shape. Since the bowl used will determine the size of the asida, use larger bowls for sharing and smaller bowls for personal asidas.

# AVOCADO & MANGO SALAD

## with Spicy Pickled Carrots & Rof Dressing

## by Pierre Thiam

MAKES 4 SERVINGS

*This refreshing, sweet, and spicy salad is an imagined recipe that takes me back to hot summers growing up in Senegal and brings together flavors and memories from my childhood in Dakar. We had three mango trees and an avocado tree in our backyard, as well as a lemon and guava. The fruits were always ripe around the same time, and we would pick and eat them directly from the tree. If I could time travel, this is the salad I would serve to my late mother, who wouldn't have believed that I had become a chef, since in Senegal, the kitchen belongs to women.*

*Mangoes and avocados are a natural pairing. They have a similar texture but very different flavors that complement each other. The dressing is inspired by a Senegalese condiment called rof, which is traditionally used to stuff the fish in thiéboudienne, our national dish. The parsley brings a particular freshness to the salad. The spicy pickled carrots are inspired by my Vietnamese uncle (Jean), who migrated along with many Vietnamese to Senegal during the French colonial times. As a kid, Uncle Jean was the only man I ever saw cooking.*

CONTINUED

## Avocado & Mango Salad, continued

**DRESSING**

2 cups lightly packed
flat-leaf parsley

4 scallions, coarsely
chopped

2 garlic cloves

1 habanero chile, stemmed
and seeded

1 teaspoon kosher salt

½ teaspoon ground
black pepper

1 teaspoon grated lime
zest, plus ¼ cup lime juice

¼ cup peanut oil,
or olive oil

**SALAD**

Two 14- to 16-ounce ripe
mangoes, thinly sliced

2 ripe avocados

1 cup grape tomatoes,
halved

1 tablespoon lime juice

2 tablespoons pickled
carrots (see recipe below)

**SPICY PICKLED CARROTS**
Makes 3 cups

2 cups coarsely grated
or julienned carrots

1 Scotch bonnet or
habanero chile, stemmed,
seeded, and finely diced

½ white onion, chopped
(about 1 cup)

2 teaspoons kosher salt

½ cup firmly packed
brown sugar

1 cup cider vinegar,
or rice vinegar

**TO MAKE THE DRESSING:** Combine the parsley, scallions, garlic, chile, salt, and pepper in a food processor. Process until finely chopped, about 1 minute, scraping the sides of the bowl as needed. Add the lime zest and juice and oil and process until smooth, about 30 seconds.

**TO MAKE THE SALAD:** In a medium bowl, combine the mango with 3 tablespoons of the dressing and gently toss. Marinate at room temperature for 30 minutes. In a separate bowl, gently toss the avocado and halved tomatoes with the lime juice and set aside.

**TO MAKE THE PICKLED CARROTS:** In a large metal bowl, combine the carrots, chile, onion, and salt. Toss well to combine and allow to sit for 30 minutes to degorge the water. Squeeze the carrot mixture between your hands to remove the water. Rinse under cold running water to remove the salt, then squeeze again to remove any excess water.

Place the sugar and vinegar in a small saucepan and bring to a boil over high heat, stirring to dissolve. Once the mixture is at a rapid boil, pour it over the seasoned carrots. Let cool to room temperature before using. Store in a sealed container in the refrigerator for up to 3 weeks.

**TO SERVE:** Arrange the avocado and mango slices on a serving plate in a concentric pattern and top with the pickled carrots in the center. Drizzle more dressing around the plate.

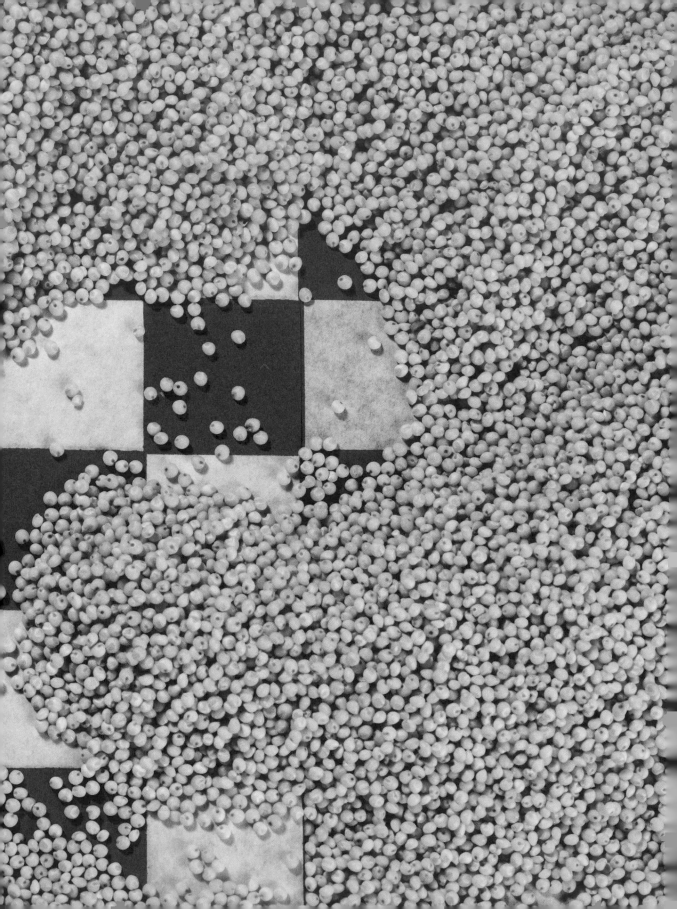

# ANJIRU MILLET

## by Njathi Kabui

MAKES 8 TO 10 SERVINGS

*This recipe was the first dish that my father, then 73 years old, made for me when he came from Kenya to Memphis to attend my college graduation. He prepared the dish with just me and him in the kitchen. The following day was the biggest day of his life. Having lost his restaurant in Kenya and then spending six and a half years in the British gulag for his struggle to liberate the country, my father felt as though his life was coming full circle. He sat in an auditorium for at least two hours to hear the name of his son being read out loud. As he sat, he reflected on his trial back in Kenya before being sentenced to detention. He felt that his struggle had been worth it.*

*As I look back, it was those six weeks my father and I spent together in Memphis that marked the passing of the torch. In that time, I learned the most I had ever learned about manhood, family history, and about the struggle for justice. Food was the common thread that tied those three pillars together.*

2 cups mung beans

4 tamarind beans

7 cups water

2 tablespoons plus
½ teaspoon salt

Sprig of rosemary

½ nutmeg seed,
finely ground

2 cups hulled millet

1 cup diced red onions

1 teaspoon minced garlic

¼ cup chopped cilantro or
parsley, plus a few sprigs
for garnish

½ teaspoon ground
coriander

⅛ teaspoon ground cloves

1½ cups butternut squash,
cut into ½-inch cubes

1 cup unsweetened
coconut milk

2 teaspoons sunflower oil,
or sesame seed oil

1 cup pea shoots

1 cup shredded red beets

Soak the mung beans overnight. Drain, then add the beans and fresh water to a medium pot and bring to a boil. Boil on medium heat until the beans are soft, about 15 to 20 minutes. Drain and set the beans aside.

Remove the outer shells from the tamarind. In a medium saucepan, boil 3 cups of the water and submerge the tamarind in the water for 30 minutes. Use a whisk and stir thoroughly for about 4 minutes. This process separates the seeds and fibrous skin covering the seeds. Strain the juice and set aside.

In a large pot, add the remaining 4 cups water, 2 tablespoons of the salt, rosemary, and a pinch of the nutmeg and bring to a boil. Once boiling, remove the rosemary sprig, add the millet, and cook on medium heat for 15 to 20 minutes, or until all the water is gone. Set aside.

In a separate pot, add the onion, garlic, cilantro, and half of the tamarind juice. Bring to a boil, reduce to medium heat, and cook, uncovered, for 2 minutes. Add the coriander, cloves, the remaining ½ teaspoon salt, and squash. Cover and cook for about 4 minutes. Add the mung beans and cook for an additional 7 minutes. Add the coconut milk and the remaining tamarind juice and cook for another 8 to 10 minutes, until the squash is tender. Turn off the heat and set aside.

To finish, add the millet to a big bowl with the oil and toss together. Serve with the mung beans, the pea shoots, beets, the remaining nutmeg, and cilantro sprigs.

Ghanian Crepe Cake (page 48)

# GHANAIAN CREPE CAKE

## with Grand Marnier Diplomat Cream & Milo Ice Cream

## by Selasie Dotse

MAKES 1 (12-INCH) CAKE

Sankofa *is a Twi word from the Akan tribe in Ghana meaning "to go back and get it" or "to return for it." The symbol is based on a mythical bird with its feet firmly planted facing forward and its head turned backward. The Sankofa symbolizes the Akan people's quest for knowledge, while never forgetting the wisdom of the past. Sankofa is about returning to one's roots, and for me, it's about returning to my culinary roots.*

*When I think of my motherland, I think of Sankofa. My mom is an amazing cook, and she cooked essentially every meal I ate growing up. I've worked with a lot of different chefs and in a lot of kitchens, but my culinary journey began in the kitchen with my mom.*

*Growing up, I never thought African or Ghanaian food could be represented in fine dining restaurants. However, cooking with Senegalese chef Serigne Mbaye in San Francisco and following other African chefs such as Eric Adjepong, Dieuveil Malonga, and Michael Elégbèdé has inspired and motivated me to go back to what I know. High on my list of favorite dishes from childhood are my mother's Ghanaian pancakes, which are similar to French crepes but sweeter. Those thin pancakes with a glass of Milo, a chocolate malt beverage similar to Ovaltine or Nesquik, would make my day. I've reinterpreted my mother's pancakes as a layered crepe cake served with Milo ice cream.*

*This moist, delicate layered cake is the perfect summertime dessert. The orange-scented cream layered between thin, buttery pancakes pairs perfectly with the chocolate ice cream. Who doesn't like cake and ice cream on a hot summer day?*

**GHANAIAN PANCAKES**
Makes 16 pancakes

4 cups all-purpose flour

1⅓ cups granulated sugar

1 teaspoon ground nutmeg

2 tablespoons salt

½ cup melted butter

12 eggs

3 cups whole milk

2 teaspoons vanilla extract

Vegetable oil, or cooking spray or clarified butter, for frying

**GRAND MARNIER DIPLOMAT CREAM**
Makes 4 cups

2 cups whole milk

½ cup granulated sugar

1 vanilla bean, split lengthwise

5 egg yolks

3 tablespoons cornstarch

Pinch of salt

2 tablespoons cold butter, cut into chunks

2 tablespoons Grand Marnier

½ cup cold heavy cream

**MILO ICE CREAM**
Makes 4 cups

1 cup whole milk

2 cups heavy cream

1¼ cups Milo or Ovaltine or Nesquik, plus more for dusting

1 vanilla bean, split lengthwise

½ cup granulated sugar

⅛ teaspoon fine sea salt

5 large egg yolks

**TO MAKE THE PANCAKES:** In a medium bowl, sift together the flour, sugar, nutmeg, and salt. Set aside.

In a blender, add the butter, eggs, milk, vanilla, and the flour mixture. Blend on high speed until smooth. Strain and let the batter rest at room temperature for about an hour or overnight in the refrigerator.

Heat a 12-inch skillet or a nonstick frying pan and lightly coat the hot pan with vegetable oil. Pour in about ½ cup of batter, depending on the size of your pan. Tilt the pan so the batter evenly coats the bottom of the pan.

Cook the pancake for 1 to 2 minutes or until the bottom is light brown. Lift with a spatula, then turn and cook the other side. Remove to a plate and repeat with the remaining batter.

Allow the pancakes to cool to room temperature by stacking them with parchment between each layer. Refrigerate until ready to use.

**TO MAKE THE DIPLOMAT CREAM:** In a 2-quart saucepan, combine the milk, ¼ cup of the sugar, and the vanilla bean and heat until it is hot and small bubbles begin to form around the edges but before it comes to a boil. Set aside.

In a stainless-steel bowl, whisk the remaining ¼ cup sugar, egg yolks, cornstarch, and salt until thick, creamy, and a pale yellow color. Whisk the hot milk into the yolk mixture and return the pan to the stove. Whisk constantly over medium-high heat until it bubbles and thickens.

Remove the pan from the heat and strain the mixture through a fine-mesh sieve into a bowl. Set the bowl over an ice bath and let the hot mixture cool to warm.

Whisk in the cold butter while the mixture is still warm. Cover with plastic wrap while cooling over the ice bath. (The plastic wrap must be touching the pastry cream.) When the pastry cream has cooled completely, stir in the Grand Marnier.

Whip the cream to stiff peaks. Fold the whipped cream into the chilled pastry cream until it is combined thoroughly. Keep chilled until ready to use.

**TO MAKE THE ICE CREAM:** In a 2-quart saucepan, combine the milk, cream, Milo, vanilla bean, ¼ cup of the sugar, and salt and heat until it is hot but not boiling.

In a bowl, combine the remaining ¼ cup sugar with the egg yolks and whisk lightly. Whisk the hot Milo mixture into the yolk mixture and return to the stove. Stir constantly over low heat until the mixture is thick enough to coat the back of a spoon.

Remove the pan from the heat and strain the mixture through a fine-mesh sieve into a bowl. Set the bowl over an ice bath and let the hot mixture cool to room temperature. Cover and chill in the refrigerator for at least 4 hours.

Churn in an ice cream maker according to the manufacturer's instructions. Set aside in the freezer in an airtight container until ready to use.

**TO ASSEMBLE THE CAKE:** Place the first pancake layer onto a serving platter and spread it with about 3 tablespoons of diplomat cream. Continue this process, layering the diplomat cream between each pancake layer, totaling sixteen layers of pancakes and sixteen layers of cream. Refrigerate the cake for at least 6 hours.

**TO SERVE:** Slice and serve with a scoop of the ice cream. Dust with extra Milo, if desired.

# CORN & GOAT'S MILK PUDDING

## with Blackberry Sorbet, Chocolate Crumble & Tapioca Pearls

## by Eric Adjepong

**MAKES 4 SERVINGS**

*For my final competition for season sixteen of Top Chef, I was meant to create a four-course meal as my final dish. I decided to tell the story of the trans-Atlantic slave trade through four courses. The story of their migration from ports in West Africa to ports in South America (particularly Brazil), the Caribbean, and the American South was manifested primarily through the ingredients I used— things like sorrel or hibiscus, cassava, Carolina Gold rice, palm wine, and others. These are indigenous West African ingredients that have become prominent in other parts of the world through trade.*

*This was the final dish, a corn and goat's milk pudding. Goat's milk is very popular throughout the continent, and I wanted to pair it with corn (abro in Twi) to celebrate these two widely used ingredients in Africa. Additionally, I used sorrel (hibiscus), which is traditionally drunk as a sweet tea in West Africa and the Caribbean, to flavor the tapioca pearls.*

### CORN AND GOAT'S MILK PUDDING
Makes 2½ cups

1½ cups corn kernels

2 tablespoons water

1 cup goat's milk

2 tablespoons cornstarch

¼ teaspoon salt

3 egg yolks, lightly beaten

⅔ cups sugar

3 tablespoons unsalted butter

2 teaspoons vanilla bean paste

### BLACKBERRY SORBET
Makes 4 cups

4 cups blackberries

1 cup water

1 cup sugar

1½ tablespoons lime juice

### CHOCOLATE CRUMBLE
Makes 2 cups

5 ounces (10 tablespoons) unsalted butter

⅓ cup superfine sugar

7 ounces (1 cup) Dutch-processed cocoa powder

1 teaspoon salt

Egg whites from about 1½ eggs

### SOBOLO/SORREL BASE
Makes 4 cups

5 whole cloves

1 cinnamon stick

5 whole allspice berries

2 pods grains of selim

3-ounce piece fresh ginger, sliced (or smashed if you like a heavy ginger kick)

Peel and juice from ½ an orange

¼ pineapple, cored and chopped

3½ cups water

4 ounces dried hibiscus flowers

1 teaspoon lime juice or more to taste

### TAPIOCA PEARLS
Makes 1 cup

1 cup small pearl tapioca

2 cups Sobolo/Sorrel Base (see recipe at left)

½ teaspoon citric acid

¼ cup sugar, plus more to taste

CONTINUED

## Corn & Goat's Milk Pudding, continued

**TO MAKE THE PUDDING:** In a blender, combine the corn kernels with the water and blend on high speed until it's a smooth consistency. Strain the corn juice and discard the solids (you should have about 1 cup).

In a medium saucepan over medium-high heat, combine the goat's milk and corn juice and whisk in the cornstarch and salt, being careful not to boil.

Place the egg yolks in a separate bowl. When the milk mixture becomes hot (but not boiling), temper the yolks slowly by whisking ¼ cup of the milk mixture into the yolks.

Add the tempered yolks to the warm milk/corn mixture and whisk to combine. Add the sugar, butter, and vanilla bean paste, stirring until the butter melts. Set aside.

**TO MAKE THE SORBET:** In a blender or food processor, combine the blackberries, water, and sugar and puree. Strain the mixture through a fine-mesh sieve, then season with the lime juice.

Cover and chill in the refrigerator until completely cold. Churn in an ice cream maker according to the manufacturer's instructions. Set aside in the freezer in an airtight container until ready to use.

**TO MAKE THE CRUMBLE:** Preheat the oven to 330°F.

In a food processor, pulse all the ingredients together until a crumblike texture. Spread the mixture onto a Silpat baking mat or parchment-lined baking sheet and rest for 1 hour in the refrigerator.

Bake for 20 minutes, then remove and allow to cool to room temperature.

**TO MAKE THE SORREL BASE:** In a large stockpot over medium-high heat, combine the cloves, cinnamon stick, allspice, and grains of selim and toast, stirring frequently, until fragrant, about 3 minutes. Add the ginger, orange peel, orange juice, and pineapple and continue to cook for 3 minutes. Add the water and bring to a boil.

Add the hibiscus to the boiling water and reduce to a simmer. Cover with a lid and allow to steep for 30 minutes. Strain and cool, then add the lime juice. (You will only need 2 cups of the Sorrel Base for this recipe; the rest can be used as tea with some sugar added.)

**TO MAKE THE TAPIOCA:** Soak the tapioca pearls in enough water to completely cover. Allow the pearls to hydrate in water for at least 1 hour.

Drain the water from the pearls. In a medium saucepan, add the pearls and sorrel base; turn up the heat until the mixture boils, whisking continuously. Stop when the sorrel base has boiled. Strain the tapioca pearls and reserve the sorrel base, returning the liquid to the pan. Rinse the tapioca pearls under cold water and then return the tapioca to the pan with the liquid. Repeat this process 3 more times with the sorrel, until the tapioca is fully cooked. Season with the citric acid and sugar.

**TO SERVE:** Ladle ¼ cup of the pudding into the center of a serving plate. Break the chocolate crumble into small pieces and arrange around the pudding. Ladle the tapioca in the negative spaces and then quenelle your sorbet and place on top.

CHAPTER 2
ART BY DEREK FORDJOUR

# JOLLOFING WITH TONI MORRISON

## by Sarah Ladipo Manyika

**Jollof**
[**jaw**-lawf]
noun: a West African one-pot dish made with
onions, peppers, tomatoes, tomato paste, palm
oil, vegetable stock, rice, cooking oil, salt;
tastiest when cooked over firewood

verb: to party, make merry, live it up, enjoy,
celebrate, bacchanal, celebrate good times

### September 6, 2019—District Six, Cape Town

"What did Toni Morrison's house smell like?"

The question comes from someone in the
audience who has followed me after the
plenary session of the Open Book Festival.
I had just been on stage along with a few fellow
contributors to *New Daughters of Africa: An
International Anthology of Writing by Women
of African Descent*. Our panel represented the
rich diversity of the landmark anthology—
a spicy mix of writers of different literary
genres, generations, and nationalities, brought
together in a place with its own complicated
racial history. On the panel, I had spoken
about Toni Morrison. Now, standing in the
foyer of the District Six Museum, surrounded
by festival attendees, this question surprises
and delights me.

### April 15, 2017—Grand View-on-Hudson, Rockland County, New York

Nadine, Toni Morrison's housekeeper, opens
the door and lets us in. Morrison is not yet
ready to receive us, so we wait upstairs in the
living room, where Morrison has said, "make
yourselves at home." Nadine is in the kitchen
chopping vegetables. Soon, there's a loud
sizzle and I catch the sharp bite of onion and
peppers, turning sweet as they fry. I can smell
tomato in there, too. It smells like home, like
jollof. Back in Nigeria, we used to eat jollof on
Sundays, after church services, and when celebrating Eid with friends at the end of Ramadan.
The best part, if you could get to it, were the
crackly bits of rice stuck to the bottom of
the pan. Jollof is both everyday and party food,
but no celebration is complete without it and
when served with fried plantains, it's heaven.
"Fish," says Nadine, when I walk over to ask
what she's preparing. "Something healthy for
Mrs. Morrison," she adds, her words lightly
seasoned with the flavor of Jamaica.

The aroma has me thinking about the one-pot
dishes Morrison writes about in her works—a
pot of turnips or maws—often simple, meager
meals to stave off hunger or to soothe. And
fish . . . I remember the "crisp sea bass" with
its "tiny flakes of white" in Miss Marie's
daydreaming of a meal shared with a past

love. I remember the precious piece of eel that ferryman Stamp Paid feeds Sethe in her escape from slavery. And what jollofing on the page when Morrison uses food in the naming of her characters—Plum, Meringue Pie, Sweetness, Chicken and Pie, and Milkman—or in describing skin tones from cream to licorice, lemonade, milk, and whey. And there is something about berries—the temptation of them, as in a deep-dish berry cobbler, toppled by inquisitively hungry children, or those other berries that "tasted like church"—"just one of those berries and you felt anointed"—delivered to one who is so close to being free of her slave masters. And when Morrison uses food as metaphor for sex, she's at her tantalizing best. From the sexual suggestiveness in the eating of an ear of corn: "How loose the silk. How fine and loose and free," to a woman's naked body "moist and crumbly as unbleached sugar," Morrison's word work is sublime. Every mention of food hints at a longing that simmers just beneath the surface.

Nadine cuts short my reverie; Mrs. Morrison is now ready. As we walk downstairs to her study, the smell of lunch accompanies us. She says to call her Toni, and in turn she calls us her friends, which feels so warm and delicious.

It's Easter Saturday, and Toni's friends and family drop by unannounced, just as I remembered it from my childhood. No invitations, but you never arrived empty-handed. We would take cakes, fruits, or vegetables when visiting. "Whadya bring me?" Toni teases her son, Ford, who is the first to arrive. "A samwich?" she asks. Not a sandwich, he says, but books. Something to satisfy a different hunger. Toni's neighbor Ned is the next to arrive, bearing an eye-popping floral arrangement as large as his hug. After an exchange of pleasantries, Toni asks Ned if he might bring her some food from his brother's restaurant.

"Seafood? You want seafood with pasta?" Ned is happy to oblige.

"Yes!" says Toni.

"Okay. Some pasta, some seafood?"

"Yes, yes, yes!" Toni enthuses.

"And a little dessert?"

"Yes!"

"Just for one? You're not having a dinner party, are you?" Ned checks.

And here is where I join in, playfully suggesting that we stay for dinner. I tell her I had planned on bringing a chocolate cake. "Hey!" says Toni with excitement at the mention of cake. "Whadya-do!" she adds, feigning indignation, when I confess to only having brought chocolates.

### August 6, 2019—Peckham, London

On the day Toni Morrison dies, I am in London. When I hear the news, I immediately set out on a walk, looking for a quiet place to process the shock. I find a church and sit outside on an empty bench. At the foot of the bench, I see a slice of fried plantain. Two days earlier, friends and I had shared jollof rice and plantain from a nearby Nigerian takeout, I Go Chop. Perhaps the plantain came from there and here it lies like an offering—a libation for the ancestors. I close my eyes and return to that afternoon when we had jollofed at Toni's house, which had smelled, quite simply, of home.

# FOODSTEPS IN MOTION

## Migration in Black Food

## by Michael W. Twitty

We have always been a people whose history was traced in foodsteps, beginning with the birth of humanity. The story of African people is, in many ways, a constant search for subsistence and satisfaction. We migrated with the herds and seasons, danced our way across the green Sahara and fertile plains, into the sacred forests and coasts. We are art in motion, gathering flora, fauna, minerals, and flavors on our way, adorning our hunger.

Across her landscape, Africa would sustain her children with more than 2,000 indigenous food plants, not to mention hundreds of fish, game, domesticated animals, insects, and birds to which was added the bounty of the globe. There were yams, sorghum and millet, cowpeas, rice, watermelons, muskmelons, greens and herbs, and fruits, both oily and sweet. On dhows and junks, across land bridges and seas, and trade routes buried under sand and humus came new resources, making Africa a greenhouse of a new world, a meeting place of food and ideas about food, brought to the place where fire and pottery and cooking first began. From her face to her heart moved plantains, mangoes, sugarcane, bananas, coconuts, and cinnamon and clove trees. There was a new foodscape, and as the generations waxed and waned, it was as if there was no line between the time this feast began and the countless seasons of harvest that led to recurring junctures of joy.

The rivers were highways of chiefdom and empire. These are the places where the herds drank and the tilapia and catfish, hippopotamus, and manatee swam. The food cultures of Kemet and Kush, Old Mali, and Songhai, and the kingdoms of the Yoruba and Edo, Igbo, and Kongo would spread indigenous cuisines with their expansions and flourishing fields. Bodies of water shrank, the searing deserts knew increase, and the movement kept going to thwart lack and ruin. Diets changed or were amended to meet the challenges of a new evening meal, prepared as they always had been, on three stones, shared among family around common bowls just before sunsets that had been reflected in the eyes of these humans longer than any other on Earth.

And yet there was trauma—new invaders came and left less than they took. Trauma moved food as fast as trade and expansion by foot and ship. The African Atlantic would represent the mass transfer of a third of Africa's population to the Western world. More bodies would arrive this way than from Europe until the 1820s, and with them, an entire seventy thousand years of eating, cooking, searching, hunger. Enslavement was the cause of movement. It meant new unfathomable pangs to come—pangs of exile, then an exhausting ache for memory beyond memory to keep the culture alive despite the whip, the gun, violations of body and spirit, and a demand to forget.

The food became the source code from village to dungeon, barracoon to canoe, caravel to colonial town, and to the plantations where sugarcane, rice, cacao, coffee, corn, indigo, cotton, tobacco, and the rest awaited their knowledge, skills, and abilities to stuff the West and resolve its desires.

We kept moving, our foodsteps taking on greater significance. Now we were to be assimilated in our tastes to Eurasia's ways, specifically its Western, Atlantic facing coast. Peaches, apples, pork, cabbages and colewort, olives, and wheat drifted into our mouths unasked for and unrequested. We took what we needed as we moved and left behind other ingredients; they were not key to remembering who we were or why we were here. Through the Middle Passage, seeds moved, not in our hair but in casks, boxes, and hogsheads; some were live plants, others dried.

The words changed with the foodsteps. Mende, Yoruba, Igbo, Ki-Kongo, Mbundu, Uldeme, Papel, Soninke merged with Portuguese, English, Danish, Spanish, French, and Dutch. A flood of foreign verbiage, but the core words and sounds remained, words and sounds for things no word in their tongues could provide. We made new culinary languages and new nations and new dishes and delicious things out of scraps, treasures, and unknown gold.

We began to rebel and inject our foodsteps with joy. Jerk and barbecue emerged. Mothers from all over Africa sat together and worked out a revolution in food—on St. Kitts and in Virginia and Maryland and over in Pernambuco and the Artibonite region of Haiti. We became architects of food in Peru, Cuba, Jamaica, Puerto Rico, Venezuela, Colombia, Georgia, and Louisiana and in Philadelphia, Manhattan, Brooklyn, and Boston. Okra soups and gumbos; fufus and mofongos; grit cakes, mashes, and mushes; and iron pots full of bones and scraps and heads and tails and torsos of game and

provisions and greens marched from labor camp to labor camp in the hands of fishermen and women, hunters and gardeners, farmers and foragers. We cooked for our captors, cooked for ourselves, and between the two, a culinary grammar and vocabulary developed to name new constellations of food crafts unmatched in the Americas.

In America, the foodsteps were thunderous. We were pushed in chains in the largest forced migration in American history—the domestic slave trade. We ran like hell. The foodsteps delivered refugees' cuisine—our food pushed beyond the coasts and core areas, to the prairie and frontier and Great Lakes. Across several centuries, little conspiracies made by sailors and crewmen, whalers, pirates, missionaries, servants, artisans, Queer seekers, orphans, and expatriates spread the foodsteps when enslavement could not. Our neighbors soaked us up, and we soaked them up—in duress and pleasure—the Irish, the Germans, the Navajo, the Lakota, the Chinese—new dishes were born in the in-between places.

Lowcountry married Louisiana.

Cape Verde married old Black Bostonian and Bajan.

Bahamian married Seminole Freedman.

We became from many, one.

Emancipation came, then westward expansion; Jim Crow led to the largest voluntary migration in American history—the Great Migration. Fried rabbit and chicken and biscuits in shoeboxes and jars of farm-made syrup and jars of succotash and pickled peaches fueled new journeys and fires within us. We used everything we had to resist and to build—new towns, organizations, unions, and everything we needed to be "modern." Despite the aggression, the violence, the nightmare days, and dystopian nights, we forced joy and passed plates out of our backdoors, opened up cafés, barbecued on the roadside. We cooked at Delmonico's, too, but nothing mattered to us more than our family reunions, cookouts and barbecues, Queer family gatherings, rent parties, Sunday dinners, Eids and Passover feasts, days for saints and their corresponding Vodun and Orisha.

We celebrated each other. We practiced culinary jazz and improvised, drawing on things we had always done since time began, classical things, endemic to Africa, and things we composed with others in mind and creative flourishes dreamed up in the void. We moved back South; we made Brooklyn into the Caribbean and Houston into Nigeria.

No matter where we go, the foodsteps will keep coming with creative fire, the character of tradition and a sense of the cool that made for a food tradition armed with a sense of empowerment and renewal that make for fertile grounds for the foodsteps of the children of Africa to come.

# IT TAKES A LONG TIME

## by Naa Oyo A. Kwate, PhD

Ackee is Jamaica's national fruit, and when paired with saltfish, it becomes the country's national dish. It hails from Ghana, where it still grows but is no longer eaten. But common lore about the plant's migration from West Africa to the Caribbean is purely fiction. In its telling, a captain in the British navy in the 1700s brought ackee to the island to nourish enslaved persons. This captain, William Bligh, who sailed the South Pacific and nearly met his end in a mutiny aboard the HMS *Bounty* in 1789, did eventually transport more than three hundred tropical fruit trees from Tahiti to Jamaica in 1793. The British called the progeny of those trees breadfruit on account of its texture, taste, and on how readily ships' crews replaced their bread with the fruit. We know Bligh did indeed execute this mission because slave owners in Jamaica beseeched the English monarchy to dispatch the starchy crop so that they might use it as feed.

But ackee? No. Bligh clearly took credit for the plant—its scientific taxonomy *Blighia sapida* bears his name. This is surely because ackee was among the plants enslaved men in Jamaica were tasked with carrying from the island's interior to Bligh's ship, whereupon he would convey the plants across the Atlantic to the Royal Botanic Gardens at Kew in London.

Ackee's name alone is evidence that an African hand bore it to the Caribbean; otherwise, it would be called something like butterfruit or eggfruit. Ackee is thought to derive from akye (pronounced AH-cheh), from the Akan. A Twi word meaning "it's taking a long time," it's a fitting description of tropical flora that takes many years to bear fruit. And even then, a new wait ensues for the fruit to ripen fully on the tree, the hallmark being skin that has opened to expose the vivid yellow arils and glossy black seeds within. Subverting this waiting period means flirting with death or else grave illness. So, threatened, you wait. *It takes a long time.*

Most likely ackee came to Jamaica because one or more individuals seized the seeds before being abducted from the Asante state, intending to plant, cultivate, and eat it wherever they landed. The seeds might also have been procured for good measure as weapons. Plucked from the fruit from the tree from the soil red with rich deposits of iron and aluminum oxides and replanted in new ground colored with the same fertility, it would bloom.

Ackee continues to traverse the Atlantic, now transported not as a botanical but as an inert object. It sails to terminals where Jamaicans live in numbers, principally the United States, England, and Canada. When, on occasion, I buy ackee, I do so the way I must when I want most foods that come directly or indirectly from Ghana—I pick up a can and put it in my shopping basket. Some tropical fruits and vegetables are available in American grocers and supermarkets—but these are perpetually expensive mistakes. Commercially available pineapple bears no resemblance to that which I bought in 2000 from a young woman near Kumasi. Never before or since have I had a pineapple like that one. I bought it from a tour bus window, knowing full well I lacked the requisite knife and cutting surface to enjoy it. And so, I waited until I arrived at the hotel. The pineapple sat patiently beside me for the rest of the day, blasting its aroma, hurting my ears. When the wait was over, I dove in, the sweetness heady, rich, synapse-breaking; the flesh exploding, littering my face with juice and making a mockery of table manners.

In America, when I buy food from home, it does not involve the senses. I'm left with a brief visual inspection for indented metal that might indicate botulism. I've never made palm nut soup from scratch. My mother told me how it's done: "Pound the fruits in a big wooden mortar with a long wooden pestle to separate the fruit from the kernel. This becomes pulp/husk and kernel. Remove it from the mortar and put it in a large bowl. Add hot water and kind of mash it while removing the kernels. Pick up a few of the husks and squeeze the liquid out. Repeat until all the husks are done. Strain the 'pulpy' liquid, maybe twice. Add this to the base simmered meat, whatever, add onion, tomatoes, and peppers. You have to pay attention to avoid it foaming and boiling over. It's a long, tedious process."

I only know how to make palm nut soup by opening a can of Trofai. In fact, growing up as a second-generation Ghanaian immigrant means that I have never had the opportunity to buy fresh, or even to see growing, many of the fruits and vegetables that are important to our gastronomy. Okro is an exception, because I grow it myself. Every year I allocate a few pots in my container garden to heirloom varieties—Cowhorn, Gold Coast, Alabama Red, White Velvet. The other pots, evidence of the seduction of seed catalogs, contain a variety of other vegetables. Okro thrives in the heat, like I do, and it relishes humidity. Penetrating, swampy, crushing heat only makes it stand upright, steadfast. The plants remember the equatorial sun that will tan you deep in the recesses of your skin even under full cloud cover.

Unlike ackee, okro does not require a long wait. Okro plants want you to pay attention, to snip their fruits at the precise moment when they are at their young and robust best. I eat them raw, right off the plant, and they are crunchy, earthy, and tender. Fresh from the stem, they are mucilaginous enough to let you know it's okro but without being overwhelming. They taste like an acerbic retort to the dishonest self-presentation of their brethren languishing in grocery produce cases. They taste like home.

# THE POETICS OF AFRO-ASIAN CUISINE

## by Tao Leigh Goffe, PhD

Cooking has become a source of refuge for me since the pandemic. I did not cook before. I never had the time. The shutting down of society in March 2020 happened to coincide with the medical leave I took from work in order to undergo invasive surgery. I began an elimination diet as part of the process of recovery. I eliminated food groups—soy, dairy, grains—slowly reintroducing them to learn what my body did not need. I was told the reason for my medical condition was, simply put, "race." Being a Black woman, according to the surgeon, was the reason for my chronic pain.

I still do not know what to do with that answer, but I could not help thinking of other maternal inheritances and mitochondrial DNA. I could not help thinking of *race,* not as a fact but as a concept and management tool of the colonial plantation. I could not help thinking of racism defined by Ruth Wilson Gilmore as group-differentiated vulnerability to premature death. If I had inherited this pain from my grandmothers, Black women from Jamaica, one who had emigrated to the UK and the other to the United States, I wondered what else I might have inherited.

As a professor and a DJ, a PhDJ, I consider the question of embodied archives and alternative epistemologies that center the sensory experience. There are not five independent senses

as we have been told by another false taxonomy of Western hierarchy. Rather there is a synesthesia, a crisscrossing and blending of the senses. For those of us who are part of the Black diaspora, we know what it means to associate a flavor with a sound, a song, a color. Diasporic memory is "wired together and fired together" like neurons, which remember a distant flavor before colonialism, before capitalism, before capture. Music and cooking are twin practices of mixing, beat matching, and remixing. As a PhDJ, I see the syllabus as a mixtape; a recipe is a mixtape, too. It is a playlist, a love letter written for another, to be experienced with or without the writer, the cook, the DJ being present.

I do not have any of my grandmothers' recipes written down. Cooking skipped a generation in my family and arrived to me late in life. The advent of the microwave and my parents being of a generation that rejected the meat they grew up eating—stew chicken, pork fried rice, and oxtail—meant that my sister and I did not grow up knowing the umami flavor of many of the foods of our West Indian, Chinese, and English heritage. And still to this day, we have never tasted meat. As children, we watched with envy at lunchtime in the cafeteria as classmates scarfed down ham sandwiches.

In disbelief at meeting someone, really a Black person, who has never eaten meat, people say with pity, "Don't you miss it?" I cannot miss something I have never tasted, never known. And yet discovering my culinary heritage from the Caribbean and South China has led me to invent and reinvent pescatarian, vegetarian, and vegan versions of dishes my sister and I were never able to order in restaurants because we don't eat meat. After all, the condition of the diaspora is to miss the taste of something you never exactly knew.

I had long written about food derived from southern US plantations and the Greater Caribbean from the abstract vantage of a historian. Yet, I had not thought to actually cook the foods I had spent many years searching for, sifting through British, Spanish, and Dutch colonial archives. Rice and curry tell a story of Afro-Asian gastropoetics, the poetry and political economy of the plantation.

As the pandemic progressed, I began to contemplate what it would mean if the food supply chains completely shut down and I could not provide food for my family. I thought of the conditions of scarcity that determined plantation recipes. Soul Food is bittersweet. It is the common palate of foodways of the Atlantic plantation and thus the Black diaspora, adapted from high-caloric fuel rationed to enslaved people to eat in order to perform backbreaking labor. Soul Food is a recipe as much as a resource for the future of Blackness itself, for survival and sustenance, for a multiplicity of Black futures. It is a culinary heritage that we can romanticize and also critique and adapt to be healthier, because it is ours. Black food is the poetics of what germinated, what grew, on the peripheries of the plantation, what Sylvia Wynter and Claude McKay write about. It is the ackee from West Africa that thrived and grew on Jamaican provision grounds, in gardens, not for European consumption.

Asian ingredients and food are also part of plantation foodways. Wontons are commonly eaten in Trinidadian cuisine for this reason.

Chow mein is eaten as a staple in Guyana, such that people forget it is indeed Chinese. Afro-Asian identity is not new. The same foodways that brought Chinese food to the West Indian plantation also brought Chinese laborers and food to Mississippi and Louisiana.

My work is animated by the forgotten catastrophe of what I call racial indenture, or the fact that at the pivotal moment of Black freedom, abolition, Chinese and Indians were brought to the Caribbean as replacement labor under brutal conditions. If we understand this colonial history, we begin to understand that Afro-Asian labor in tension and tandem led to much of the Caribbean cuisine eaten today. A centuries-long process has left us with patties, curry goat, doubles, buss-up shut, and dal puri roti. Fried rice was eaten on the plantation alongside callaloo and ackee.

These delicious dishes, signatures of the Caribbean, are New York icons. As a Black British person, I barely noticed a difference in the food culture from London to New York because of Black Atlantic currents that intimately connect Brixton to Brooklyn. A quarter of New York City is of Caribbean heritage, and so Jamaican beef patties are a mainstay of Manhattan pizza parlors and hotdog carts.

I might be breaking all the rules, but I continue my work tracing the recipes that the embodied archive reveals and inspires. What is food but an archive of global desires? The necessity of eating was and continues to be a process of understanding the difference between the cravings for what we desire and what we cannot live without. Food is the sustenance of our survival, and the recipes tell a colonial narrative of inheritance that is also a family history for Black and Asian people. From the plantation to the present, our ancestors made us a mixtape of flavors across the continents. It is the taste of something we will never exactly know. It is a recipe for reinvention in times of scarcity, for fashioning the future, for survival.

# PIQUE HOT SAUCE

## by Reina Gascón-López

MAKES 1½ CUPS (375ML)

*Pique is a homemade pepper vinegar sauce that's popular in Puerto Rico and often sold at street-side kiosks. It also has a permanent home at the lechoneras, whole pig barbecue stands with their adjoining dining tables that show up throughout the island. The cooks at lechoneras share many techniques with the barbecue pitmasters of the South, particularly in the Carolinas, with their method of slow roasting whole pigs. And it's no surprise, since this method of barbecue originated in Puerto Rico from the indigenous Taíno people, another reminder of just how closely our cultures are connected and intertwined throughout the diaspora.*

*Traditionally, Puerto Rican cuisine isn't a spicy one, so we keep pique on hand for anyone looking for a little extra heat in their food. I love using this pique on barbecue and in stews, braises, and soups; both the acidity and heat work well with cutting through something rich. This recipe is one that I've adapted from my maternal grandfather's favorite pique sauce. I use the peppers (along with homegrown ajices dulces) that are available to me here in Charleston, since it's difficult to find more traditional Caribbean items. If you can't find ajices dulces, simply omit them. I use them for extra flavor, but since they're sweet, they don't contribute to the heat of the sauce. If you want this to be on the very hot side, play around with a variety of chile peppers, until you find the combination that is to your liking.*

**1 small serrano chile,** stemmed, seeded, and cut in half

**1 small red Anaheim chile,** stemmed, seeded, and thinly sliced

**2 aji dulce chiles,** thinly sliced

**2 large garlic cloves, sliced**

**2 sprigs of oregano**

**2 teaspoons black peppercorns**

**⅔ cup distilled white vinegar**

**⅔ cup water**

Carefully place the chiles, garlic cloves, and oregano sprigs into a clean, empty bottle with a plastic cap. Using a small funnel, pour in the peppercorns, vinegar, and water. Cover the bottle with its cap and gently shake to distribute all the ingredients evenly.

Next, remove the cap from the bottle and, using a small nail or pushpin, carefully poke two or three holes into the cap to allow air and fermentation gas to escape. This will also serve as a way to shake the pique onto your food without drowning it in pepper sauce.

If the bottle you're using doesn't have a cap that can be easily punctured, you can simply cover the bottle with some plastic wrap that has been cut with a slit or a small piece of thin cheesecloth instead.

To store, place the bottle in a cool, dark area like a pantry or cabinet and check occasionally. Covering the holes with a paper towel or napkin, give the bottle a gentle shake every day or two.

The pique will be ready in one week and should be slightly orange or yellow in color. This pepper sauce only gets better the longer it sits; I suggest keeping it at room temperature for up two weeks, but you can definitely keep it stored in the fridge for longer.

**TIPS:** When preparing, make sure to use gloves to avoid getting any of the oils from the chiles on your skin or accidentally on your face. To store, an empty and clean pint-sized liquor bottle with a plastic cap works well.

# BAJAN FISH CAKES

## by Sarah Kirnon

MAKES 30 TO 35 FISH CAKES

*Fish cakes so nice, Blackmailer made a song about them. These fish cakes are the perfect combination of savory, crispy, fluffy, and light! A fried fritter filled with shreds of cod (saltfish) and packed with fresh herbs, this Bajan treat is an island favorite, commonly served at parties and events or just any time. You've been warned: these are addictive! My grandmother would call the accompanying sauce Marry Rose Dressing, and I still refer to it as such.*

**FISH CAKES**

½ pound saltfish, boneless if you can find it

10½ cups water

1 small shallot, finely chopped

4 garlic cloves, finely chopped

1 tablespoon Bajan pepper sauce, or any other hot sauce as long as it has a kick

1¼ cups all-purpose flour

2 tablespoons baking powder

1 egg

½ cup whole milk

2 tablespoons butter, softened

¼ cup finely chopped scallions (from about 2 or 3 scallions)

A few sprigs of thyme, flat leaf parsley, or oregano, leaves picked from the stems and finely chopped

Freshly ground black pepper and white pepper to taste

Salt to taste

About 8 cups vegetable oil for frying

**MARIE ROSE SAUCE**

½ cup mayonnaise

2 tablespoons ketchup

1 tablespoon fresh lime juice

2 tablespoons Tabasco sauce for flavor and color

1 teaspoon sugar

Pinch of salt

Lime wedges for squeezing

**TO MAKE THE FISH CAKES:** Place the saltfish in a saucepan with 6 cups of the water. Bring to a boil for a few minutes, then pour off the water. Add another 4 cups of the water and bring to a boil a second time, then simmer for ½ hour. Check the saltiness of the fish; it should be salty but not overly so. If it is still too salty, you may need to boil it up a third time with fresh water.

Drain the water and shred the salt fish with your fingers or a fork.

Combine the shredded fish with the shallot, garlic, pepper sauce, flour, baking powder, egg, milk, the remaining ½ cup water, butter, scallions, herbs, pepper, and salt in a medium bowl and stir vigorously until a thick batter is formed. You can also use a stand mixer, fitted with the dough hook.

In a large heavy-bottomed pot, heat the oil until it reads 370° to 375°F on an instant-read thermometer.

Working in batches, deep-fry tablespoonfuls over medium heat, about six at a time, until golden brown. Monitor the heat carefully to avoid burning the outside of the fish cake before the middle is fully cooked. Use a slotted spoon or spider during cooking to turn and move the fish cakes. Each batch takes about 4 to 6 minutes to cook. Drain on paper towels.

**TO MAKE THE SAUCE:** In a medium bowl, whisk together the mayonnaise, ketchup, lime juice, Tabasco, sugar, and salt.

To serve, place the fish cakes on a serving plate and serve hot with the sauce, along with some lime wedges for squeezing.

# JAMAICAN-STYLE ACKEE & CALLALOO PATTIES

## by Tao Leigh Goffe, PhD

MAKES 6 OR 7 PATTIES

*The foodways of British imperialism and 1960s diasporic migration brought the "patty" to New York. One of my grandmothers traveled similar routes, migrating from Jamaica to New York in 1967. Myself a migrant to New York, I was inspired to invent my own Jamaican patty, a vegan one with ackee and callaloo. Extra turmeric and curry powder give it the glow of the Golden Krust chain restaurant that sells patties across the boroughs. Few realize that the gold is turmeric, an Indian spice that arrived in Jamaica from Bihar and Uttar Pradesh. And while a patty is not an Indian pastry, it bears a resemblance to a samosa, even though it is more closely related to the English pasty. Cornish pasties were designed for the masses, British miners who needed a contained lunch. The buttery pastry culture of Great Britain converged with Indian spices to make what is now arguably a Black food. I've been told its West African cousin can be found in Nigeria, the meat hand pie. To eat a patty is to consume a Black world to which Asian cookery was central.*

*Thinking of the high fat content in pastry that served laboring people in the nineteenth century well, I tried a vegan remix. I substituted butter with coconut oil. Then I filled my patty with the best vegetarian West African–derived comfort foods of Jamaica: ackee and callaloo. Be careful if picking from a tree; like another West African transplant to the Americas—cassava—ackee can be a deadly poison if the skin and the seeds are consumed. Eating ackees before they are ripe leads to the Jamaican vomiting sickness, which has a storied record in the British colonial archive and was part of the arsenal of enslaved Africans. While ackee and callaloo are not always easy to find, replacing them with hardy greens such as kale or spinach and tomatoes works, too.*

### FILLING

1 tablespoon coconut oil

½ cup diced yellow onion

2 large garlic cloves, minced

⅛ teaspoon cinnamon

¼ teaspoon allspice

½ teaspoon cumin

½ teaspoon garam masala

½ teaspoon ground coriander

½ teaspoon turmeric

¼ teaspoon curry powder

½ teaspoon garlic powder

⅛ teaspoon cayenne pepper

½ teaspoon pink Himalayan salt, plus more to taste

½ green chile or Scotch bonnet pepper, seeded and minced, to taste

½ cup shredded callaloo (if using canned, use 1 cup), or 1 cup hardy greens like kale or spinach

1 (19-ounce) can of ackee, or diced tomatoes

Black pepper to taste

1 tablespoon minced fresh thyme

### PASTRY

2¾ cups unbleached flour

2 teaspoons turmeric powder

1 teaspoon curry powder (Caribbean or British brands preferable)

½ teaspoon pink Himalayan salt

¾ cup coconut oil, chilled

2 teaspoons white vinegar

½ cup cold water

Coconut or vegetable oil for brushing

West Indian hot pepper sauce for serving

CONTINUED

## Jamaican-Style Ackee, continued

**TO MAKE THE FILLING:** In a medium sauté pan over medium-low heat, combine the oil, onion, and garlic and allow them to sweat and take on a little color, then add the spices, salt, and chile. (As they say in Trinidad, you should parch the spices, cooking them to activate the oils.) Sauté, stirring occasionally, for 8 to 10 minutes or until the onion and garlic are caramelized.

Stir in the callaloo, reduce the heat to low, cover, and cook for 10 to 12 minutes or 5 to 6 minutes for kale or canned callaloo. Add the ackee and cook for an additional 10 minutes; do not overstir. Season with additional salt, pepper, and thyme and set aside to allow the flavors to marry.

**TO MAKE THE PASTRY:** In a large bowl, combine the flour with the turmeric, curry powder, and salt and mix well with your fingers like a rake. Add the oil and mix with your hands until it's fully incorporated and the mixture feels like fine sand, about 10 minutes.

Combine the vinegar with ½ cup cold water and mix well. Hydration of the dough is important. Then, without overworking the dough, add the vinegar mixture by the tablespoon, while stirring, just until the dough comes away from the sides of the bowl and begins to feel like wet sand on the shore of a beach. Add additional tablespoons of water as needed. Knead the dough and roll into a tight ball. It should look yellow and be hydrated. Cover with plastic wrap and let rest in the refrigerator for at least 2 hours.

**TO MAKE THE PATTIES:** Preheat the oven to 400°F and remove the dough from the refrigerator. Use the internal fan setting if your oven has one. Wait for the dough to soften at room temperature so that you can roll it with a rolling pin.

Lightly dust a clean surface with flour, roll out the dough until it is about ⅛ inch thick. This will require some elbow grease because the vegan crust is not as pliable as a traditional butter pastry crust. Cut 6-inch circles from the dough (you can use a bowl if

you don't have cookie cutters, running a sharp knife around the bowl). Spoon 2 tablespoons of the filling onto the center of one side of each circle, leaving about a ⅛-inch border. Caution: You will be tempted to overstuff; don't. Fold the other half over to make a semicircle, press to seal, and if you do not have a crimper, a fork works well enough to close the parcel of pastry. Press hard to make an imprint and seal the pastry; you should notice the dough bounce back.

Transfer the patties to a parchment-lined baking sheet, brush with oil, and bake until you see the golden turmeric-spiced crust begin to brown, about 25 minutes. Remove from the oven and let cool for 5 minutes. Jamaican patty shops often feature signs warning that hot patties should be left to cool lest you burn your mouth with the delicious curry filling. Enjoy with hot pepper sauce.

**DIASPORA TIP:** If you do not have access to callaloo, you can try substituting with spinach or other hardy greens. While there is no substitute for ackee, tomatoes, another fruit miscategorized as a vegetable, work well with greens for the filling.

# CREAMY GRITS

## with Jalapeño-Scared Maitake Mushrooms & Sautéed Chard

## by Rahanna Bisseret Martinez

MAKES 4 SERVINGS

*I am Black, Mexican, and Haitian American. The Mexican side of my family identifies as Mexican, but beyond that as people of the Native Mexican nations, the Purépecha and the Otomi. I've grown up learning the history of my people from stories, which you cannot find in books. Now many scholars share these beliefs; that our original people and our gods, in Mexico, were Black. And while this is still debated and argued among some, I wonder who benefits when Black and Mexican people see themselves as different from each other?*

*There are so many legacies of the Mexican and Black communities spanning across North America. My story is just one. In the 1920s, my mother's maternal family emigrated from Mexico City to Chicago. Her father escaped the brutality of the Papa Doc regime in the 1960s and left Haiti for New York City. My father's family migrated from Baton Rouge, Louisiana, to Marin County, California, in the 1940s as a part of the Great Migration. Plants have a migration story, too, and few ingredients are as central to Black and Mexican unity and prosperity as corn. This recipe is a celebration of this important food and its ancient knowledge.*

**CREAMY GRITS**

1 cup organic grits (if using stone ground, like the blue grits pictured on page 75, soak them overnight to create a creamier dish in less time)

¼ cup unsweetened oat milk cream (coconut, nut, or soy cream will work, too)

1 tablespoon olive oil

1 tablespoon kosher salt

**JALAPEÑO SAUCE**

1 quarter of an unpeeled yellow onion

1 jalapeño

3 unpeeled garlic cloves

1 teaspoon Meyer lemon juice (regular lemons will do just fine, too)

1 tablespoon olive oil

⅓ cup chopped cilantro

8 ounces maitake mushroom (cremini and portobello will work but won't have the umami of maitake)

**RAINBOW CHARD LEAVES AND PICKLED STEMS**

1 bunch of rainbow chard (about 7 stalks), with leaves and stems

2 tablespoons neutral cooking oil (such as grapeseed, avocado, or canola)

Salt and pepper to taste

1 cup water

1 jalapeño

1 cup white vinegar

1 garlic clove

¼ yellow onion

2 tablespoons sugar or maple syrup

1 tablespoon oil

**TO MAKE THE GRITS:** Cook the grits according to the package instructions in a large, heavy-bottomed pot. The cook time can range from an hour to two hours, depending on the age and quality of the grits. Stir the grits occasionally and check to see if more water is needed. It is important to make sure no grits are sticking to the bottom of the pan. When the grits are tender, remove from the hot burner and pour in the oat cream, oil, and salt, stir well, and cover. Set aside.

**TO MAKE THE SAUCE:** Place a cast-iron skillet over medium heat. Once heated, place the onion quarter, jalapeño, and garlic cloves into the skillet. Some people prefer to place the veggies on a piece of tinfoil on the bottom of the pan. Either way, you are looking to char

CONTINUED

## Creamy Grits, continued

the outside of each item and slightly cook them. The garlic will likely be done first, after 4 or 5 minutes.

Place each item in a bowl as they char and place a lid over them. When the charred veggies are cool to the touch, remove the outer skin of the onion, remove the stem of the jalapeño, and peel the garlic. If you are very sensitive to spice, slice the jalapeño in half lengthwise and remove one half's seeds and white veins; it will be much milder. In a blender, blend the onion, jalapeño, and garlic with the lemon juice, olive oil, and cilantro until smooth.

Clean the mushrooms with a damp towel and break apart at the stem into 2-inch pieces. Place the mushrooms in a bowl and pour the jalapeño sauce on top; let sit for at least 15 minutes.

**TO MAKE THE CHARD:** Place the chard shiny side face down on a cutting board and slice the stems and ribs away from the green leafy parts. Place the green leafy parts in a pile and cut into thin strips. Transfer these to a bowl, toss with the oil, and season with salt and pepper.

Cut the chard stems into matchstick-size thickness. In a medium saucepan, combine the water, jalapeño, vinegar, garlic, onion, and sugar and bring to a boil. Then, remove the pan from the heat, add the chard ribs, and let sit, uncovered, for a minimum of 10 minutes.

Place a medium cast-iron skillet over medium heat, add the chard leaves and sauté, using tongs to move them around quickly in order to keep their bright green color. Transfer to a bowl and set aside.

In the skillet, add the oil and lightly swirl to coat the entire bottom of the pan, then place over medium-high heat. Take the mushrooms and shake off any extra sauce back into the bowl. Too much sauce on the mushrooms will cause them to steam instead of sear. Once the pan is hot, add the mushrooms and cook for about 5 minutes on each side, until they are tender to the bite and nicely caramelized.

**TO SERVE:** Spoon the grits onto a large platter and top with the mushrooms, chard, and pickled stems.

# JOLLOF RICE WITH BEANS

## by JJ Johnson

MAKES 6 SERVINGS

*Every culture has its own version of a one-pot rice dish—jambalaya, paella, and so on—and West Africa's take on the dish belongs with the best of them. From Senegal to Mali, Nigeria, Cameroon, and Ghana, jollof is a beloved favorite. Every cook gives the dish her or his own spin, but what remains consistent is the bright red color that comes from the tomato paste and palm oil. To that base, you can add proteins like chicken or fish. Plantains in jollof give it a sweet vegetarian spin. At my restaurant, FIELDTRIP, it plays the same role that mainstays like a hamburger or spaghetti and meatballs might play somewhere else.*

**TOMATO SAUCE**

2 tablespoons vegetable oil

½ Spanish onion, chopped

Kosher salt to taste

1 tablespoon chopped garlic

1 teaspoon chopped ginger

2 bird's eye chiles, seeded and chopped

¼ cup tomato paste

3 ripe plum tomatoes (about ½ pound), chopped

**RED BEANS**

1 cup dried adzuki red beans (or red kidney beans)

4 cups cool water, plus more as needed

4 garlic cloves

1 bird's eye chile

1 Spanish onion, chopped

Kosher salt to taste

Freshly ground black pepper to taste

**JOLLOF RICE**

2 cups jasmine rice

1 tablespoon olive oil

2 cups Tomato Sauce

1½ cups Red Beans

3 cups water

½ teaspoon kosher salt, plus more as needed

Black pepper to taste

**TO MAKE THE TOMATO SAUCE:** Heat the oil over medium heat in a large saucepan. Add the onion and sprinkle with salt. Cook until the onion is soft and translucent, 3 to 5 minutes. Add the garlic, ginger, and chiles and cook for an additional 2 minutes; make sure they do not brown. After the vegetables are softened, stir in the tomato paste and cook for 5 to 8 minutes. Make sure to incorporate the tomato paste with the vegetables to ensure even cooking of the paste. Transfer to a blender and pulse to combine. Add the tomatoes and puree until the mixture forms a smooth sauce. Add a little bit of water if the sauce is too thick or chunky. Season with salt.

**TO MAKE THE BEANS:** In a medium saucepan, combine the beans, water, garlic, chile, and onion over high heat. Bring to a boil, then quickly lower the heat to a very gentle simmer. Cook the beans over low heat until they are tender, about 1½ hours, adding more water as needed to keep them submerged by at least 1 inch. Make sure to stir the beans occasionally while they simmer to make sure they don't cook unevenly or burn on the bottom. Taste the beans frequently, testing their texture and flavor, as they start to become tender after about 1 hour. Season with salt and pepper after they begin to soften. Remove the beans from the heat once they are creamy and soft but before they begin to lose their shape. Cool them in their cooking liquid and then transfer to a nonreactive storage container. Remove and discard the chile.

**TO MAKE THE RICE:** Combine the rice, oil, tomato sauce and beans in a large saucepan. Add the water, salt, and pepper and bring to a simmer over medium heat. Cover the pot and cook for 35 to 45 minutes, until the rice is tender. Let the rice sit, covered, for 10 minutes after it's done cooking. Then fluff with a fork. Serve immediately.

# DIRTY SOUTH HOT TAMALES

## with Cilantro Sauce

# by Bryant Terry

**MAKES 15 TAMALES**

*One of my favorite childhood food memories is getting hot tamales with my dad from the "Tamale Man" near the Crystal Palace Skating Rink on South Third Street in my hometown, Memphis. Those spicy, unctuous little packages are at the top of the list. Back then, I had no idea that there was a long history of African American tamale making in the Mississippi Delta. Several years ago, I ran across an oral history project by the Southern Foodways Alliance (SFA) and learned that hot tamale making in the South reaches back at least to the early twentieth century. There are various theories about its origins. According to Amy C. Evans, SFA Oral Historian, tamales could have come to the Mississippi Delta in the early 1900s when Mexican migrant laborers worked the cotton harvest, or during the U.S.–Mexican War a hundred years before that. It's also possible that tamales date to the Native Americans' Mississippian culture.*

*When I was creating this recipe, I discovered that hot tamales were one of my dad's favorite childhood snacks, too. He told me about a blind married couple, Mr. and Mrs. Haynes, in his South Memphis neighborhood, who made them at home. Mr. Haynes would walk around the neighborhood pushing a cart heated by charcoals, selling to his loyal customers. According to my dad, "When my friends and I saw Mr. Haynes pushing his cart from a distance, we would run to our houses, grab two quarters, buy some, and eat them on a nearby porch."*

*These plant-based tamales nod to Southern hot tamales by using grits instead of masa or corn meal. Pork or beef is replaced with jackfruit, a tropical tree fruit grown in Asia, Africa, and South America. Delicious cilantro sauce adds more flavor and heat (adjust the jalapeño to suit your taste).*

## CILANTRO SAUCE
Makes about 1 cup

2 garlic cloves, minced

3 tablespoons extra-virgin olive oil

¼ teaspoon ground coriander

¼ teaspoon coarse sea salt, plus more as needed

1 cup tightly packed fresh cilantro leaves

2 tablespoons fresh lemon juice

½ jalapeño

## CREOLE SEASONING
Makes about ¼ cup

1 tablespoon garlic powder

1 tablespoon paprika

2 teaspoons coarse sea salt

2 teaspoons freshly ground black pepper

2 teaspoons onion powder

2 teaspoons chili powder

2 teaspoons red pepper flakes

1 teaspoon dried thyme

1 teaspoon dried oregano

¼ teaspoon cayenne pepper

## FILLING

40 ounces canned green jackfruit, in brine or water

¼ cup extra-virgin olive oil

1 cup ¼-inch diced yellow onion

½ cup finely chopped celery

½ cup ¼-inch diced green bell pepper

1 heaping teaspoon minced garlic

1 teaspoon creole seasoning

¼ teaspoon kosher salt, plus more as needed

3 tablespoons tomato paste

1 tablespoon Bragg Liquid Aminos

1 cup vegetable stock

**TAMALES**

Corn husks

2 cups yellow grits, soaked overnight

5 cups vegetable stock

1 teaspoon salt

½ teaspoon chili powder

½ teaspoon smoked paprika

⅛ teaspoon cayenne pepper

½ teaspoon baking powder

2 tablespoons grapeseed oil

**TO MAKE THE CILANTRO SAUCE:** In a small skillet, combine the garlic, olive oil, coriander, and salt. Bring to a simmer over medium heat and cook just until the garlic is fragrant, about 1½ minutes. Remove from the heat and let cool. Transfer the oil mixture to a blender. Add the cilantro, lemon juice, jalapeño, and ¼ cup water and blend until smooth. If necessary, season with additional salt to taste. Set aside.

**TO MAKE THE CREOLE SEASONING:** Combine all the ingredients in a mortar or spice grinder and grind into a fine powder. Store in an airtight container at room temperature for up to 6 months.

**TO MAKE THE FILLING:** Rinse the jackfruit well and drain in a colander. Transfer to a clean kitchen towel and squeeze tightly to remove as much moisture from the jackfruit as possible. Next, sort through the pieces and separate the ones with a tough fibrous center from the rest of the fruit. With a sharp knife, remove the firm core from each piece and discard. With two forks, pull the remaining fruit apart into small pieces. Transfer to the towel and squeeze again to remove any remaining liquid. Set aside.

In a large skillet over medium-low heat, warm the olive oil. Add the onions, celery, and bell pepper and cook, stirring occasionally, until the vegetables begin to soften, about 5 minutes. Stir in the garlic, creole seasoning, salt, tomato paste, and liquid aminos. Cook, stirring constantly until it is aromatic, fully incorporated, darker in color, about 2 minutes. Stir in the vegetable stock and add the reserved jackfruit. Simmer, stirring occasionally, until starting to thicken, about 20 minutes, Season with salt to taste. Remove from heat and set aside.

**TO MAKE THE TAMALES:** In a large bowl, soak the corn husks, weighted down with small plates so they are fully submerged, while you make the tamale masa.

Strain the grits in a fine-mesh colander. In a medium saucepan over medium-low heat, bring the stock to a simmer. Whisk in the grits, cayenne, smoked paprika, chili powder, and salt, turn the burner down to low and cook until liquid is fully absorbed and grits are tender, about 15 to 20 minutes, whisking every 3 minutes or so to prevent grits from sticking. Pour the grits into a bowl, stir in the baking soda and grapeseed oil, transfer to the refrigerator, and let cool completely for 30 minutes. The grits should have a spreadable consistency similar to fresh ricotta.

On a cutting board or clean counter surface, place a piece of corn husk so the longer sides are on your left and right, and the widest side is at the top. Spread ½ cup grits onto the center of the husk, leaving a border around the grits, 2 inches from the sides, 3 inches from the bottom, and 1 inch from the top. Place ¼ cup filling in the center of the grits. Fold the sides of the husk up to meet each other, gently pressing grits together to seal in the filling. Next, fold the sides over together to the right, then fold the bottom of the husk up. Repeat until all the grits have been used.

Fill a steamer stock pot with enough water so that it just reaches the bottom of the steam basket. Bring to a boil, then turn burner down to low, and place tamales on the steam basket standing up, so that the part of the tamale that is open is facing up. Cover and steam for 50 minutes. Check the water level in the pot every 20 minutes or so, adding more if needed. When done, turn the burner off, uncover the pot, and let tamales rest for about 10 minutes.

Serve the tamales with the cilantro sauce on the side.

# POULET YASSA OSSO BUCO

## with Jollof Rice & Maafé

# by Dadisi Olutosin

MAKES 4 SERVINGS

*There's an inextricable connection among cuisines throughout West Africa, and in each of them, you'll find Arabic, European, and Asian influences. Much of this is due to a history of colonization. When I initially came up with the concept for this dish a few years ago, it was for a dinner highlighting African cuisines at the James Beard House in New York. My first question was: which dish could I prepare that would not only highlight traditional West African cuisine but also integrate European cooking techniques and ingredients? One of my favorite dishes to make and eat is the Senegalese dish poulet yassa. I wanted to use elements from both Nigeria and Senegal along with Italian influences for this dish. Poulet yassa is a very humble and flavorful dish that could be considered everyday fare. When combined with maafé, also known as groundnut stew and made from peanuts, and jollof rice (ceebu jën or benachin), a highly contested dish in terms of who makes it best throughout West Africa, it becomes a dish elevated from the everyday. Preparing the chicken in the style of Italian osso buco is what brings everything together and makes this dish a true fusion of West African and European cultures.*

### POACHING LIQUID

4 cups purified or distilled water

2 cups chicken broth

1 teaspoon peppercorns

1 bouquet garni

1 bay leaf

### POULET OSSO BUCO

4 bone-in, skin-on chicken thighs

Butcher's twine

6 cups Herbal Poaching Liquid (see recipe at left)

¼ cup Dijon mustard

2 tablespoons olive oil

2 tablespoons unsalted butter

Salt and pepper to taste

### YASSA

2 tablespoons olive oil

2 large carrots, thinly sliced

2 large Spanish onions, thinly sliced

4 oil-cured olives, pitted

1 teaspoon lemon juice

Salt and pepper to taste

¼ teaspoon cayenne pepper

### JOLLOF RISOTTO

1¼ cups Arborio rice

2 cups reserved Herbal Poaching Liquid, plus more as needed

2 bay leaves

Salt to taste

1 large red bell pepper, finely diced

1 Scotch bonnet chile, stemmed, seeded, and thinly sliced

2 plum tomatoes, finely diced

1 large shallot, finely diced

4 garlic cloves, thinly sliced

1 teaspoon palm oil (may substitute olive oil)

1 tablespoon tomato paste

2 teaspoons smoked paprika

### MAAFÉ

¼ Scotch bonnet chile, stemmed, seeded, and minced

1 teaspoon garlic powder

1 teaspoon onion powder

1 cup low sodium chicken broth, plus more as needed

Sea salt to taste

½ teaspoon ground black pepper

2 tablespoons unsweetened creamy peanut butter

Microgreens or edible flowers for garnish

CONTINUED

**TO MAKE THE POACHING LIQUID:** Combine the water, chicken broth, peppercorns, bouquet garni, and bay leaf in a large stockpot and bring to a simmer.

**TO MAKE THE OSSO BUCO:** Roll the chicken thighs tightly with all the skin folded inward and then tie off with two 8-inch-long pieces of butcher's twine, spaced 1 inch apart, to keep the skin in place around the entirety of the thigh. Once this is done, place the chicken thighs in the poaching liquid, cover, and poach for up to 15 minutes on medium heat. The goal is to ensure the chicken is cooked through while remaining flavorful and tender. After the thighs are cooked, take them out of the poaching liquid. Set them aside and allow them to rest. Strain the poaching liquid and reserve for the jollof.

Once the thighs are cool enough to handle, cut them in half with the bone marrow exposed. If you have a small saw, use it, so that the cut is clean and not jagged; then transfer the thighs to a container and gently apply a good helping of Dijon mustard to the chicken and refrigerate for 30 minutes.

In a sauté pan, add the oil and butter and place over medium-high heat. Add the chicken and sear on all sides until golden brown. Set the pan to the side, season with a little salt and black pepper, and allow to rest for 5 minutes.

**TO MAKE THE YASSA:** Heat the olive oil in a sauté pan and add the carrots and onions. Cook over medium heat until soft and tender; you don't want to caramelize them. While sautéing, add the olives and lemon juice, season with salt, black pepper, and cayenne to taste. Once the vegetables are tender, take off the heat and set aside.

**TO MAKE THE RISOTTO:** In a medium pot, combine the rice, 2 cups of the reserved poaching liquid, bay leaves, and a small amount of salt.

In a medium saucepan, combine the bell pepper, chile, tomatoes, shallot, garlic, oil, tomato paste, and paprika. Stir and simmer until all the ingredients are incorporated. The flavor profile we're going for is smoky and spicy. Once this is done, place the stew in a food processor or blender and blend until completely smooth. Pour the blended stew through a mesh strainer into a bowl. Add the rice to the stew, cover the pot, and simmer until the rice is done. You can add more poaching liquid if needed to achieve a creamy consistency. Once the rice is done, let it rest.

**TO MAKE THE MAAFÉ:** In a medium saucepan, combine the chile, garlic powder, onion powder, and chicken broth and bring to a simmer over medium heat. Season with the salt and pepper. You want the sauce to be savory but not too overwhelming. Once the mixture comes to a simmer, slowly add the peanut butter and stir until completely incorporated. Lower the heat to low and cook until it thickens enough for you to test by streaking your finger across the sauce; it should separate completely without dripping. If the sauce becomes too thick, add more broth but not too much; you don't want it to be soupy.

**TO ASSEMBLE:** This dish is plated in layers. Using a 2-inch ring mold, place the risotto in the center of the mold at about an inch in height, then place a half inch of yassa on top of the risotto. Then drizzle the maafé around the perimeter of the ring mold and garnish the perimeter with the microgreens; use your creativity as to how you'd like it to look. Last but certainly not least, place the chicken osso buco atop the yassa and risotto, still within the ring mold, then gently remove the ring mold and voilà, your dish is finished.

# DOUBLES

## by Isaiah Martinez

MAKES 10 SERVINGS

*Doubles, the most popular street food in Trinidad and Tobago, are my favorite dinner party entrée and hands down, the best version of a naturally vegan taco. I love them because of the warm spices and because their heavy filling can be lightened up when served as a taco or sandwich with a spicy herb sauce or sweet tangy sauce. They're also very easy; you can make the bread and the curry mixture a day ahead and warm up the bread in the oven along with the chickpeas. This recipe is super forgiving and super delicious.*

**BARA**

½ to 1 cup warm water

¼ teaspoon sugar

1 teaspoon dry yeast

2 cups all-purpose flour

½ teaspoon kosher salt

1 teaspoon turmeric powder

½ teaspoon ground cumin

½ teaspoon ground black pepper

Vegetable oil for frying

**FILLING**

2 cups dried chickpeas, soaked overnight

1 tablespoon canola oil

1 onion, diced

3 garlic cloves, crushed

2 tablespoons curry powder

1 tablespoon ground cumin

½ pound small Yukon gold or new potatoes, peeled and quartered

1 small butternut squash, diced

1 Scotch bonnet chile, or 2 to 3 habanero chiles

Salt and pepper to taste

**TAMARIND SAUCE**

¼ cup tamarind paste (fairly easy to find online or in a specialty grocery store)

½ cup jaggery or cane sugar

**CUCUMBER CHUTNEY**

1 tablespoon hot pepper sauce (for authentic taste, buy a Caribbean pepper sauce)

1 cup grated cucumber

Cane vinegar to taste

4 sprigs of shado beni or cilantro, minced well

**TO MAKE THE BARA:** In a medium bowl, mix the water with the sugar and yeast and let it get bubbly, 2 to 5 minutes. In a separate bowl, mix the flour with the seasonings. Fold the flour mixture into the yeast mixture and knead until it's soft and smooth, 2 to 3 minutes. Place the dough in an oiled bowl and set it in a warm area to rise until it's double in size, 1 to 2 hours.

Separate the dough into ten portions, rolling each one into a ball, and then, on a floured surface, flatten each to a ¼-inch thickness.

Fill a cast-iron skillet halfway with the oil. Heat until the oil reaches 350°F on a candy thermometer, then drop in the bara and cook for 1 minute on each side. They will puff up slightly. Remove the baras from the oil with a slotted spoon and place on paper towels.

**TO MAKE THE FILLING:** Rinse the soaked chickpeas well, then drain. Add the chickpeas to a large pot, cover with fresh water, and bring to a boil. Cook the chickpeas until just tender, then drain off most of the liquid, reserving enough to just cover the beans.

In a large deep skillet, add the oil, onion, garlic, curry, and cumin and toast until fragrant on medium-low heat for 5 to 10 minutes, then turn off the heat. Add the potatoes and squash to the skillet, coating the

CONTINUED

## Doubles, continued

ingredients in the curry mixture, then deglaze with the reserved bean liquid, making sure the ingredients are covered. Add the chile (keep whole). Simmer on low heat until all of the ingredients are tender, 30 to 45 minutes. Season with salt and pepper. This filling always tastes better the next day.

**TO MAKE THE SAUCE:** Gently warm the tamarind paste in a saucepan, adding the sugar and ¼ cup water at a time, until the sugar has dissolved, being careful not to reduce it; this shouldn't take longer than 5 minutes.

Cool the sauce and serve at room temperature or cold.

**TO MAKE THE CHUTNEY:** Mix the pepper sauce and cucumber. Season with the vinegar. Add the herbs last and mix well. (Don't add salt because it will break down faster that way.)

**TO SERVE:** Place a bara on a plate, spoon some chickpeas over it, and top with the tamarind sauce and chutney.

# FLAN DE ARROZ CON DULCE

## by Paola Velez

MAKES 8 TO 10 SERVINGS

*To me, rice is one of those life-changing crops. It's a staple found on restaurant menus and home tables across every island in the West Indies. But as popular and ever present as rice is, it is not a crop that was native to the West Indies. The sad reality is the presence of rice in the West Indies is a direct result of colonization and the trans-Atlantic slave trade. This haunting truth broke me, but it also inspired me because rice was one of the ways our descendants found to stay connected to their culture and traditions, even as they were ripped from their homelands and dispersed across the Americas. In the Caribbean, rice is our connection to our ancestors. This flan recipe uses rice pudding as a base to create a decadent, dreamy dessert. You'll get to learn how to make two desserts for one!*

**ARROZ CON DULCE**

2 cups cooked short-grain sticky rice

1 (16-ounce) can unsweetened coconut milk

½ cup firmly packed dark brown sugar

½ teaspoon kosher salt

⅛ teaspoon black pepper

⅛ teaspoon ground nutmeg

¼ teaspoon cinnamon

½ teaspoon vanilla extract

**CARAMELO**

1 cup granulated sugar

¼ cup warm water

**FLAN**

1¾ cups heavy cream

½ cup granulated sugar

3 eggs plus 3 yolks

¼ teaspoon kosher salt

1 teaspoon vanilla bean paste

1 cup Arroz con Dulce

Puffed rice for garnish (optional)

**TO MAKE THE RICE PUDDING:** In a saucepan, combine the rice, coconut milk, brown sugar, salt, pepper, spices, and vanilla and boil on low to medium heat. Stir constantly to make sure that the mixture doesn't stick to the bottom of the pan. Cook for 20 to 30 minutes, until thick. Set aside to cool before making your flan.

**TO MAKE THE CARAMELO:** Pour the sugar and water into an aluminum pot and stir; the mixture should look like wet sand. Over medium-high heat, cook the sugar until it's a light golden brown (310° to 320°F, if using a candy thermometer). This mixture should be *light* golden brown and not dark brown like traditional flan. Pour the caramel into a 9-inch round cake pan and allow it to flow all the way to the sides of the pan. Set aside.

**TO MAKE THE FLAN:** Preheat the oven to 350°F. Pour the cream and sugar into a medium bowl and whisk to incorporate. In a separate bowl, whisk the eggs and yolks, then pour the cream mixture into the whisked eggs in a steady stream until no yolks are visible. Add the salt and vanilla bean paste and whisk to combine. Mix in 1 cup of the cooked rice pudding and whisk again. Pour this mixture into the caramel lined cake pan.

Prepare a water bath (baño maria) by placing the cake pan in a roasting pan filled with enough water to reach halfway up the sides of the pan. Transfer the pan to the oven and bake for 45 minutes or until your flan is set and not jiggly. Remove the pan from the oven and let the flan sit at room temperature until it has cooled slightly. Refrigerate overnight, covered with plastic wrap, before unmolding.

**TO SERVE:** Unmold the flan onto a serving plate. Top the flan with an even layer of puffed rice. Enjoy!

# NANA'S SWEET POTATO PIE

## by Jenné Claiborne

MAKES 2 PIES

*Sweet potato pie is my favorite food. Even as an adult, even as a vegan, even as someone who otherwise seldom enjoys pie. Every bite of sweet potato pie reminds me of my favorite childhood holiday memories—my family around the table, dancing to Christmas and soul music for hours, hilarious holiday mishaps, and the importance we placed on dressing to the nines for dinner in our own dining room. It took me years to perfect this vegan sweet potato pie and to craft something that tastes as delicious as my nana's famous pie. The texture is perfectly creamy yet firm, with just the right amount of sugar and spice, and the crust is just right: flaky and light. Even my own nana approves of this recipe.*

**SIMPLE FLAKY PIECRUST**

2½ cups all-purpose flour

1 teaspoon salt

1 tablespoon sugar

½ cup plus 2 tablespoons well-chilled vegan butter or vegan shortening, cut into ½-inch cubes

½ cup plus 2 to 4 tablespoons ice cold water

**FILLING**

3 cups pureed sweet potato

1 cup pureed butternut squash

½ cup firmly packed light brown sugar

½ cup cane sugar

½ teaspoon salt

⅜ teaspoon ground cloves

2 teaspoons cinnamon

½ teaspoon nutmeg, freshly ground if possible

1 teaspoon vanilla extract

1 cup plain unsweetened soy milk (I use Westsoy brand)

4 tablespoons arrowroot powder

**TO MAKE THE PIECRUST:** In a medium bowl, whisk together the flour, salt, and sugar until well combined. Add the butter with a pastry cutter and mix until it resembles coarse meal, almost pea sized.

Slowly add the ice water, 2 tablespoons at a time. Gently stir with a wooden spoon or your hands. Once the dough begins to hold together, form it into two tight balls. Flatten them a bit (this will make it easier to roll out later) and wrap each one in plastic wrap or parchment paper. Place them in the refrigerator for at least 1 hour.

Remove the chilled pie dough from the fridge. Let it sit on the counter for 10 minutes to soften. Flour a clean, smooth stone surface and place one of the dough balls onto it. If you don't have a stone surface, use parchment paper.

Use a floured rolling pin to roll the dough flat; it should be about ⅛ inch thick and wide enough to comfortably fit over your pie dish with at least 2 inches of overhang.

Fit the dough into a pie dish and up the edges. Roll out the remaining crust. Place the piecrusts in the refrigerator to chill for at least 30 minutes until firm.

**TO MAKE THE FILLING:** Place all of the filling ingredients into a blender and blend until smooth.

**TO ASSEMBLE THE PIES:** Preheat the oven to 350°F. Fill the crusts with the filling and bake for 50 minutes. Remove the pie dishes from the oven, let them cool for at least 30 minutes, then set in the fridge to chill for a few more hours or overnight before serving.

RELIGION, FAITH &
LIBERATION THEOLOGY

# CHAPTER 3
ART BY DEMETRI BROXTON
PHOTOGRAPHED BY DAVID SCHMITZ

# BLACK GOD IN THE GUMBO KITCHEN

## by Michael Otieno Molina

### How She was enslaved:

Pinch in potent sin. Dash faith with doubt.
Bake hate; fold in fear. Grate greed; twist in
toil till every drip of hope is wrung out. Fold
in fear. Bake hate in the funk of 400 years of
kill or be killed. When each dome done risen,
then them hogs can get to eating their own
chitterling fill and belch war into Eden like
the demons of free will . . .

### How She got free:

She gashed his grabbing hand good with
a shiv of wood

to remind him that he had never touched
Her and never would.

She served him White Toade soup seasoned
with crushed up snake heads

and leaves plucked from rash-ivy vines.

In two days time, he swallowed his tongue.

She vanished into the sunk sun.

The whole town was lucky She was done . . .

### How She built a home:

Exacting order.

Everything in its place.

Cast iron pots She restored

hung from the ceiling here.

The oak bed He'd built over there

crowned with a nest of cotton stuffed
with goose down

and lined with fur of hare.

In front of the black stove pipe He dug
up—the one She oiled clean—

were two cedar rocking chairs smelling
like live woods full of wren.

She made one room into a kitchen,
bedroom, den . . .

### How we sang at Her Second Line:

Black God in the Gumbo Kitchen?

Hey, where the gumbo?

Black God in the Gumbo Kitchen!

Hey, with St. Malo!

Black God in the Gumbo Kitchen?

Hey, where can I go free?

Black God in the Gumbo Kitchen!

Hey, in the Plaquemines!

Black God in the Gumbo Kitchen?

Hey, where the jambalaya?

Black God in the Gumbo Kitchen!

Hey, in Atchafalaya!

Black God in the Gumbo Kitchen?

Hey, where we want be?

Black God in the Gumbo Kitchen!

Hey, where we go free!

# FOOD & FAITH

## by Scott Alves Barton, PhD

I have given you, my father, the offering of meat, the heated sacrifice, for many days, for many years:

Food for the gods is as old as humanity. Across the globe, ancient cultures have prepared comestible offerings to their divinities to ensure good harvests, fertility, success on the battlefield—or lasting peace, wealth, and well-being. Ancient Egyptians gained access to the gods and the dead through offerings that kings gave to Osiris, the lord of the underworld. In turn, Osiris might give bread, beer, meat, or fowl to ka, the spirit of the deceased. Devout Babylonian mourners honoring the deity Tammuz wept in grief as they sowed, or interred, seeds "to die" so that they might spring up as corn in another season. Metaphorically, these tears cleansed the mourners and nurtured the seeds. For many cultures, it was not food but blood that was the purest sacrifice, the brio or "the life of every creature is its blood," according to Leviticus 17:14. Failed offerings implied corruption among the leaders or shamans, fostering cause for revolt. If water is life, blood is life's vital force.

Within the many West African and African diasporic religions, clergy and practitioners use food to communicate with their gods: orixás. Offerings are made in honor of the trickster figure Exú/Papa Legba/Elegguá, the interlocutor to all deities. The essence of foodstuffs or sacrificed animals "feeds" the gods as a kind of sacred banquet, with the foods organized according to those favored by each deity. Ideally the deities reciprocate by aiding and ministering to the faithful. Offertory foods and prepared dishes are divided into three meal types: comidas secas (white/cool or vegetal foods), honeyed foods, and colorful/hot (palm oil, blood, and viscera foods). The offerings require specific menu, ingredient, and preparation protocols, as well as a divine response that the meal was well received. Some may see a direct link between these West African food offerings and the Christian Eucharist, which symbolically reveres Christ's sacrifice for humanity, thus

"GROUND MEAT, FINE GROUND MAIZE, COOKED MEAT, GROUND MEAT, FINE GROUND MAIZE. THIS WILL BE THE OFFERING OF MEAT, THIS WILL BE THE OFFERING OF MEAT FOR MANY DAYS, FOR MANY YEARS, FOR MANY DAYS TO COME, FOR MANY YEARS TO COME."

—*The Olson Codex* (Dennis Tedlock, 2017, page xiv)

placing the faithful in God's debt. Abraham's faith was tested when God commanded him to sacrifice his son Isaac on Mount Moriah as a "burnt offering" equivalent to the sacrificial animals cited in Genesis 22, Leviticus 9:1–4, and the Quran 22:36–22:37. Neither their meat nor their blood reaches God. What reaches Him is your righteousness.

Today, wheat breads, communion wafers, wine, fruit, and juice are standard in Abrahamic religious offerings and animal sacrifice is no longer canonical. Likewise, the ritual cleansing of shrines and supplicants, the songs and prayers, and the methods of slaughter that mark foods as blessed and clean or profane and unclean take the place of ceremonial practices, where prayers are whispered into the ears and mouths of the animals to be carried to the ears of the deity, alongside the sounds of ritual sacred drumming, dancing, and prayer songs. . . .

Growing up, my family meals began with one or two sentences sacralizing our food, bringing us under God's care: "Bless this food to our use and us to Thy service," or "For what we are about to receive, may the Lord make us truly thankful. Amen." Early on, when I grabbed for a favored item from the table, I was admonished to wait for grace. I can imagine that Clifford, my agnostic father, mouthed the words or sat silent. In his eyes, saying grace was a facile and "compleat" package for a young person to engage with the sacred—no ritual baths or personal or animal sacrifices.

What I did not appreciate then was that I was also honoring the colonizer, since faith came into my life through my mother's Bajan heritage via the Church of England. Following my family's genealogical trail, the Yoruba-based Candomblé custom of lifting the prepared food and saying *Ajeum* (the food is ready), *Ajeum-bo* (please come and partake in the meal), or *Ẹ wá jẹun, À gba ibire* (come and eat; you will be rewarded) may have been

spoken by my great-grands. And even more questions around this ancestral link arose when my parents visited me at work, where Paula, my Haitian colleague, rose from her desk and bowed and genuflected, placing her head on the floor at my mother's feet, taking everyone aback. Paula and I had never spoken of faith. It was apparent that for her my mom was "sainted," according to Vodun beliefs. And what about my mother's faith? Was it the West African deities overlaid with Christian saints and the Holy Trinity or taken directly from her colonial Episcopal upbringing? A Vodun initiate (whom I did not know as such) saw my mother as a *mambo* (or priestess) in the tradition of Haitian Vodun practice. For someone who never overtly exhibited any reference in her spiritual beliefs to those aligned to West African traditional religions and who was a devout Episcopal, this was revelatory.

For Muslims, saying grace may be bifurcated. When a meal is cooked: *Allahumma barik lana fima razaqtana waqina athaban-nar* (O Allah! Bless the food You have provided us and save us from the punishment of the hellfire). And when beginning to eat: *Bismillahi wa 'ala baraka-tillah* (In the name of God and with God's blessing).

Many Jews begin their blessings by burning a nubbin from the loaf in symbolism of the burnt offering before breaking and sharing bread that blesses God, the gift of food, and the community gathered to share it: *Barukh ata Adonai Eloheinu melekh ha'olam hamotzi lehem min ha'aretz* (Blessed are You, Lord our God, Ruler of the universe, who bring forth bread from the Earth).

The Iroquois mealtime prayer is: *We return thanks to the corn, and to her sisters, the beans and squashes, which give us life. We return thanks to the bushes and trees, which provide us with fruit. We return thanks to the Great Spirit, in who is embodied all goodness, and who directs all things for the good of his children.*

While Zen Buddhists ask:

*First, let us reflect on our own work and the effort of those who brought us this food. Second, let us be aware of the quality of our deeds as we receive this meal. Third, what is most essential is the practice of mindfulness, which helps us to transcend greed, anger, and delusion. Fourth, we appreciate this food, which sustains the good health of our body and mind. Fifth, in order to continue our practice for all beings, we accept this offering.*

Finally, the Bhagavad Gita states:

Aham Vaishvaanaro Bhutva Praaninaam Dehamaashritha Praanaapaana Samaa Yuktaha Pachaamyannam Chatur Vidam

"Becoming the life-fire in the bodies of living beings, mingling with the upward and downward breaths, I digest the four kinds of food" (14th verse, 15th chapter).

Saying grace is a gateway linking food and faith. It opens a world of connections and imagined correspondence that are moderated and adjudicated through gustatory taboos and prohibitions. These are central to many faiths, defined in Deuteronomy, Leviticus, and the initiation rites that honor one's orixás. Showing me what you don't eat reveals your faith.

Food is everywhere in worship and yet rarely attended to in religious scholarship. Commentary on food is usually dismissed as a sign of mere folk naiveté with no impact on doctrine or high worship. The association between food and spirituality has diminished in most Western societies, except as direct victuals of communion. Coke and Pepsi drinkers are usually unaware of the sacred implications kola nuts inscribed in West African and diaspora culture. In northeastern Brazil, the street vendor's black-eyed pea fritter is the favored food of the orixá and Iansã, whether prepared by African-Brazilian Candomblé novitiates, Baianas de Acarajé, Evangelicals, or atheists. Historically, the faithful ritually washed the consecrated ground occupied by their stalls, offering the first cooked fritters to the orixás Exú, Xangô, and Iansã and fried fish to Iemanjã. These are just a few of the customs that link the secular and the sacred in northeastern Brazil.

Here in the United States, we can still "go a piece a way" with our ancestors, by embracing the deities through our inherited culinary culture. Consider Hoppin' John, the black-eyed pea and rice pilaf made for good luck on New Year's Day. Are southerners aware of its roots as a sacred dish? Black-eyed peas are favored foods for Ògún and Ọṣun. Ògún, the orixá of iron and technology, is known for his virtuous morals, nurturing nature, prosperity and his ability to "open doorways" (opportunity). Ọṣun embodies the fresh water that we drink and affects the destinies and fertility of all beings. Reminders like these of a connection to the spiritual world are still present in our food if we attune ourselves to them.

# THE SPIRITUAL ECOLOGY OF BLACK FOOD

## by Leah Penniman

Our ancestral grandmothers in the Dahomey region of West Africa braided seeds and promise into their hair, before being forced into the bowels of trans-Atlantic slave ships. They hid sesame, black-eyed pea, rice, and melon seed in their locks. They stashed away amara kale, gourd, sorrel, basil, tamarind, and kola seed in their tresses. The seed was their most precious legacy, and they believed against odds in a future of tilling and reaping the earth. They believed that their descendants would exist and that we would receive and honor the gift of the seed. With the seed, our grandmothers also braided their esoteric and cultural knowledge. For our ancestors, the earth was not a commodity but a family member. They did not tuck a seed into the ground and expect it to grow without the requisite prayer, offerings, song, and propitiation. They did not see themselves as masters of creation but as humble members of a delicate web of sacred beings.

There are those among their descendants who remember the legacy of that seed and honor the spiritual ecology of this lineage. Through traditional African festivals, rituals, and sacrifice, they work to maintain balance in our world.

The Vodun harvest festival of Manje Yam is one such manifestation of that remembering. Last November, at Soul Fire Farm, an Afro-Indigenous training farm in upstate New York,

friends and family gathered to honor the spirit of the yam. They pulled the bright tubers from the heavy, cool earth to the sound of the drum, washed them gently, and rested them on a white sheet to the east of the gathering space. The community members took turns approaching the yams with reverence, to offer thanks for the good yield and successful harvest. They poured offerings of palm oil, rum, and cornmeal to the yam spirit Njoku, the sovereign of all crops, according to Igbo and Vodun tradition. While pouring, they sang, *"Peye peye wan peye!"* a Kreyol song reminding the community of its duty of reciprocity.

Offerings and prayers complete, they covered the floor completely with banana leaves, representing the surface of the water that the magic boat of the loas crosses to reach the holy city of Ife. Banana leaves were selected because they perpetually self-renew from the roots, mirroring the eternal nature of the divine. Many community members were new to the ritual of Manje Yam, so they shifted with awkward anticipation before taking the mystic journey across the sea to visit the land of their ancestors. One at a time, they saluted the four directions and kissed the ground to the West. Then, each lay down on the banana leaves and rolled themselves toward the yams in the East, the land of Ginen, their ancestral home, where the loa would fortify them spiritually for the year ahead. After the ritual journey back across the Middle Passage to receive the blessings of their ancestors, the community could prepare and eat the new yams.

Since it is forbidden to eat the new yams in bitterness, relatives and friends took time to settle quarrels and make peace. Folks drifted off in pairs to ask one another for forgiveness and renew their commitments to harmony. The Igbo believe that quarreling on a yam farm, throwing a yam in anger, eating yams with others whom you despise, or defecating near the yam desecrates the yam spirit.

In restored peace, they cooked the yam with salted fish and passed the pots of kwi over the heads of those present. The fish represented the bounty of the sea, and the yam represented the bounty of the land. Bellies satisfied and hearts full, they dreamed forward to the Haitian New Year's Day festival of soup joumou and to the spring Souvenance festival to honor the spirits of nature.

Of course, the festivals honoring nature are just one manifestation of the holistic spiritual approach of African traditionalism. Fundamentally, Vodun, Yoruba, Igbo, and related faiths view the Earth as sacred. "The basis of Yoruba religion can be described as a worship of nature," explains Professor Wande Abimbola, the global spokesperson, or Awise Agbaye, of Ifá. In the Yoruba religion, it is believed that divinities, known as orisas, changed themselves into forces of nature, such as thunder, lightning, rain, rivers, oceans, and trees, after they completed their work on the Earth. Oya became the Niger river. Sango became thunder, lightning, and rain. Olokun changed herself to become oceans, while Osun and Yemoja became the Osun and Oogun rivers, respectively. There are at least sixty-four trees whom the Yoruba people worship as divinities. Every hill, mountain, or river of Yorubaland is a divinity. Numerous birds and animals are sacred to the Yoruba people, who

worship or venerate them. The Earth itself is a divinity. We human beings are divine through our *ori* (personal divine nature) and *emi* (divine breath encased in our hearts) that are directly bestowed on humans from Olodumare, the supreme god.

To acknowledge that we as humans are not the most powerful force in nature and to act accordingly is not always easy. For example, when the founders first came to the land that would become Soul Fire Farm, they were very excited about the potential for renovating an existing overgrown swamp into a pond for swimming and irrigation. According to tradition, they were required to ask permission before moving earth and disturbing the ecosystem. So, they used a simple divination tool called obi abata to determine whether the spirits of the land wished for the pond to be dug. The response was a firm no, as revealed by the patterns made by the obi. Year after year they asked, receiving and honoring a no for eight years. On the ninth annual divination, the spirits of the land responded yes, provided that certain safety features were put in place to protect children and also that the residents committed to regular offerings to Nana Buruku, the grandmother of the universe, whose energy dwells in forest wetlands. Soul Fire Farm now has a beautiful pond and remains in a harmonious relationship with the land, which spares her compliant human guests of accidental tragedy, poison ivy, and most biting insects.

In traditional African faiths, reciprocity is the law of the universe. When people honor the divine forces of Nature, they are taken care of. For example, according to Ayo Salami's compilation of verses of *Odu Ifá*, the farm is a place of refuge from violence. The chapter Owonrin Obara teaches, "The warfare in the city does not get to the farm. When everyone heard about Cricket's house on the farm, they paid him homage. He shrieked, 'the warfare in the city did not get to the farm.'" It is possible that in our exile from the red clays of the South to the paved streets of the West and North, Black people left behind a little piece of our souls. Forced by structural racism into overcrowded and under-resourced urban neighborhoods, many of us have grown up with profoundly traumatizing exposure to violence. Ifá invites us to reclaim the gift of rural land as a haven of peace, even as we do the essential work of uprooting violence from our urban communities. Ifá invites us to pick up the bundle of seeds handed to us by our ancestral grandmothers, tuck them into the waiting ground, and reap a harvest of healing and liberation.

# A PLACE ALL OUR OWN

## Uncovering Traditions of Sovereignty in the Black Church

### by Rev. Dr. Heber Brown III

In the waning months of the Civil War, as Union General William T. Sherman led his troops through Georgia and toward South Carolina, the question emerged of what to do with the growing number of formerly enslaved Africans from the state who had now been freed from chattel slavery through military action. The proposed solution would actually come from Black people themselves.

On January 12, 1865, General Sherman and Secretary of War Edwin M. Stanton met with twenty Black Christian ministers and lay leaders to hear their views regarding what to do with those who were newly freed. The spokesperson for the group, Baptist minister Rev. Garrison Frazier of North Carolina, said, "The way we can best take care of ourselves is to have land and turn it and till it by our own labor. . . . We want to be placed on land until we are able to buy it and make it our own." Four days later, General Sherman issued Special Field Order No. 15, which confiscated 400,000 acres of land from Charleston, South Carolina, through Georgia (including the state's sea islands) and ending at the Saint Johns river in Florida. The land was apportioned to Black families in 40-acre segments.

When given the chance to articulate a pathway to communal self-determination, Black Christian ministers did not hesitate to point to land stewardship and ownership as the necessary ingredient. In fact, they not only

## "FORTY ACRES AND A MULE."

wanted land but they also wanted to live in communities of their own that were separate from white people. (Only one of the ministers present at the meeting voiced a desire to live in a racially integrated community.)

Black ministers continued to see the significance of land and the primacy of communal self-determination as a key expression in the practice of the Christian faith, even after that fateful meeting in 1865, even after President Andrew Johnson revoked the order and returned the land to the white owners later that same year.

Throughout the 1900s, various Christian ministries embraced and employed similar approaches. The Peace Mission Movement was one such ministry. Founded by Mother and Father Divine, the International Peace Mission movement came into prominence during the Great Depression, in part, because of their land- and labor-based communes and cooperatives. In 1935, movement member and domestic worker Clara Budds purchased the ministry's first of many farms in upstate New York, opening the door for the ministry to create a food supply chain that stocked the shelves of their cooperatively run businesses throughout the state. As Divine's influence grew, the ministry expanded across the country and followed similar patterns of farming and embracing cooperative economics as part of its religious obligation.

Some thirty years later in Detroit, Michigan, Rev. Albert B. Cleage Jr., inspired in part by the Peace Mission movement, began casting a land-based vision to his congregation—the Shrine of the Black Madonna. A contemporary and close comrade of Malcolm X, Cleage was very much aligned with the Black Power spirit of his era. He outlined the details of his vision in his 1972 publication *Black Christian Nationalism: New Directions for the Black Church*. In this work, he set forth a reinterpretation of Christianity that embraced Jesus as a Black revolutionary, saw Black people as the "chosen people" of the Bible, and forcefully critiqued the Black Church, arguing that it should be restructured into an institutional base for Black Power and for the building of a Black nation within a nation. Farming was central to the plan. He proposed an interregional, land-based solidarity economy that would allow Black people to "distribute goods raised in rural counties of the South on Black farms in northern urban centers, where Black people are now dependent on white merchants for their produce." Citing the systematic ways in which Black people were (and are) being oppressed, Cleage argued that the Black community needed its own system of governance, along with a Christian theology that provided spiritual fuel for the Black Church to be transformed into an institutional engine that would operate in service to the Black Freedom Struggle.

The Peace Mission movement and the Shrine of the Black Madonna are but two of many examples in a long tradition of the kind of Christianity that runs counter to the more popular expressions that the general public is more familiar with.

To those who have had any kind of interaction with or membership in Black Church communities, the preachers and practitioners who flaunt material possessions and individual, capitalist achievements as signs of God's favor are well known. We've watched televangelists rise to celebrity status at the expense of their local communities floundering in state-sponsored squalor. We've been wounded by the ways Black Churches have demonized those who don't believe or don't practice spirituality in ways that precisely align with what Western white theology has dictated since the days of chattel slavery. Perhaps one of the greatest sins committed by this presentation of the Black Church and Christianity is that it obscures other models of practice of this faith. It's this way or the highway. This could not be further from the truth!

Rev. Garrison Frazier (and the nineteen other religious leaders who met with General Sherman), Mother and Father Divine, Rev. Albert B. Cleage Jr. and countless other women, men, and churches stand as hidden monuments to a storied legacy of Christianity: a practice of the way of Jesus that embraces the Black radical tradition and understands God as being on the side of the oppressed. The way they lived out the tenets of this faith provides me—a Black pastor—with a model for ministry that does not require that I leave my Blackness, my spiritual curiosities, or my commitment to the freedom struggle outside the doors of the church.

These ancestors inspired me to establish the Black Church Food Security Network (BCFSN) in 2015 during the Baltimore uprising. That period of social upheaval created an opportunity for us to solve one of our fundamental concerns: access and agency with regard to nutrient-rich food. In the spirit of asset-based community development, BCFSN organizes and mobilizes the existing resources of Black Churches to create Black-led food systems. We help churches start gardens on their land and help them buy in bulk from Black farmers. We also assist with logistics related to the delivery, storage, preparation, and preservation of the food we purchase. We are bypassing the system to help meet one another's needs; co-creating food value chains along the way.

The Black Church community's rich history of land and food-based ministries is propelled by a desire for freedom and communal self-determination. Even if we have forgotten this, it is part of our heritage.

With all of the land, kitchens, vehicles, classrooms, money, and facilities that Black Churches own, it only seems right that we join those outside the church who are actively working to advance Black food and land sovereignty. While the church does not have all the answers, we do have many of the basic ingredients that can serve as a catalyst for some of our wildest and most revolutionary dreams.

# CARE & REST IS OUR LIBERATION

## by Tricia Hersey

I was eight years old the first time I saw the Holy Spirit show up in a body. While holding my breath, Sister May softly fell onto the red carpeted floor of the sanctuary. I still remember the shock of seeing her eyes rolling back in her head, while her light blue ruffled skirt floated above her knees. She began speaking in tongues, while lying on her back on the floor of our small family church outside of Chicago. I wasn't afraid watching her body transform. Instead, I was mesmerized by what was happening around her: the other women circling in all-white clothing, as they placed a crisp white sheet over her legs. The circle clapped wildly while chanting, "Jesus, Jesus, Jesus," over and over again. It went on for at least two hours without any breaks. The energy would rise, until the room was almost buzzing, and then it went back down to a quiet silence. The only thing you could hear was the constant chanting. It was relentless and powerful. Sister May rested on the floor while being cared for like a fragile infant by a circle full of Black women. In and out of consciousness, I witnessed her face shift from tense and determined to relaxed and contented. As the chanting and speaking in tongues stopped, I stood up from my seat to put my entire attention onto Sister May and how she would emerge from under the white sheet and back to her seat across from mine. She appeared shiny to me, as she slithered back to the wooden pews. Her face was covered in tears, as she smiled and hummed the hymn now being sung by the entire congregation. In unison, all forty people in the congregation began to slowly sing, "Yes, Lord. My soul says yes!" I kept my focus on Sister May as I joined in with the singing, slightly disappointed that the spectacle was ending. I felt held and comforted as I sat closer to my mama while she sang loudly.

Power and divinity exist in Black bodies. Our liberation is deeply connected to the portal of healing, a portal we can tap into when we rest. Our bodies are a site of liberation. I began experimenting with the idea of rest as resistance and reparation in 2013. I believe wherever our bodies are we can find rest, ease, and liberation. Part of our decolonizing resides in knowing that rest is our divine right. We are divine. Our bodies are divine, and from this power, we can craft spaces of rest.

James Cone is the father of Black liberation theology, and he is one of the reasons I entered divinity school. His analysis of Christianity from the lens of Black Power and his radical truth telling about the beauty of living in a Black body propelled me to experiment with the philosophy of deliberate and intentional rest. This theology asserts that the liberation of the Black community is God's liberation.

This deep knowing of God seeing me, Sister May, and all of those blessed with the gift of a Black body makes the idea of divine rest sweeter. This calling, illuminated in part by Cone's work, grounds the message of The Nap Ministry.

I'm interested in the interrogation that happens in the private and connected moments in our bodies, in our homes, and in our souls. I am curious about how Black people can tap into the subversive nature of our survival to imagine a New World centered on liberation. We can imagine a world without white supremacy and capitalism. We can daydream our way to freedom. Deep change begins and ends at the root. Deep sleep, rest, and daydreaming produce an alternative world in the midst of our current reality. Rest disrupts and makes space for invention, imagination, and restoration. We can receive an inspired message from our ancestors while we are resting. We can be made new, like Sister May, who got close to the burning flame of the Holy Spirit, her body liberated and anointed by interconnected community care.

By resting, we refuse to donate our bodies to a capitalist system. Rest is resistance because it disrupts and pushes back against the values of capitalism and white supremacy.

Both of these toxic systems refuse to see the inherent divinity in human beings and have commodified and used bodies as tools for production, evil doing, and destruction for centuries. Grind culture has made us all human machines, willing and ready to donate our lives to a capitalist system that thrives by putting profits over people. Rest is resistance because it disrupts the lie that we are not doing enough. It screams, "No, that is a lie. I am enough. I am worthy now and always, because I am here and from God." Watching Sister May and the circle of women holding radical space for divine intervention will always be my guiding star. This is ingrained in my mind as true resistance.

"IN THE ACT OF WORSHIP ITSELF, THE EXPERIENCE OF LIBERATION BECOMES A CONSTITUENT OF THE COMMUNITY'S BEING. IT IS THE POWER OF GOD'S SPIRIT INVADING THE LIVES OF THE PEOPLE, BUILDING THEM UP WHERE THEY ARE TORN DOWN AND PROPPING THEM UP ON EVERY LEANING SIDE."

—James Cone

# LATE FALL SHOEBOX LUNCH

## by Amanda Yee

*In* The Fire Next Time, *Baba Baldwin is quoted as saying, "I remember anyway, church suppers and outing, and later, after I left the church, rent and waistline parties where rage and sorrow sat in darkness and did not stir, and we ate and drank and talked and laughed and danced and forgot all about 'the man.' We had the liquor, we had the chicken, the music, and each other, and had no need to pretend to be what we were not." And that is my prayer as a blessing for this meal: I pray that whether you are coming or going on your journey or whether your journey is physical or simply the places you find in this book, that Jocelyn's cinnamon roll pound cake is so rich and heavy on the tongue, your darkness is too delighted to stir; that while you crunch on a wing or a thigh of the buttermilk fried chicken, music graces your ears, causing you to exclaim: "Turn that up! That's my jam!" as you sway to your tunes. I pray that the sun shining on your face from a window half rolled down causes you to break into laughter as you dunk persimmon spears into fluffy goat cheese dip; and that if only for a moment, the heat from these inferno hot ranch kale chips distracts you from "the man." I pray that here, at this meal, you only need to be, because you know that here, on this journey, your being is the only thing that really matters. Be sustained. Be sustained. Be sustained. Amen.*

**NOTE:** If you are *not* pairing the items together as a shoebox meal, you may want to consider adding some sort of chile flakes to the goat cheese dip—it will bring the snack to a whole nutha level. However, if you are pairing everything together, the inferno hot kale chips are so spicy, they may knock the taste out of yo' mouth or slap you into next Tuesday, or whatever else your momma or grandmomma and them used to say. Alls I'm saying is, if you don't want to be cryin' real tears on your road trip ('cause you wasn't ready), proceed cautiously with spice everywhere else! Be careful when handling the Carolina Reaper Powder; it can cause severe skin and eye irritation!

"Twentieth-century African American travel culture was profoundly shaped by the historical oppression of Black communities' rights to free movement. From the 1890s until 1965, Jim Crow segregation laws legitimized the isolation of public spaces, schools, transportation, restrooms, and restaurants exclusively for white people. 'The vast majority of the country was composed of white spaces where black people were forbidden or unwelcome,' Dr. Gretchen Sorin wrote in her article, 'The Negro Travelers Green Book.' For the Black traveler, accessing food along journeys was nearly impossible. In response, Black women would arm Black travelers with 'shoebox lunches.' At times faceless and unsung, these women—family members, church attendees, or businesswomen—would find ways, both legal and illegal (as hawkers) to cook delicious meals with limited resources, making a way out of no way." —Bryant Terry

# BUTTERMILK FRIED CHICKEN

MAKES 4 SERVINGS

**CHICKEN**

4 cups buttermilk

4 or 5 dashes of hot sauce (page 66), or store bought

1 tablespoon garlic powder

2 tablespoons Old Bay Seasoning

2½ to 3 pounds whole organic chicken, cut into 8 pieces

**DRY MIX**

1½ cups cornstarch

1½ cups all-purpose flour

3 tablespoons garlic powder

2 tablespoons dry mustard

⅓ cup Old Bay Seasoning

1 teaspoon salt, plus more as needed

½ teaspoon pepper, plus more as needed

8 cups canola oil for frying

**TO PREPARE THE CHICKEN:** In a large container, combine the buttermilk with the hot sauce and spices and stir until well combined. Once the buttermilk and spices are incorporated, fully submerge the chicken pieces in the buttermilk. Place the lid on the container and allow the chicken to marinate in the refrigerator for at least 8 hours, but 12 to 18 hours is ideal. (After 24 hours, the chicken will fry up with dark spots that look burned.) Pull the chicken out of the refrigerator at least 1 hour before frying and allow to reach room temperature.

**TO MAKE THE DRY MIX:** In a large bowl or large brown paper bag, combine the cornstarch, flour, and spices. Be sure to taste the flour mixture and adjust accordingly. If it needs a little oomph, add more Old Bay or more salt and pepper. The chicken will lose some of its flavor when being fried, so it's okay if the flour mixture tastes a little strong.

**TO FRY THE CHICKEN:** When you are ready to fry the chicken, place a rack over a baking sheet lined with parchment paper, so there is a gap between the two. Place the rack and the baking sheet on the same middle rack in the oven and preheat the oven to 300°F.

In a large heavy-bottomed cast-iron skillet or pot, pour in the oil until the pot is three-quarters filled. Heat the oil on medium-high heat, until it reaches a temperature of 375°F on an instant-read thermometer, then reduce the heat to medium.

While the oil is heating, remove a piece of chicken from the buttermilk and dredge in the flour mixture. If using a brown paper bag, shake vigorously until the chicken is well coated. Set the pieces aside on a rack lined with parchment paper. Repeat this process until all the chicken is generously coated. Work quickly, since the chicken will absorb the flour if it sits too long. Be sure to check in the nooks and crannies of the chicken pieces to make sure they are well floured. (This will ensure that the chicken will be crispy everywhere.)

Once the oil reaches temperature and all of the chicken pieces are coated, place the chicken, one or two pieces at a time, in the hot oil. Start with the thickest pieces first, since they will take longer to cook. Go from breasts to thighs, from thighs to drumsticks; and from drumsticks to wings.

Fry for 3 to 4 minutes on each side before flipping. Once the chicken skin is a golden brown on all sides, 6 to 8 minutes, use a pair of tongs to place the pieces in the oven on top of the rack. Allow to finish in the oven, while you fry the other pieces, about 15 minutes. The wings should be ready straight out of the fryer.

The chicken should reach an internal temperature of 165°F on an instant-read thermometer at the thickest part, and the juices should run clear.

If packing for a picnic or a road trip, allow the chicken to reach room temperature before storing so that it maintains its crispiness. Chicken should be packed loosely in a container lined with paper towels and may be refrigerated overnight.

# PICKLED PERSIMMON SPEARS

## with Honey, Walnut & Goat Cheese Dip

MAKES 4 SERVINGS

2 large firm Fuyu persimmons, peeled

1⅓ cups apple cider vinegar

½ cup water

⅓ cup firmly packed brown sugar

1 tablespoon kosher salt

2 tablespoons bourbon

½ vanilla bean

1 tablespoon green peppercorns

2 cardamom pods

2 thick orange peel slices

3 or 4 sprigs of thyme

1 garlic clove

**HONEY, WALNUT, AND GOAT CHEESE DIP**

16 ounces goat cheese, softened

½ cup heavy whipping cream

⅓ cup toasted walnuts, crushed

1½ tablespoons ground sage

⅓ cup honey

Salt and pepper to taste

**TO PREPARE THE PERSIMMONS:** Cut off the tops and cut into five or six spears or wedges. Set aside.

In a medium saucepan on medium-high heat, combine the vinegar, water, brown sugar, and salt. Bring to a rolling boil, 5 to 10 minutes. The liquid should reduce by a third.

While the mixture is boiling, begin to pack a sanitized 16-ounce Mason jar with the bourbon, vanilla pod, peppercorns, cardamom, orange peel, thyme, and garlic. Stack the ingredients around the jar, as well as on the bottom of the jar. For example, the vanilla pod and thyme sprigs can stand upright around the jar, while the peppercorns can just be placed on the bottom of the jar.

Once the jar is packed, stack the persimmon spears or wedges in the jar.

Pour the vinegar mixture over the persimmons, until the liquid reaches the brim. Screw on the lid and refrigerate overnight. If the persimmons are sticking up past the liquid, fold a piece of parchment paper into a square and stick it on top of the persimmons before screwing on the lid; this should keep them submerged.

The pickles will be ready to use the next day and are good for up to 2 weeks.

**TO MAKE THE DIP:** In a stand mixer or in a medium-size bowl and hand mixer, combine the goat cheese, cream, walnuts, sage, and honey. Whip on medium-high speed, until the mixture is well incorporated and fluffy, 3 to 5 minutes. Season with salt and pepper.

Store in a sealed container.

# INFERNO HOT KALE CHIPS

1 pound kale, preferably lacinato, washed, thoroughly dried, and stems removed

2 tablespoons avocado oil

½ teaspoon kosher salt

¼ cup raw cashews

3 tablespoons brewer's yeast

3 tablespoons dried milk powder

1½ tablespoons dried dill

1 tablespoon dried chives

1 tablespoon dried parsley

1½ teaspoons garlic powder

1 tablespoon onion powder

2 to 5 tablespoons Carolina Reaper Chili Powder or the hottest chile powder you can find

2 tablespoons apple cider vinegar

Preheat the oven to 300°F. Line two baking sheets with parchment paper and set aside.

Tear the kale into medium- and large-size pieces. A large piece should fit in the palm of your hand; a medium piece is a little smaller than that.

In a large bowl, toss the kale in the oil and salt, until the leaves are a bit less fibrous, about 3 minutes.

In a food processor, add the cashews and pulse, until the cashews are like coarse sand, then set aside.

In the empty food processor, add the brewer's yeast, milk powder, and spices and pulse until the mixture is of an even consistency. Wear a mask while you are doing this, since the spice will kick you in the face. Also, you may wish to open a window.

Sprinkle the vinegar over the softened kale and toss gently. Using a pair of food-safe gloves, sprinkle the spice mixture over the kale and follow with the cashew dust, making sure to coat all sides. (Be careful not to touch any parts of your body, until you have thoroughly discarded the gloves and washed your hands.)

Place the chips on the prepared baking sheets and bake in the oven for 5 to 6 minutes before flipping and baking on the other side for an additional 5 to 6 minutes.

When the chips are done, they should be crispy but still retain their shape. Allow to cool before storing.

To store, place uncooked rice in the bottom of a sealed container. Loosely place the chips on top of the dry rice and cover with the lid. Alternatively, place the chips loosely in a paper bag and fold the bag tightly shut. The chips will stay good for about a day.

# JOCELYN'S CINNAMON ROLL POUND CAKE

## by Jocelyn Delk Adams

MAKES 12 TO 16 SERVINGS

*When my mama was growing up in Winona, Mississippi, she long awaited the day when she would be old enough to take the Winona train all the way to Chicago to visit her favorite auntie. When she came of age in high school, her parents, my Big Mama and Big Daddy, finally gave their approval. In preparation for her travels, Big Mama would make my mama a special lunch sack of fresh fried chicken and pound cake. These lunches would make those long trips feel more like home. You see, Big Mama bought crates of live chickens from her friend's hatchery, then she would wring the chicken necks, and finally drop them in scalding water so she could pluck the feathers before frying them to golden brown perfection. And as if that wasn't special enough, the dessert was even more memorable. Big Mama's pound cakes were famous in Winona. There would be an endless stream of doorbell rings from fellow neighbors asking her to bake them one. Made with the simplest of ingredients, each bite melted from its tender, sweet, buttery deliciousness.*

*One of her favorite cakes to bake was a moist sour cream pound cake. My cinnamon roll cake is a fun twist on that classic. It starts with a wonderfully balanced cake batter that's swirled with a brown sugar–cinnamon spice. Drizzled with a cream cheese icing, it will remind you of those pillowy soft and fluffy cinnamon rolls you may have indulged in for breakfast.*

### CAKE

1½ cups (3 sticks) unsalted butter, at room temperature

2½ cups granulated sugar

6 large eggs, at room temperature

3 cups cake flour, sifted

1 teaspoon salt

½ teaspoon baking soda

1 cup sour cream, at room temperature

2 tablespoons vegetable oil

1 tablespoon vanilla extract

### CINNAMON SWIRL

⅓ cup unsalted butter, melted

⅓ cup firmly packed light brown sugar

1 tablespoon all-purpose flour

1½ teaspoons cinnamon

1 teaspoon vanilla extract

### ICING

2 ounces cream cheese, at room temperature

2 tablespoons unsalted butter, at room temperature

1½ cups confectioners' sugar

¼ cup milk (can be whole, 2%, or even refrigerated coconut)

1 teaspoon vanilla extract

**TO MAKE THE CAKE:** Preheat the oven to 350°F. Liberally prepare a 12-cup Bundt pan with nonstick baking spray or liberally butter and flour the inside of the pan. Set aside.

In the bowl of a stand mixer fitted with the whisk attachment, beat the butter for 1 minute on high speed. Slowly add the sugar and cream for an additional 5 minutes, until very pale yellow and fluffy. Add the eggs one at a time, combining well after each addition and scraping down the sides and bottom of the bowl as needed. Turn down the mixer to its lowest speed, scrape down the bowl, and slowly add the flour in two batches. Add the salt and baking soda. Add the sour cream, oil, and vanilla. Scrape down the sides and bottom of the bowl and mix the batter until

CONTINUED

just combined. Be careful not to over mix. Set the batter aside.

**TO MAKE THE CINNAMON SWIRL:** In a small bowl, whisk together all the ingredients until well combined. Set aside.

**TO BAKE THE CAKE:** Pour one-third of the batter into the prepared pan. Drizzle half of the cinnamon swirl over the batter. Using a butter knife or skewer, swirl the mixture through the cake batter. Repeat with the rest of the cake batter and cinnamon swirl. Top with the remaining batter. Bake for 85 to 95 minutes on the upper-middle rack, or until a toothpick inserted into the center of the cake comes out mostly clean. Let cool in the pan on a wire rack for 10 minutes, then invert onto a serving plate. Let cool to room temperature. Lightly cover the cake with tinfoil or plastic wrap so it does not dry out.

**TO MAKE THE ICING:** Clean the mixer bowl and whisk attachment. Beat the cream cheese and butter for 2 minutes on medium-high speed. Turn down the mixer speed and carefully add the confectioners' sugar in two batches, scraping down the sides and bottom of the bowl as needed. Once the sugar is fully incorporated, turn up the mixer to medium-high speed and add the milk and vanilla. Beat until the icing is smooth and pourable. Drizzle the icing over the cooled pound cake.

Keep, covered, in the refrigerator; bring to room temperature before serving.

# SHOEBOX ASSEMBLY

### MAKES 4 SHOEBOXES

**4 shoeboxes**

**4 hankies filled with salt, pepper, and 2 toothpicks each**

**Parchment paper**

**Twine**

**4 (4-ounce) Mason jars with lids**

**4 (6-ounce) Mason jars with lids**

**4 small brown paper bags**

**TO ASSEMBLE YOUR SHOEBOXES:** Line each box with one or two pieces of parchment paper. Place a hankie of salt and pepper in the corner of each box.

If you'd like to go old school, use parchment paper to wrap one or two pieces of chicken and tie with twine. Place the chicken in the center of each box.

Evenly distribute the goat cheese dip among four 4-ounce Mason jars. Screw on the lids, wipe the sides, and place one container in a corner of each shoebox. Repeat the same steps for the persimmon spears but place them in the 6-ounce jars. Place the spears next to the dip.

Wrap four pieces of the cinnamon roll pound cake (page 111) in individual pieces of parchment, tie with twine, and gently place in an empty space in each box.

Place the kale chips in small brown paper bags and gently place in any open space; keep away from the chicken so the oil doesn't rub off on them.

Write a sweet note to your loved ones on the inside of each box lid, place the lids on the boxes, and secure with twine.

Enjoy your journey!

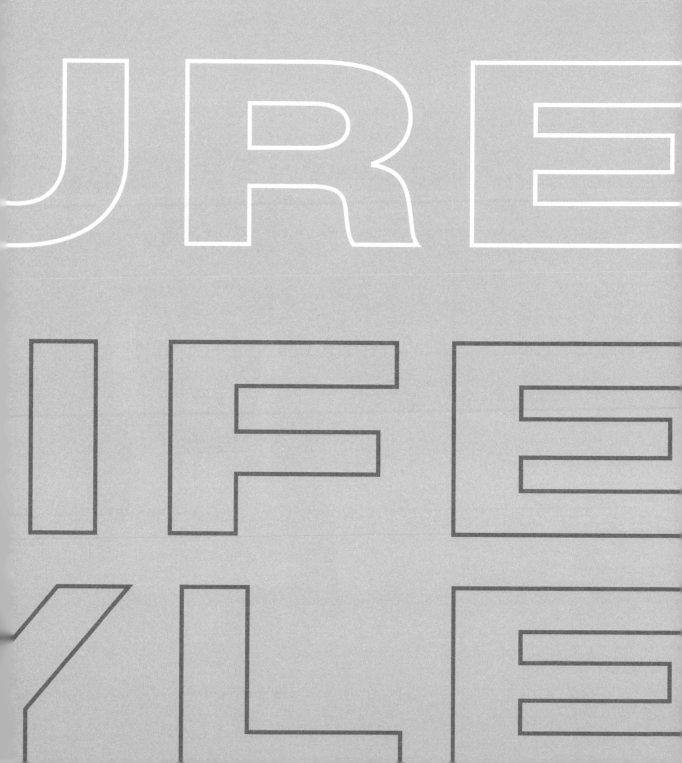

INTERMISSION
ART BY JADE PURPLE BROWN

# TAKE FIVE

## by Osayi Endolyn

I had just completed my junior year in high school in 1999, when Marie St. Louis died. She was mother to my uncle Marc by marriage. I didn't know her well. But you didn't have to know Marie intimately for her to be memorable. Boston-born with heritage going back to Jamaica, she was a fiercely loyal New Yorker with high-octane energy and a spirited turn of phrase to match. A founding member and executive for Festival Productions Inc., the groundbreaking live-concert producer launched in New York in 1954, she booked talents like Ella Fitzgerald and Duke Ellington. Over nearly four decades, she shaped and executed the grand jazz concert experience now well-known to so many fans of live music.

I remember Marie as lithe, sophisticated, intently curious, and unable to suffer fools. She had a beautiful irreverence about her that I sensed could sting those close to her at times. But her willingness to live unconcerned with convention was apparent even to me.

One Christmas, when she came to visit me in Los Angeles, she gifted me with a GM-logo, click-in leather seatbelt that had been refashioned as a belt. The band of the belt was studded with twenty-two beer bottle caps: Newcastle, Bud Light, Miller, Foster, you name it. Of course, she'd found it in some cute vintage spot in a part of New York City this Southern California girl knew nothing about (by that point I had only been to the city once). "It's so edgy!" she exclaimed. Every other adult in the room was silent. I had no interest in underage drinking; I was that kind of straight-A school nerd. But, of course, I loved the belt

and, of course, I wore it everywhere, and, of course, I loved the implication that I might know something about the brands around my waist. Maybe the student of the month could be edgy, too! I loved that Marie saw me that way or at least thought passively enough about my potential to project such coolness. The belt hangs on a nail in my Brooklyn kitchen today, and I believe Marie, as a woman who took great care with her fashion and beauty, would be thrilled that the thing still fits.

It might have been that same Christmas visit, when Marie talked about going to Vietnam. She was an avid and intrepid traveler, in part because of her work, but more so, I believe, because she was the kind of lady who didn't want to be *told* anything about the world. She wanted to see the world and decide for herself. Then, trust, she'd let you know what was so. The mind blurs, but I recall that she had recently undergone treatment for the cancer that would eventually overpower her thin frame. There were murmurs about whether she should go in her state of health. "What are you going to do in Vietnam?" someone asked.

"Walk," she said, flatly. If there was a romantic tone to her reply, I don't remember it. A few years later her words would jump out at me.

I never knew Marie's home in Chelsea, but I got a sense of the world she created for herself because of the worlds she helped define elsewhere. Festival Productions originated with the iconic Newport Jazz Festival, and the team developed countless programs like the New Orleans Jazz and Heritage Festival and the heralded Playboy Jazz Festival, hosted at the Hollywood Bowl in Los Angeles. My uncle Marc spent some of his New York–based youth working as a production assistant, learning the deft machinations of how talent actually gets on stage ready to satisfy an audience of thousands: it takes a village. Today, he's one of the music industry's most sought-after tour managers. And it's because of this legacy that for several summers between high school and college, I found myself running around in a sweaty staff T-shirt with headphones and a walkie-talkie, working as a PA for the West Coast arm of Festival Productions at the Playboy Jazz Festival.

Among many ad hoc requests, my job was to wait behind the artist check-in for talent to arrive, then usher these acts to their dressing rooms. At their call time, I was one of a team of people making sure everyone who was supposed to be on stage was on stage. Playboy, as the two-day June festival is colloquially referred to, thanks to a decades-long sponsorship and Hugh Hefner's affection for big social affairs, and let's tell the truth, all things Black culture, is a unique outdoor concert in that acts perform on a revolving stage.

It remains a beauty to witness because this way, the music never stops. An oft-quoted jazz adage I learned from my aunt Patrice Rushen (a trailblazing pianist and composer, Marc's wife, and Marie's daughter-in-law) goes like this: "The music never stops, you just have to stop playing."

So, while Wynton Marsalis and the Lincoln Center Jazz Orchestra are killing it for the crowd, the stage crew on the flip side of the iconic bunny partition is setting up for Nancy Wilson or Chick Corea. The acts play off as the stage rotates, and boom, there'd be Etta James, Roy Hargrove, Herbie Hancock, Arturo Sandoval, or Patrice and friends cueing up their first tune as the rotating stage comes to a stop. The day begins at 2:00 p.m. and goes until about 11:00 p.m., or whenever the noise ordinance kicks in for the folks in Hollywood Hills. The Hollywood Bowl seats about seventeen thousand. Up top, there's the grassy space, where it's effectively general admission. Regular seats cascade around the rest of the amphitheater, until you get closer to the stage where there are the boxes—cordoned-off sections where small groups can sit together. This is *the move* for people in the know and with the cash, who want to make a full day or weekend of drinking, dancing, eating, and watching the world's best jazz artists. Bring a picnic or have the Bowl's catering partner serve you, and do absolutely nothing but enjoy your goddamn self.

Backstage, where I spent most of my time, and from the side view of the stage and box seats where credentialed staff could peek, it was a who's who of Hollywood, especially Black Hollywood. I spent as much time watching people relax and socialize as I did hustling down to the basement dressing rooms or across the venue to trailers, looking for a drummer or trumpeter or bassist. Artist check-in, artist ushering, being a teenage PA prone to distractions as I could sometimes be—was a more political affair than one might expect. Nearly everyone wants you to already know who they are—musician, spouse of the musician, manager or agent or lawyer to the musician, celebrity guest or friend or significant other of the musician. It means balancing deference and respect to young folks with too much bravado just starting out and not being too precious with older acts who, as Sammy Davis Jr. sings in "Mr. Bojangles," are at the top of their game, but who really knows for how much longer. It is impossible for me to think about Marie without also considering such big names and buoyant scenes and the entertainers and industry vets who knew her fondly. She carried the aura of a woman, a Black woman, who knew she had helped create the very thing you presumed had always existed. Black culture, in all its expressions, comes from Black people. And while jazz festivals around the world can be stunning in their multicultural representation, I understood then that such developments were rooted in Black music, Black sound, and Black style.

In 2001, I took my first trip to Paris. Then a sophomore at UCLA, I had been studying French since I was thirteen, and was thrilled for the month-long visit. I was traveling alone but would connect with friends from school at various points during my stay. As I rode the train into the city from Charles de Gaulle airport, I noticed something about the France I was seeing compared to the one I'd been taught about during the previous six years. I saw Black people just like me every-where. I saw brown people of Arab descent everywhere, in the same quantities that I saw Latino people everywhere in LA. These folks were out here! One of the best meals I had was bùn thit nu'óng and cha gio at a Vietnamese restaurant in the Marais. I was reminded that just as the United States had benefited from Vietnamese immigration, France had long reaped the pleasures of that culture as well. At nineteen years old, I was stunned that the France that had been shaped for me over years of conjugation exercises and cultural study had been so convincingly white, so full of pastry and fromage. And the whole time, I realized, there had also been Africa, and Asia, and mafe, and tagine, and dumplings. I couldn't help but stroll everywhere, often simply staring at the people. And I ate.

I would wake in the morning and walk from the Marais, where I had holed up in a friend's apartment, to Montmartre, or toward the Arc de Triomphe, or out by Place de la Bastille. I had enough pain au chocolat to match my weight. I learned what steak tartare was. And I befriended this guy Jamal, who worked in a currency exchange booth. He and his girlfriend invited me to their home, where they served crepes and Moroccan mint tea, traditionally steeped, sweetened, and then poured into narrow gold-accented glasses. I even encoun-tered an expatriate jazz musician named Sulaiman Hakim, who I soon discovered had gone to high school with Patrice in Watts. He immediately took me under his wing as an uncle, and with that paternal affection, I saw any hope of a fling with the man who'd brought me to the jazz club that night instantly vanish (*dommage*). When I returned to California the next month, I sat down with my grandmother Ruth, who wanted to hear about my first solo trip abroad. I began to recount my experiences, but as we talked, she seemed to be waiting for something.

"You went to the Louvre?" she asked. I shook my head no. Grandma, a serious collector of art on her own international travels, expressed dismay. "You didn't go to the *Louvre*? Osayi!"

"Grandma," I began. I tried to explain that the France in book pages and in cinema was not the one that I observed. I had not avoided learning about history, much of which was looted from the very cultures whose food and hospitality I had enjoyed. It was that I was getting a more accurate lesson than anything I could have acquired from a whitewashed academic curriculum.

"What all did you do then?" Grandma asked in this way where she'd tuck her chin downward and drop her voice in playful seriousness. She understood me.

In that moment, I thought of Marie. I thought of the occasions where I had seen Black people in my family, and Black people at the Playboy Jazz Festival, and Black people in Los Angeles and Paris dressed up maybe, resplendent always, determined only in their commitment to ease and joy. I imagined Marie strolling while in Vietnam, her curiosity never sated. I didn't know then I, too, would travel the world, blur-ring the line between work and pleasure, often alone, feeling free.

I smiled at Grandma and said, "I walked."

# BEYOND THE TREE LINE

## by Rashad Frazier

For too long, Black people have been told, explicitly and subliminally, where we do and do not belong. Even outside of man-made walls, natural landmarks have been exploited and declared to be political and social boundaries in order to exclude "others." "Others," meaning nonwhite folks. Although there are laws prohibiting things like segregation, even in the 2020s, there is still a general fear among many Black folks of exploring the outdoors past their front porch. A fear often expressed as, "We just don't do that." A fear manifested in declaring that hiking, camping, and mountain climbing are "white folks' stuff."

I don't blame my people for their anxiety, because I understand its source, but I do plan to inspire us all to overcome them. My latest venture, Camp Yoshi, is one way I mix my love of all things food and nature. Through exhilarating guided outdoor adventures and thoughtfully curated culinary experiences, I aim to democratize and diversify access to Mother Nature. In times like these, we need the opportunity to experience her beauty and benefit from her healing powers. I've designed Camp Yoshi to be a catalyst for building this much-needed bond between Black people and the outdoors.

I was lucky enough to begin forming a relationship with the outdoors early on. Growing up in North Carolina in the '80s, I vividly remember my dad and uncle speeding through the waters of Lake Norman in a brand-new Seacraft, a cold beverage in hand, the Isley Brothers blasting, and a pistol next to the steering wheel. Back then, my understanding of connecting with nature came from those two Black men and from the rest of my family, who were living their best lives on that lake, which was roughly twenty-five miles from Charlotte. Since 1986, summers there primed my brother and me for future adventure in a way we couldn't have realized at the time.

Although we were fortunate enough to have adults in our life who exposed us to nature beyond our backyard and local parks, my exploration as a youngin' had its limits. I was made aware from early on that the tree line of the forest, just past our side of the lake, was where we were unwelcome, unsafe, and therefore not allowed to go. This human-made social boundary set in us a fear that was ever-present, and that was its purpose. By the '80s, this boundary was no longer reinforced by law, but the legacy of Black trauma at the hands of white folks still echoed throughout our community. Micro-aggressions and threatening behavior were enough to keep us inside our respective communities and away from those kinds of invisible lines.

Even now, my family back home has bouts of anxiety whenever we embark on an outdoor excursion. A detailed itinerary, emailed beforehand, that outlines all locations (so they can be Googled, making their histories and demographics known ahead of time), is required to ease their minds enough to feel comfortable venturing outside of city lines and into the wilderness. (I assume this experience is much less common for white folks.) Many times, their only living threats when going out into nature are wild animals and other creatures that bite and sting. As long as they know they aren't on anyone's hit list, their concern for being shot and even hanged (yes, even today), should be little to none—as it should be for everyone.

I got to see beyond the tree line when I was seventeen and going into my senior year of high school. A local nonprofit had awarded me and ten other Black teens an opportunity to see America via a cross-country adventure—exploring some of America's most prized national parks and monuments. It took me another fifteen years before I could connect with nature like that again.

I would've sworn "Reunited" by Peaches & Herb was playing in the background the next time I got out into the wilderness. I was in my early thirties, and my brother had invited me to attend Overland Expo in Asheville, North Carolina. Completely boundless and by far the most liberated I'd felt in the outdoors up to that point, that trip was the first of what would become a yearly tradition. The feelings of freedom and joy, matched with the vastness of the places we'd visited gave us confidence. A newfound fearlessness and a sense of belonging had finally entered our psyches and replaced the anxieties that had been harboring there for so long. I didn't have the words for it at the time, but the incomprehensible sensation we had on that trip was the feeling of breaking generational trauma. It became clear and undeniable to me from that point on that the wilderness makes you better.

I lived in New York City for twelve long years, but in 2019, I moved to Portland, Oregon, a city with so much access to natural sites that it feels like a real-life Shangri-la. And that was

a wrap. That knowledge, that the wilderness is crucial to my well-being, was reinforced in my mind—over and over again. I've never looked back.

As a father and as a Black man, it's more important than ever that I know how to recharge: how to heal my mind, body, and spirit—all of which are tested and tried on the daily. Many of us live with precepts of what self-care looks like, but these camping trips and outings help me reshape what healing and resetting feels like. I return a better man. A better husband. Hell! I return feeling like a superhuman badass ready to take on the world, despite knowing good 'n' well the odds are still stacked against me at every turn. This is a fact, which I can't forget but one I cannot allow to hang over my head, blocking my light. Fortunately, through these trips to the outdoors, I've learned that my battery is solar-powered. In order to recharge, I must get out and let natural light shine on me.

Many would say 2020 and beyond has been a long series of disappointments, but when I flip my perspective a bit, I see it's also been a beautiful and rare opportunity to get outside and explore beyond our own backyards. Covid has forced us all to rethink travel and getting away. Where do we go to recharge our batteries? Where do we go to heal? Where do we go to disconnect so we can reconnect? For me, I found my strength out in the sun with my brother years ago, and I want to be a plug for other Black folks to discover that same power.

# BEAUTIFUL COFFEE TO THE PEOPLE

## by Summer Sewell

Keba Konte, the founder of Oakland-based Red Bay Coffee, says specialty coffee is seen as "white" and therefore not for the Black community. But it should be ours. "All coffee plants have Ethiopian DNA. This didn't start in Seattle. It didn't start in Europe with espresso. It started in Africa," Keba says. "You can't have espresso without coffee."

The coffee plant originated centuries ago in a region called Kaffa, on the plateaus of southwestern Ethiopia, where coffee still grows wild today. In Ethiopia, coffee is central to the culture—used in wedding ceremonies and stored in homes as green beans, then roasted, ground, and eventually poured for guests.

"I've been trying to spark a Black coffee movement, and in order to do that, we had to remind Black people, 'Yo, this is your shit,'" Keba says. "You should claim it because people are making billions on it. It's a whole industry. I want to inspire Black people to participate and claim coffee as their inheritance because it is our heritage. That's the opportunity and the struggle."

Oakland—birthplace of the Black Panther Party in the 60s, now an epicenter of mass gentrification—is the headquarters of Red Bay's café and roastery. Red Bay, one of only a few Black-owned coffee companies in the United States, also sells coffee via retail throughout the Bay Area and cruises a Mercedes Sprinter van converted into a coffee bar to locations in San Francisco and Oakland. Around the corner from the roastery is their newest addition: a three-story former bank building from 1930 that includes a coffee bar and lab. A local muralist painted one side of the building to read: "Beautiful Coffee to the People," which is Red Bay's motto.

Beautiful coffee starts with fair conditions and livable wages—that's a given, Keba says. But beyond that, beautiful coffee means welcoming in those who have traditionally been left out of enjoying it. To make sure it is clear that the doors of Red Bay's cafés are open to anyone, but especially to Black people and Oakland natives who have watched their neighborhoods become occupied by places that aren't welcoming of them, Red Bay's roastery also serves as a venue featuring music and artists that resonate with pre-gentrified Oakland. Events there often reach capacity.

"We really flex our culture in our community in such a powerful way," Keba says. "People show up who didn't drink coffee before. It is a way to make coffee culturally relevant. We turned a lot of people on to coffee who weren't drinking it at all or who were drinking crappy commercial coffee. That's the impact of that public space."

Keba creates a space where Black people can show up and feel as if it was built for them, unapologetically. "Nappy hair, just lounging. They don't have to contort themselves to be in there," Keba says. The welcome goes beyond the expected photo of a farmer holding coffee beans in cupped brown hands. Black people see their reflections at Red Bay in the person roasting the coffee, the person pouring it, the person ringing up the guests, and the person contemplating the living wall of plants in the shape of Africa (see pages 20–21) as they wait for their charcoal latte. This is all minus any pretense or expectation. Keba never requires anyone to buy coffee in order to be there. He's saying: "Black people, this leisure, the luxury of waiting for a pour-over, the smooth body and fruity notes of the King's Prize blend from Ethiopia—this is all for you."

It is working. Fifty percent of Red Bay's café clientele are Black. And throughout the country, young people of color are responsible for the growth in consumption of specialty coffee. Black people of all ages have closed the gap over the last decade, finally catching up after decades of consuming less coffee than all other groups; they are now consuming as much specialty coffee as other people of color, and more than whites. This kind of uptick keeps the supply chain, which starts with Brown and Black farmers—or what Keba has renamed the "value stream to decolonize the process"—healthy.

Keba says there are people in the specialty coffee industry who assume he's not really an expert. But he's put in the legwork, from his first endeavor, a popular coffee shop called Guerilla Café that opened in 2006, to watching YouTube videos and talking with Ethiopian elders in Oakland, to traveling to Africa to learn how to roast coffee. In 2013, the year before he launched Red Bay, he spent his evenings in his mini-roastery dojo, a converted garage behind his Fruitvale Victorian, experimenting with beans. "I was out here trying

to learn these secrets," Keba laughs. "I was building my case for African Americans' role in coffee; I was trying to understand the secrets of coffee. I went into it naive, thinking, this is a single ingredient, how hard can it be? But to get the most out of it, you have to understand it on deep levels."

George Washington Carver, the pioneering Black agricultural scientist and botanist, peers out of a framed photo in the dojo. A piece of paper with a quote of Carver's, "If you love something enough, it will reveal its secrets to you," rests among the yam, beans, potatoes, and peanuts on an altar Keba created for him. Keba refers to Carver as an American hero and savant who is not given enough credit, despite introducing the concept of crop rotation to address starvation in the Jim Crow South.

As Keba looks to Carver for inspiration, Oakland can look to Keba. He says, "There's an admiration in our community when you're not just seeking a job but creating your own path. Ownership is something that is praised because it speaks to determination and liberation. It's symbolic of being off the plantation. People in the Black community admire that."

# THE COOKOUT

## by Adrian Miller

The phone rings, I answer, and I hear these words: "What's going on, brother? I'm having some people over at the house. If you're free, why don't you roll through?" Nothing else had to be said in terms of what I was invited to (answer: a cookout), by what time I should be there (answer: whenever I feel like it), and what I should bring (answer: whatever I want to). In a September 2015 article for Deadspin.com, Michael Harriott—a journalist, podcast host, poet, and prolific social-media poster—helpfully defined the cookout for those who aren't in the know: "At a Black cookout (yes, if there's more than seven Black people there, the name automatically changes from 'barbecue' to 'cookout'), only the meat and the grill is supplied by the host. Everything else is brought by attendees—and no, this is not 'potluck.' Black people don't do potlucks."

I'm really glad that Harriott brought up the subject of barbecue. One of the most enduring linguistic tragedies in the English language is the continued confusion of the words *barbecue* and *cookout*. Fortunately, Black folks haven't been so quick to get things twisted. Building on Harriot's previous definition, a cookout tends to be an intimate, and often impromptu, gathering in someone's backyard. In addition to the eating, there's plenty of socializing and playing games. A cookout can certainly happen in other places like a public park, but it usually involves more planning and puts the host perilously on the road to a barbecue. To understand this difference, one must better understand what barbecue was, as a cooking process and as a social event, before the 1900s.

In the seventeenth, eighteenth, and nine-teenth centuries, barbecue in the American South was pretty much cooked the same way, regardless of location. The ideal setting for a barbecue was a rural open-space area with beautiful trees and a spring nearby. Enslaved African Americans performed a series of labor-intensive steps: clearing the designated area of debris, chopping down the trees and the wood necessary for cooking, burning that chopped wood into coals, digging a trench to fill with those burning coals, killing and butchering the whole animals that would be cooked, piercing the animal carcasses with sharpened poles so that they might be periodically flipped during the cooking process, seasoning the meat by regularly basting it with a sauce primarily made of vinegar and red pepper, making the side dishes and beverages, and then serving the whites attending the barbecue. Only after all that work had been done and the whites had finished with their meal could African Americans enjoy the barbecue.

As a social event, the early days of barbecues were much like a cookout. Family and friends got together in small numbers to eat food, play games, consume alcoholic beverages, and shoot their guns. Eventually, any life event, like a funeral or a wedding, became an excuse to host a barbecue. As barbecue grew in popularity as a type of food, barbecue as a social event also grew in size. One reason is that the traditional way of cooking barbecue was scalable. As long as the host had enough labor (typically from enslaved African Americans), food, and space, a barbecue could meet the needs of a hungry crowd of any size. At first, it was the wealthy who realized barbecue's promise to draw a multitude and keep them happy, but politicians and preachers got in on the act by the 1820s. Barbecue became the main culinary attraction at political campaign rallies, civic events of all kinds, and multiday religious events called camp meetings and revivals, where thousands of people attended. Whole-animal cooking demands community because a lot of food is created, and these events were a smash hit with the general public.

The cookout emerged as the smaller, private-party clapback to the grand public spectacle that barbecue had become. The cookout is about cooking smaller cuts of meat instead of a whole animal and about cooking it in a shorter period of time (for example, grilling at a high temperature rather than cooking for several hours at a low temperature, nick-named "low and slow"). In fact, the easier that something is to cook (like chicken wings, hamburgers, hot dogs, or hot links) or some-thing that is premade (such as bread, coleslaw, potato salad, or a red-colored drink), the more that item will be welcomed. Convenience is the cookout's main vibe.

Cooking outdoors is a large part of African American culinary tradition. For much of our history, African Americans had no choice but to cook outdoors because of inadequate housing. In antebellum America, the physi-cal condition of enslaved people's dwellings varied wildly in the North and South. Much depended on the whims of the slaveholder. Generally, enslaved families lived in simple one-room or two-room structures. Instead of a separate room as a kitchen, enslaved cooks usually prepared food in a fireplace. If the slaveholder built on the cheap, they cooked outdoors. In terms of cooking, options weren't much better when African Americans moved from the rural South to urban areas during the Great Migration. Many urban apartments had no kitchen at all, and tenants had to pay extra for "kitchen privileges," so they could

cook food in a kitchen shared by all of the tenants in a building. As an alternative, African Americans turned to alleys and public parks to do their cooking. In time, the cookout became synonymous with backyards, and it soared in popularity when African American home ownership rates improved dramatically after the 1950s.

A problematic aspect of cookout history is that of white surveillance. When it came to making barbecue, people liked to watch. Nineteenth century newspaper accounts show that guests at the grandiose barbecues often arrived early just to see African Americans doing this unique culinary craft. In the antebellum South, whites also liked to watch for the purpose of monitoring the activities of enslaved African Americans. The smaller the gathering, like a cookout, the more nervous racist whites grew. Why? Because they suspected that these small gatherings were not about eating and social-izing but about planning a slave rebellion. Slaveholders had reason to worry. At a small barbecue in late August 1831, an enslaved man named Nat Turner organized a dramatic and nearly successful insurrection in southeastern Virginia. The paranoia of some whites grew so thick that in a few jurisdictions, antebellum barbecues hosted by enslaved African Africans became illegal.

After Emancipation, white anxiety never abated when it came to African Americans assembling for any purpose. The African American–hosted political barbecues held in the 1870s and 1880s were no exception. Racist whites were not happy about Blacks flexing their newfound political rights. Many tried to intimidate Black voters by showing up at the rallies to violently disrupt them. Many Blacks died during these altercations, even though they were just minding their own business and trying to participate in the democratic process.

The Black-barbecue-as-trouble-making-vibe persists in the United States and came into sharp relief in late April 2018, when a white woman called the police on a Black cookout-in-progress at a public park surrounding Lake Merritt in Oakland, California. Their "crime" was using a charcoal grill in an area where such use was banned, something the family, and others, had been doing for years. The event was part of a larger wave of whites, as private citizens, privately policing Black people or calling law enforcement for minor infractions instead of for legitimate emergencies. Oakland's Black community responded a couple of weeks later in the same park with a massive "Barbecuing While Black" event.

Thousands of people turned out with their barbecue grills to cook delicious food while listening to music, playing games, and socializing with members of their community. The fact that a cookout was simultaneously a party and a community protest reinforced its stature in Black culture.

Which brings us back to Michael Harriot. His helpful article defined the cookout and explained its ground rules, especially in terms of food and conduct. Though intended for white audiences, Harriot's article reminds all of us that anyone can become family at the cookout.

# THE RARE BIRD

## by Renée Wilson

*I am the color green*

*The rare bird indeed*

*Who sees the heart in every one of you*

*Take me to your hearth*

*Take me to your home*

*Embrace with me the union of grace*

*Embrace with me the union of joy*

*Embrace with me the union of love*

*You are the color green*

*The color of all hearts*

*You are the rare bird indeed*

*Sing sweetly in the dark*

*And seek for your heart*

*Allow your awakening to come*

*Welcome it all*

*Bless this life and this gift*

*For you and I are One*

# THE ESSENTIAL LESSONS PARIS TAUGHT ME

## by Klancy Miller

**Leisure**

noun: time free for relaxation or enjoyment
—*Oxford English Dictionary*

I was very lucky to get a Parisian do-over. In college, I spent the spring semester of my junior year studying in the City of Light. It was my first time living outside of the United States, and it was mostly a bummer. For about five months, I felt lonely, cold, broke, and the opposite of chic. I had my first panic attack in the Jardin du Luxembourg. When I returned to the States, I made a vow to myself that I would go back to France (as soon as possible) and have a much better experience.

And so, four years later, I moved to Paris to attend Le Cordon Bleu and earn a Diplôme de Pâtisserie. I knew that I would learn everything about French pastry; but what I didn't

anticipate was that Paris would teach me about pleasure—savoring it, experiencing it on a daily basis, and sharing it with others.

By day, I was a culinary student. We watched our chef instructors prepare a confection, and then we would head into the kitchen to make the same thing. During the first week, our teacher told us that we must always consider how a pastry or dessert looks—does it look appetizing or beautiful? He instructed us to walk around the city and study the displays at all of the *pâtisseries* in order to train our eyes. His advice was a serendipitous gift that turned into my first lesson about pleasure.

The best way to appreciate Paris (and its sweets) is to become a *flâneur*. Edmund White explains the term best in his wonderful book *The Flâneur: A Stroll through the Paradoxes of Paris:* "A flâneur is a stroller who aimlessly loses himself in a crowd, going wherever curiosity leads him and collecting impressions along the way." I strolled constantly in Paris. After class, I walked along the Rue de Vaugirard in the 15th arrondissement to Boulevard

## "TO ERR IS HUMAN. TO LOAF IS PARISIAN." —Victor Hugo

Pasteur. From there, I would take a right onto the Rue de Sèvres and walk until I reached my favorite grocery store in the world—La Grande Épicerie de Paris. If Bergdorf Goodman and the late Barney's morphed into supermarkets, they might resemble La Grande Épicerie de Paris. When I walked into this grocery store, I always felt a sense of calm and awe (to borrow a phrase from Baudelaire: "*luxe, calme et volupté*"). The aisles are lined with beautiful products and there's so much to look at: grapefruit jelly with gold leaf, dozens of varieties of artisanal lemonades in assorted colors, a sumptuous pastry section, great wines from every region of France (and the world), a delicious takeaway section, gorgeous produce, and my favorite, smoked duck breast. A true *flâneur,* I often went to La Grande Épicerie just to browse and soothe my eyes. I would leave the store, walking along the Rue de Sèvres, until I got to the Rue du Bac and then to the Rue de Grenelle, where I drank in the beautiful window displays at Christian Louboutin, Sonia Rykiel, Yves Saint Laurent, and others. Often, I walked to Pierre Hermé for a kouign-amann or a passionfruit macaron. Or, I would indulge in one of my new favorite habits, an aperitif at Café de Flore or the café Les Éditeurs. In Paris and all over France, the aperitif, also known as *l'apéro,* is both a time of day and a predinner drink. In having an *apéro* with friends or by myself, I learned the art of savoring the moment, drinking it in, not rushing things.

In school, I was learning to use my senses while making food, learning by sight when a pastry cream is cooked, learning by smell when a caramel was nearly burned, getting the feel of *viennoiserie* when making croissant dough. After class, I learned the senses are the conduits of pleasure outside of the kitchen, too, and that I could bring my sensual self to life in lots of different ways—from dressing well to spending time in parks, having dinner parties, going to museums and to the movies, exploring the city, enjoying idle moments, romancing myself, flirting. Even

though I was studying food, I learned a new vocabulary for leisure and pleasure. *L'art de vivre* (the art of living), *ça sent les vacances* (it smells of vacation), *faire l'amour* (make love), *bien dans sa peau* (good in one's skin), *en mai, fais ce qu'il te plaît* (in May, do what pleases you), and of course, *flâneur.*

As I write this now, I'm in Brooklyn, in quarantine because of Covid. I have several work projects due. One of the things I've been thinking about, one of the things I've been thinking about repeatedly since my time in Paris, is how to re-create the feeling of ease, pleasure, and leisure I often experienced in the City of Light (even when I worked in a restaurant that was blessedly closed on weekends). Some of my all-time favorite elements of leisure: spending time in nature; socializing with friends; not rushing; having picnics; taking naps; listening to music; spending time with a lover; going to the movies; window shopping; strolling anywhere; exploring my city, neighborhood, or wherever I find myself; enjoying art; lighting candles and relaxing in my home. I intentionally make time to tap into some of these elements to feel less like a work robot and more like a sensual human being who loves freedom and respite. To celebrate that freedom and respite, here's my recipe for a Kir Royale.

# KIR ROYALE

### MAKES 1 COCKTAIL

**1 ounce crème de cassis**

**5 ounces dry Champagne, or a sparkling white wine such as Blanc de Blancs or Prosecco**

Pour the crème de cassis into a Champagne flute and top off with the dry Champagne.

# RAISING ATTICUS

## by Jessica Moncada Konte

MAKES 1 COCKTAIL

Like many folks I know, I was completely transfixed with Misha Green's original HBO series Lovecraft Country. This show, which features so much of our Black history, culture, queerness, and magic, inspired me so deeply I was moved to make a collection of lovecraft cocktails. The first in the series is a spirit-forward (no pun intended) cocktail featuring an unusual trinity; Uncle Nearest 1856 whiskey, Smith & Cross rum, and Xila agave liqueur. Sip well and speak with your ancestors.

1¼ ounces Uncle Nearest 1856 whiskey

¾ ounce Xila agave liqueur

¾ ounce Smith & Cross Jamaica rum

½ ounce (shy) Byrrh

4 dashes of Jamaican #2 bitters

1 cinnamon stick

1 (2-inch) grapefruit peel

1 (2-inch) blood orange peel for garnish

Add the whiskey, agave liqueur, rum, Byrrh, and bitters to a mixing glass along with the cinnamon stick, grapefruit peel, and ice. Stir for 30 seconds. Strain into a cocktail glass. Garnish with the blood orange peel.

# MY SUMMER GETAWAY

## by Kristina Gill

MAKES 1 COCKTAIL

There is a restaurant here in Rome named Marigold, whose owners, Domenico and Sofie, forage for special items—flowers, herbs, porcini mushrooms, certain seafood—to make their dishes stand out. One of the flowers they collect each year is the elderflower, which they use to make a wonderful elderflower cordial. I use it to make a beverage with lime juice or another tart citrus, and just a touch of lavender bitters. It reminds me of sunny summer days, when winter is at its darkest.

3 tablespoons, plus a little more (1½ ounces) St-Germain

Juice of ½ lime, plus more to taste

½ cup chilled seltzer, or carbonated water

2 or 3 drops of lavender bitters

Lime wedge

Pour the St-Germain, lime juice, and seltzer into a glass, over ice if you prefer, and stir lightly. Add the bitters. Garnish with a wedge of lime.

# GOOD BONES

## by Shannon Mustipher

MAKES 1 COCKTAIL

*Inspired by the genesis of rum and the liberation from colonialism, this drink calls on the story of Haiti. It was here that the first uprising against colonial powers took place, inspiring a chain of events that emboldened other colonies to follow suit.*

*Meanwhile, Haiti never deviated from the tradition of distilling clairin—the moonshine of rum, produced according to a methodology that has not changed in more than two hundred years. This recipe plays homage to this rum tradition, while incorporating a vitamin-rich juice to create a libation that is the epitome of a restoration, restoring health to the bones.*

*Making rhum arrangè ("arranged rum") is a tradition in many homes in the French-speaking Caribbean. As on many islands, infusing rum with fruits and spices served as a means to soften and make a spirit more palatable, as well as to preserve fruit and showcase the maker's signature style and creativity. Sirop de canne is a simple syrup made from fresh pressed cane juice.*

**RHUM ARRANGÈ**
Makes 1 liter

1 liter rhum agricole blanc (preferably 50% ABV or above)

3 pears, cut into quarters

2 apples, cut into quarters

1 vanilla bean

3 tablespoons sirop de canne

**COCKTAIL**

2 ounces Rhum Arrangè (see recipe at left)

1 ounce soursop juice

½ ounce guava juice

½ ounce honey syrup (use 1 part honey to 1 part hot water)

¾ ounce fresh lime juice

Generous sprig of mint for garnish

**TO MAKE THE RHUM ARRANGÈ:** Add the pears, apples, vanilla bean, and syrup to the rum, ensuring that they are completely covered by the liquid. Seal, shake to agitate, and store in a cool, dark place for a minimum of 3 weeks at room temperature, tasting weekly until you reach the desired flavor. The optimal amount of time is 9 weeks. Each time you taste it, give the bottle a shake to blend the flavors as they are being extracted.

Store the rhum arrangè indefinitely in a cool place away from direct sunlight.

**TO MAKE THE COCKTAIL:** Combine all ingredients in a cocktail shaker with ice, then shake to mix. Pour into a Collins glass over crushed ice. Garnish with a mint sprig, then serve.

**NOTE:** You can use essentially any fruit or spice to make rhum arrangè; follow the guidelines of fruit and spice to rum ratio outlined above. In Martinique, ingredients commonly used in rhum arrangè include bananas, pineapples, mangoes, passionfruit, cinnamon, cloves, and nutmeg. For the best results, use a rhum agricole bottled at 50% ABC or higher: the higher alcohol content will allow for a more vibrant extraction of flavor from the maceration. I recommend using La Favorite, Rhum J.M, Rhum Neisson, La Maison & Velier Clairin le Rocher, or Barbancourt Blanc.

# VERMOUTH SPRITZ

## by Stephen Satterfield

MAKES 1 COCKTAIL

2 ounces vermouth

1 ounce lime juice

½ ounce sparkling water or bone-dry sparkling wine, plus more as needed

*For the entirety of my adult life, including a decade in which it was my vocation, wine has been at the center—of my pleasure, curiosity, and personal ideology. The language of terroir gave me a relationship to place, rooted in the land. To this day, it is the simplest and most reliable form of indulgence, superseding my otherwise wavering attention.*

*On the subject of reliable and accessible daily indulgences, I present to you, vermouth (sounds like* vermooth*), a wine in the family of aperitifs. Aperitifs, linguistically speaking, are derivative of the Latin* aperire, *or to open, and that's exactly what it does. Vermouth is the beginning of something good, usually a meal, or at the very least, an evening.*

*Vermouth is a grape-based wine imbued with herbs and botanicals. It's fortified, usually with a neutral, unoaked brandy, yet it maintains a low ABV that makes it easy to say yes to the next one. It is, after all, just the beginning. My favorite way to do vermouth is as an effervescent indulgence, which accurately describes my mood after the first sip. Say hello to the vermouth spritz.*

In a pint glass, add the vermouth and lime juice over ice. Stir a few times until the liquid chills, just slightly, then pour into a wine glass over a large ice cube. Stir again, briefly, then top with the bubbly water, just enough to add an effervescent expression. Enjoy and adjust as you see fit.

**NOTE:** There are all kinds of vermouths, from dry to sweet, but for this recipe, some of the brands that work best are Cocchi Vermouth, Carpano Antica Formula, and for a more bitter iteration, Carpano Punt e Mes.

# CHAMPAGNE COCKTAIL

## by Nicole Erica

MAKES 1 COCKTAIL

As a sommelier, I rely heavily on being able to pull out very subtle nuances and fragrances of wine. Often, these will transport me back to my childhood and my mother's collection of ethereal Italian and French perfumes. Because of this, I've always been fascinated by the link between palate and memory.

I have sensory memories that extend to experiencing wine. Whenever I smell cedar in a wine, it immediately transports me to this little miniature jewelry box that I had as a kid. Champagne, Laurent-Perrier, specifically, is uniquely divine. It's a snapshot of the terroir, in this case an abundance of chalk, layered with Kimmeridgian soil or fossil deposit–rich soil. It is single-handedly the most important vehicle to showcase the highly regarded and carefully selected Chardonnay, Pinot Noir, and Pinot Meunier grapes. It truly captures the beauty of Mother Earth—from the topsoil, the positioning of the vineyard for sun exposure, and the scarcity of water that allows for it to truly be magnificent.

Calvados also hails from France, specifically Normandy, and exhibits the most luscious apple and pear notes. It's an absolutely stunning brandy to accent such an elegant Champagne with its crisp, firm acidity—the hint of toast is not from oak but from the extended time it's given to develop with the reserved wine from two or three vintages. So as not to mask such fine ingredients, I suggest simple garnishes that lend a hint of fresh citrus oil, spices that complement apple and pear, and then finally bitters, a flavor profile I've grown to love. The star anise is as captivating as a floating flower as is the geometric cinnamon stick. However, both contribute lovely spices and aromatics to entice the senses. This recipe showcases my love for simplicity—utilizing only a few amazing ingredients to truly capture the senses. Enjoy!

5 ounces Laurent-Perrier Champagne

2 star anise pods

4 or 5 dashes Angostura aromatic bitters

½ ounce Calvados

1 cinnamon stick

1 Cara Cara orange

Allow the Champagne to chill in the refrigerator for 3 to 4 hours or in an ice bucket for 25 minutes before assembling the cocktail.

Pour the Champagne into a large voluminous wine glass, like a Burgundy glass. Add the star anise. Add the bitters, then the Calvados. Stir well with the cinnamon stick, then drop it in. Slice a thin orange wheel and shave a thick orange peel, twist lengthwise, and drop both in. Allow those ingredients to rest and chill in the fridge for 15 minutes in order for the flavors to marry like soup. No ice required or necessary, since it would only take away from the delicate Champagne. Quaffable once removed from the fridge!

# GRAPE-TARRAGON SPRITZER

## by Bryant Terry

MAKES 4 TO 6 MOCKTAILS

*The anise-like flavor of tarragon syrup and sweet grape juice go well together in this refreshing, modern drink. Topping off the concentrate with sparkling water and adding frozen grapes will make it a standout at summer parties.*

**TARRAGON SYRUP**
Makes 1 cup

1 cup raw cane sugar

¼ cup packed minced tarragon

½ cup water

**SPRITZER**

1½ pounds red seedless grapes (preferably organic)

3 tablespoons freshly squeezed lemon juice

¼ cup Tarragon Syrup (see recipe at left)

4 cups sparkling water, chilled until almost frozen

Sprigs of tarragon for garnish

**TO MAKE THE TARRAGON SYRUP:** Combine the sugar, tarragon, and water in a small saucepan over low heat. Stir well until hot to the touch and the sugar is completely dissolved, about 3 minutes. Let cool and refrigerate until ready to use.

**TO MAKE THE SPRITZER:** Put 8 ounces of the grapes on a large plate and freeze for at least 3 hours, until completely frozen.

Remove the remaining grapes from their stems. Put them in a blender and process until completely broken down. Strain through a fine-mesh sieve into a serving pitcher, pressing the solids to extract as much liquid as possible (compost the solids). This should yield about 1¼ cups of juice.

Add the lemon juice and the tarragon syrup and mix well. Add the sparkling water and stir *gently* to combine.

**TO SERVE:** Put a handful of frozen grapes in each glass, pour in the blended liquid, and garnish with a sprig of tarragon.

CHAPTER 4

ART BY EMORY DOUGLAS

# RICE!

## by Gail Patricia Myers, PhD

3,000 years ago, my people grew rice along
the Niger River.

Black hands sowed the seeds.

In water, planted paddies of trials and error.

In water, solid seeds grew sufficient lines,

Scattered inside a chaff interior.

Eventually, behold the gold.

Rice!

Tall golden stalks threshed and winnowed.

Stubble trails ready for mounds of fluffy
bouquets of

fragrant rice.

Once cooked, rice filled fed bellies and souls.

Satisfied tongues singing to the wind.

Full hands talking to beating drums,

offering to Spirit what is theirs,

offering to everyone what they can eat.

And what they can keep.

These were my people.

The rice people first.

The rice people,

brutally captured and traded

for rice to grow empires' culinary
commodities.

To build their empire, set their foundations,
nails into their walls.

But we lay the rows, planted the rice,

Hands unwilling but forced through
migration.

People who labored but never ate the fruits.

Be it indigo, tobacco, sugar, cotton,

Rice building framed the empires.

But their hands could never see.

Their bent bodies tall, short, planted,
pulled, plucked, harvested,

winnowed the dragging fluff,

wafted the shackled rice

that drained into the sea,

with six million quieted hearts,

along the sinuous transatlantic pathways,

Grains of rice beneath the sea,

six million flickering lights,

six million faces, fading into mirages.

We eat from a pot of warm rice.

We know to remember to never

forget the lines beneath the sea.

Six million souls sacrificed.

The sea paid the price.

The coastal South Carolina sea people
grew rice.

With no taste of liberation.

No time to sleep.

But this was the dish.

The dish from which we grew

strong, knowing uninterrupted 3,000 years
of rice,

Knowing the toil of the rice.

Wind knowing. Rice knowing.

Because we knew rice,

We knew wind.

The many voices of wind.

Because we knew rice, we knew the beauty
of water.

Understood water intonations.

*Like the curves of waves and the pulse*
*of currents.*

*We knew the hums from the four directions.*

*They said, "You are also water. You are*
*also wind."*

*They knew this was true.*

*We are truth.*

*The rice people knew truth, they knew wind.*

*They felt deeply the swelling clouds falling*
*like rain.*

*Rain for rice. Clouds sacrificed for rice.*

*Rain overflowed covered fields and paddies,*

*Yet the leaves remained dry on the trees.*

*There was no water for the roots.*

*We thirst for juices that liberate souls.*

*We hunger for a dish that tastes like rain.*

*When it rains, I think of rice people in my family.*

*Growing up in my house, we ate rice every day.*

*My mom says my dad wanted rice every day.*

*My mom also said, his mom probably ate rice*
*every day,*

*And her mom too.*

*My father was a South Carolina low country*
*Geechee,*

*which makes me a Geechee.*

*In my house, growing up, we ate rice every day.*

*This is our dish.*

*In spite of how our dish was made*

*We have not shame to feel.*

*We make this dish in joy from*

*Trials and tribulations from all those years*

*feeling the mirages of six million lights,*

*hearing the wafting of wind's songs singing*
*the knowing.*

*Songs that keep us free, in spite of the talk*
*of liberation.*

*The empires' tongues talk of liberation*
*but we*

*never taste a scent of rice or the wet of rain.*

*The rice people first.*

*They knew the water and the rain,*

*And fished every day along coastal shores.*

*In my house we ate rice every day.*

*We also fished, and I learned nearly early*

*How to fish along water's edge on a*
*backwater creek*

*with snakes crawling, minding their own*
*business,*

*with my wooden reed fishing pole*

*with my aunties and uncles.*

*We fished and ate rice*

*as a testimony to our knowing.*

*It was the dish we made, knowing rice*
*and rain.*

*Rice tasting like survival.*

*Fish comforting like water.*

*We bleed our ancestors' blood.*

*We give to Spirit what is theirs.*

*We keep what we can eat,*

*And know what to leave in the fields.*

*We are rice people first.*

*We see beauty in the wind,*

*We taste truth in the rain.*

*For this dish we made to remember*

*the six million souls beneath the sea.*

*We are rice . . .*

---

This poem is dedicated to my Gullah Geechee
ancestors and all the rice people of the world.
In gratitude!!!!

# FEEDING OURSELVES IN DANGEROUS TIMES

## Lessons of Love, Food & Freedom Farmers

### by Monica M. White, PhD

*Critical fabulation is the theoretical underpinning for this fictional meeting between three women, whose paths did not cross in history. Three wayward lives come together in this imagining, in a multiverse, where time is not linear and multiple realities are possible.*

It was March 2020. Ms. Shirley Sherrod had invited Ms. Fannie Lou Hamer to lunch. In the 1960s, Ms. Hamer had founded Freedom Farm Cooperative, 680 acres of affordable housing, community gardens, commercial kitchens, and fields upon fields of food crops in Sunflower County, Mississippi. The two women had known each other, and about each other's work, for a long time, but they lived half-a-day's drive away and had not seen each other in years.

Ms. Sherrod welcomed Ms. Hamer on the porch of the mansion at Resora. In 2012, she and her husband, Rev. Charles Sherrod, had been able to buy the former Cypress Pond Plantation after the U.S. Department of Agriculture paid out more than a billion

dollars in damages to Black farmers who had suffered material damage due to the nakedly racist policies of the agency. Resora was their new name for it. The two women embraced. Ms. Sherrod had questions.

Ms. Hamer was her foremother. Both women had dedicated their lives to providing resources for the Black community in the rural South, where most members had agricultural skills and knowledge of growing cash crops like soybeans, tobacco, and corn, but they had little knowledge of food production and lacked health care, quality education, clean water, and safe housing. Both wanted Black rural families to have access to safe and affordable housing, nutrient-rich foods, and quality health care and education. Both had fought on the front lines to demand access to the basic necessities of life, and they had also fought for the right to be heard, seen, and included in decision making.

Ms. Sherrod wanted to know, first, how had Freedom Farm been able to do so much with so little? She and Rev. Sherrod had founded New Communities decades before: 5,735 acres, housing five hundred families and growing food and raising cattle to support the wellness of those families and others in Lee County, Georgia. In 1970, it was the largest single tract of land owned by African Americans. It, like Freedom Farm, was a vision created in response to a community that needed food and sustenance. And it paid off—their efforts ameliorated the ill effects of poverty and diet-related illness and disease and provided social resources that were especially necessary in a community facing oppression through food and, by extension, bad health. This work was inspired by Ms. Hamer's earlier project to combine land, food, and freedom for the many Black families that needed it. Her project, like New Communities, was not an emergency food program. Both were planned to be sustainable and self-sufficient.

The lunch menu included a wild lettuce salad with shaved cured ham, chèvre, salt-preserved hen egg, and dressed in a vinaigrette of brandied pear preserves. The next course was a savory mélange of foraged poke salad and field peas, braised in a stock of roast pork bones and a refreshing glass of dried golden-rod sun tea, sweetened with Sapelo Island purple cane sugar. The peas are an heirloom cowpea variety known as "creme 40," some of Mrs. Sherrod's favorite from her youth in Baker County, Georgia. The pork bones were from forest-raised heritage hogs, salted and roasted before they made the broth braise for the greens and peas.

The main course included a coal-roasted quail stuffed with local satsuma citrus and glazed with North Carolina sorghum syrup, yard sage, toasted peppercorn, and topped with crushed groundnuts, a healthy serving of corn grits from South Carolina with heavy cream, butter, and salt. For dessert they enjoyed a slice of sweet potato cinnamon buttermilk pie.

As they sat down to eat, the doorbell rang. It was Celia, making a delivery of some fresh produce that she'd just harvested from a Black agricultural cooperative, where she serves as farm manager. Celia was a young sister—forty years their junior—and they decided to include her. Like Ms. Sherrod, Celia had questions. The third generation at the table, she looked at these civil rights icons, Titans both of them, with innocence and optimism, and she asked them why they had embraced food production. She, too, had embraced it, but she knew that hearing their answer would affirm her own commitment.

"Food," said Ms. Hamer, in the voice that had commanded the attention of the nation in 1964, soothed the nerves of organizers and activists with her hymns, and had articulated the vision of Freedom Farm and won scores of funders for it in its early days, "is necessary for survival. With the passage of the Voting Rights Act of 1965, I returned to Sunflower County and realized that the right to vote was insufficient to a healthy, happy, whole life. Voting alone does not include the right to accessing nutrient-rich food, safe and affordable housing, health care, and a quality education."

Sherrod joined in: "We knew that we had to have access to land. We'd both experienced and witnessed the dispossession of land for Black farmers and had seen how many farmworkers had left the South for promises of a better life." She turned to Ms. Hamer and winked. "We knew differently."

Hamer responded: "Yes, as I've always said, EVERYTHING comes from the land. If you leave the South, you lose the ability to feed yourself . . . and with that, you do not have the basics you need to demand your own civil and human rights."

Sherrod added: "Participating in food production, distribution, and preparation allows you to build the capacity to provide for your community, and a well-fed community can do lots of things. We wanted a food system that was regenerative, instead of one like the current system that operates as extractive."

Celia was taking notes. She asked another question about something she knew in her bones but could not articulate: "Why is the collective necessary?"

It was Sherrod who answered: "In our organizing, we had seen how vulnerable individual Black farmers were to the well-established systems of oppression. We'd seen how powerful cooperatives and collectives had been historically, and we realized that we could do so much more together. We had more economic options, so we could pool our efforts together to care for each other."

Celia thanked them both for giving her a history lesson that she had been denied in school. She remembered that she had other food deliveries to make.

As her pickup carried her down the driveway of Resora, she turned on the radio. The station had a breaking news report, and all she remembered hearing was the word Covid-19. As she listened, she realized why the lessons that she had just been taught were so important. She felt a range of emotions that she struggled to contain. Little did she know that a new era was beginning and that Celia and all those like her would need to draw on the legacies of Sherrod and Hamer as they met it. Farming and collective action would gain new urgency. She would not forget their teachings.

# BLACK FOOD AS RESISTANCE
## Land, Justice & Black Liberation

## by Dara Cooper

*And who will join this standing up*

*and the ones who stood without sweet company*

*will sing and sing*

*back into the mountains and*

*if necessary*

*even under the sea*

*we are the ones we have been waiting for*

*—June Jordan*
(from "Poem for South African Women," *Directed by Desire: The Collected Poems of June Jordan.* Copper Canyon Press, 2005)

In the wake of recent massive uprisings in response to state-sanctioned violence on Black life and the pain of so much Black death, I think back to a time when a workshop facilitator asked us to describe when we had felt most *free*. I closed my eyes, and a vivid image of acres upon acres of land with beautiful Black people surrounding a fire appeared. I could hear drums playing, laughter, and very animated storytelling. The delicious food we were eating was grown on that land, stewarded by local people. We engaged in political education and debate and challenged each other in healthy ways. We were nourished, held, felt safe, and cared for, and we focused on the highest interest of the collective. We were free, creating different imaginations of regenerative relationships with each other, as we designed systems for the well-being of our communities. The taste of that vision felt *delicious*.

That image is a combination of land-based experiences I've had with food justice communities all over the country—in community gardens, in yurts, on eco-campuses, in abandoned lots taken over and converted into liberated zones, and in remote rural areas with no electricity or reliance on fossil-fuel consumption. Black people have been experimenting with freedom dreaming for a very long time. From Black foodways and Black culinary brilliance to Black cooperative infrastructures and food justice experimentations, Black food work is expansive and genius. Black people have made incredibly important interventions against the violence we've experienced via the food system, despite so many odds.

Violence in this country is profound, nuanced, and deep. It permeates virtually every aspect of the Black experience. While facing some of the highest rates of incarceration, police brutality, unemployment, wage and wealth theft, forced land removals, displacement, and some of the highest rates of food- (and stress-)

related illnesses ever, the assaults Black people experience are incessant. Since the leading causes of death for Black people in this country are heart disease and cancer, violence for Black people is sudden and immediate (as we see in police murders), but they are also more often experienced in very slow, measured, and deliberate ways.

These slow deaths have so much to do with what I've come to identify as nutritional violence and food apartheid—separate and unequal food sources that have left so many Black communities devastated, with little to no healthy, quality food options. We know through the important work of scholars such as Naa Oyo Kwate at Rutgers, Ashanté Reese at the University of Texas at Austin, and Angela Odoms Young at the University of Illinois, along with so many others, that there is structural malice behind nutritional violence. These systems have shaped the conditions in our communities and explain our food and health outcomes. We know there is a direct correlation between race (particularly Blackness) and the quality of food. Dr. Kwate and colleagues conducted a study in New York City, for example, and found that "the percentage of Black residents was the strongest predictor of fast food density" (*The Journal of Urban Health*, 2013). Which is to say that fast food and junk industries have preyed on Black communities, while the means to feed our communities nourishing foods have been systematically stripped away from us.

In the documentary *Soul Food Junkies*, the poet and professor Sonia Sanchez says that you can go into any grocery store in Black communities and the vegetables look as if they're "having a nervous breakdown." This illustrates one of the many flaws with advocating for simple proximity to a grocery store as the solution to so-called "food deserts." The problem with the narrative (and false solutions behind) "food deserts" is it doesn't address the systemic assaults against our communities and the disinvestment from resources (such as land and capital) our communities need to thrive. This leaves Black people vulnerable to corporate-controlled food sources devoid of nutritional value. The absence of food for sale alone is not the problem: it's the kinds of food available.

Considering the ceaseless harm Black people have endured via the food system, the solutions have to be rooted in justice, food justice, specifically. Justice is not about individual choices and choosing to eat "better." The *justice* component in food justice means our communities not only have access to good food but also the means to produce good food and control all aspects of the food system. We can't rely on corporations to continue feeding our communities poisonous foods. Justice requires addressing and repairing the harm waged against Black communities and restoring our role as earth stewards, land keepers, growers, seed keepers, distributors, leaders, and healthy consumers with better options for nourishing our communities.

Despite enslavement, exploitation, and the extrajudicial murders we've endured, Black people have resisted against violence in creative and profound ways. And still, one of the most intimate ways in which we experience violence and assert our resistance is through our food. Our resistance looks like the reclamation of our rightful place as leaders within our own food systems. The ways in which we've created beautiful meals to feed our loved ones despite it all, the markets we've created to counter the Jim Crow foods that saturate our communities, the cooperatives we've created to pool our limited resources, the burning of corporate (sterile) seeds donated to us in our most vulnerable moments are all forms of protest and resistance that lead us to what we know as food justice.

As Black communities continue to rise up against violence in all of its forms, reclaiming the nourishment of our communities is essential. In the legacy of our foremothers and freedom fighters, we have a clear path forward to step into our leadership and actualize our full freedom dreams. Black food as resistance, rooted in justice, can be incredibly delicious. It gets us that much closer to the taste of actual *freedom*.

# REFLECTIONS OF A GARDEN CHILE

## On the Village & Homestead

## by Gabrielle Eitienne

At the top of 2018, I made my reverse migration from New York back to North Carolina after almost a decade away. This decision was based on what I now acknowledge as a call back to the land, a call placed by my ancestors, who knew this land well. It was with open arms that I was welcomed back by my family and community. This community, fondly known as St. Mary's, is located on the line between Apex and Holly Springs, its soils are red clay and its population once mostly Black and kin. This community raised me, my mother, and my grandfather. My move home was a way to reclaim some things while preserving our familial foodways and deep ties to land stewardship.

My first stop would be Uncle Lynn's and Aunt Laura's. I melodically knocked on the door, and their daughter, Barbara, answered with a squeal of excitement. Barbara's skin is the color of honey, and her thin coiffed hair sat up on her head. "Girl, you look just like Von." This is a phrase I hear a lot these days, and because my mother is a stone-cold fox, I smile, every time. I walked in through the kitchen, where Uncle Lynn sat with his legs crossed as if he belonged in someone's magazine, selling something. The chain of his pocket watch sat atop his chinos, which held in his beige and navy plaid shirt. He looked up through his glasses and smiled a smile that sang welcome home. His voice was small like his frame, and his wit sharp, even at the glorious age of eighty-six. I gave soft hugs, as I made my way into the living room, where Aunt Laura sat by the window. The light came in and sat on her smooth cheekbones. Her skin was the color of dried cottonwood, and her hair lay in soft gray plaits. She had just returned home from the doctor, and her feet were elevated on an ottoman, with a plaid fleece blanket draped on her lap and legs. I sat on the plush couch beside Barbara, as the news hummed below our conversation. I talked about New York for a while and then somehow got on the topic of food. My Aunt Laura was known as a great cook, and although I had never had her coconut custard pie, my grandfather's description of it was so vivid that I believed I had. I liked the way she pronounced okra—OAK-ree—and laughingly both complained and celebrated how thick my hair was. That visit would be the first but definitely not the last. Their home was situated diagonally across the road from us, in view from our living room window. Next door to them were my cousins Wade and Netta, with their home full of antiques, the kind you put out and show off, collector's items that roused my inner child and ignited my imagination. Behind their home was a barn, designed and built by them, with massive accordion doors concealing the antiques that were too large for the house. Most impressive, my cousin Wade went to his room and brought back a large piece of tanned paper the color of a real-life treasure map. Little did I know, it was. This paper was a hand-drawn map of the original neighborhood, each lot outlined and numbered. As I looked over this heirloom, he explained that his mother, my great-great Aunt Issabell, had helped to sell most of the lots in this community—helping to shape a village of kinfolk and friends, people who would look out for one another. There were people like Ms. Annaclyde, now ninety-one, who had started an "outreach club" that several women, including my grandmother Artris P. Woodard, would become a part of. These women would hold yard sales and other fundraisers to buy necessities like groceries and clothing for others in need.

I frequent Ms. Annaclyde's home, which is made of cinder bricks painted taupe, hemmed in dark brown, and bordered by giant elephant ear taro plants. These visits usually include watching episodes of *The Young and the Restless* and the passing of wisdom and casual conversation during commercial breaks. I walk home through her backyard, where the woods connect to what is now our garden, which sits on about an acre of land that is managed by my great-uncle Andrew. This is my grandfather's youngest brother. He's the farmer, artist, and arguably the chef—although the one who is ordained in chef's whites is Herbert, the eldest brother and the herbal/astrological hobbyist. I want to cook like them, their hands heat resistant. I once witnessed Uncle Herbert eat fire from the palm of his hand, or was it molten gravy? Either way, they are the type of hands that move pots from one stove eye to the next with no mitt and who uncover and let billowing steam waft directly from vessels and don't blink. Those hands put themselves in those meals, and you can sense the experience of them if you are lucky enough to get a plate.

Great-uncle Andrew's kitchen is where I used to spend most evenings—right by his side over the stove, the sink, or a tin tub, as we shelled peas, mashed bronze muscadines for wine, or cut up pears for preserves. Growing up, I knew little of who he really was. I knew he smelled of beer most times and that his voice and anecdotes made me laugh. However, I wouldn't come to learn that these things, small observations, were in part by-products of a not-so-easy life. One Sunday, over a pot of simmering cabbage-collards, he started to share that he had been drafted into Vietnam in his twenties, had lived in Germany for a portion of his adulthood, and then had returned home to farm for thirty years. I also learned that his labor had been exploited by a local farm, where he was paid very little but managed a lot. I discovered, too, that he is our family's griot, made some of the most incredible woodwork, and could throw a little Deutsch your way to see if you'd really been listening. All of this I learned right there across the street at the same house where he'd lived my entire life.

I vividly remember the first fall season I spent in the garden with him and Pop. My grandfather Mayfield, now eighty-four, is the resident mechanic and engineer. His mechanic shop, once known as Woodard's Garage, sits behind our home, surrounded by massive oak trees and truck parts. Answering the phone and greeting customers as they fulfilled invoices with my grandmother was my very first job. The shop is now mostly used for what my grandfather calls piddlin, which means fixing something on his own time, making robotic parts for my aunt's STEM competitions and working his magic on our old-school Farmall tractors. Since I've been home, it has served as a community film screening space, and most recently as a pick-up location for our CSA "Tall Grass Food" box, born in the pandemic and inspired by the work happening right here on our homestead.

Pop stands at around 6 feet 4 inches with a close cut the color of oak ash and a pair of those indestructible hands I mentioned earlier. My grandfather is the middle son of Andrew Jackson Woodard, the great-grandfather whom I never met but learned so much about in the kitchen and field with his three sons. There were lessons in wine making, pit cooking, barbecue alchemy, and figuring shit out, all passed down from him. Though memories of their mother, Cora Lee, are few and far between because she passed away when my grandfather was only twelve, there is one that I hold close. Whenever the symptoms of her blood disorder would flare up, she would send a then-ten-year-old Pop to the community clay bank to collect her medicine from the earth itself.

Another lesson I learned was how to reimagine the word *wealth*. Over a span of three days during one winter week in 2018, I witnessed at least two handfuls of folks drive up to get their holiday greens. One instance that stands out was when Mr. and Mrs. Wilson made their way down our rocky driveway, and even before they could get out of their car, my uncle had pulled a half-rusted hacksaw from the bed of his pickup truck and made his way to the collard patch. After a few moments of deliberation, he walked back toward us, holding two large emerald collards in one hand and his handcrafted walking stick securely in the other. As he approached the Wilsons, I asked whether I could take a portrait of the two of them holding the larger-than-life brassicas, and they stood, still smiling, as I attempted to freeze us in time. Soon after, Mrs. Wilson reached into the car to retrieve a few singles, which my uncle slid into his leather wallet without counting as the Wilsons turned out of the driveway. I could sense that these transactions were more than an exchange of goods; the pride my uncle took in feeding folks is what educated me on what drove his work. This would end up being my uncle's last holiday season in our community. As silly as it may have seemed to the Wilsons that I wanted their portrait with the collards,

it's that portrait and many others like it that have become monuments for the lessons I've learned right here at home.

The reflections below are snapshots from the months leading up to the displacement of several long-standing members of my community. The highs and lows of town hall meetings, where town council members would pretend to know nothing about the impact this highway extension was going to have on their rapidly declining Black population. I felt such pride, a pride mirrored back to me by my mom, my older brother, Antony, and my big cousins Tricia and Nicole, when we stood up and told our truth about this place we call St. Mary's. And what sorrow we all felt, as we watched these homes being demolished, one after the other. Hold this feeling, if you can, as you read these reflections.

*November 27, 2018*

*As a kid, I remember being ashamed of where I'm from. My 13-year-old self, wishing our house was bigger . . . car was newer, completely unaware of how blessed I truly was. I moved to San Francisco for college and didn't see myself ever looking back. It was this time last year, that I started feeling pulled back home, and after seven years in New York, where I had made an entire life, I packed my things into a rented minivan and drove nine hours back to the home my youth had taken for granted. I made this move with the intention to keep what we have, reclaim what we'd lost, and stand with the community that raised me in the midst of gentrification and other changes. This wasn't an easy decision; however, I'm reassured every day that it was the right one.*

*March 18, 2019*

*Our elders are our direct link to who we are. They embody our history and culture, and they keep us grounded . . . if you think for a second, you're hot sh\*t, sit down with* *your grandparents. The groundedness is aligned with encouragement to continue to seek; you don't know it all. As a student of the ol'school, I have to stand up and stand with our elders. I ask the community to stand with me tomorrow night at town hall, 7:00 p.m., as we will share our history as we work toward some equitable solutions to protect and preserve our spaces.*

*March 20, 2019*

*Our home seems to stretch into all eternity. It's massive, starting at our back door, across into Uncle Andrew's kitchen, then through a small cove of pines into Uncle Lynn's living room, where Aunt Laura and Barbara sit on the plush couches filled with cotton and clouds. It then extends over to Wade's barn full of antiques and dreams. From there, it reaches forward in all its comfy, roomy wideness and wraps around the McNeil's, and pours into Ms. Annaclyde's mangled grapevine, through the fruit trees, and into her/our living room. That's only the first floor, by the way.*

*April 19, 2019*

*Three years ago, while I was living in Brooklyn, I had a conversation with my grandfather about a vision to continue the work he had started at his mechanic shop. This work would look different from fixing 18-wheelers and creating parts but would be rooted in the same creativity and wonder that he builds from. I was serious but was not in the position to do the things we discussed. He grinned in support, in semi-disbelief because I'm his "big dreams" grandbaby. Well, on New Year's Eve, 2017, I packed everything into a Toyota minivan [that was rented with faith], hit the high-way, and returned to the home that I had grown up in. My grandfather's grin slightly changed . . . this Saturday night, 4/19, will be my first step into this work, which honors our intergenerational legacy as creatives,*

*designers, and most importantly—dreamers. Y'all know I love to tell a good story, so I'll be screening my first documentary film inside the shop. Pop has helped me clean and prepare for this all week, and I know this is only the beginning of what our family has in store. I hope you'll join us sometime.*

*May 10, 2019*

*This home you built. Under a sky that seems to understand you. Frame you, shield you, provide a moon to light your porch at night. You worked for this home. Sacrificed so much. We lost so much. We lost your wife, my grandmother, our lifeline. You both worked so hard for this. Who dares diminish its worth? Appraised, based on a market that never understood the worth of a Black man or his work, or his family, or their well-being, while I contemplate our worth, based on numbers too low, numbers that won't soothe my angst, numbers that won't ever truly understand our compensation. I'll imagine that today never ends. Today, while we are where we are, in this—whole—sense of who we are, I'll stand with you and this home.*

# OKRA & SHRIMP PURLOO

## by BJ Dennis

MAKES 4 SERVINGS

*Okra purloo is a dish that resonates in the hearts of most Gullah Geechee folks. It speaks the language of the diaspora. Forced labor produced Carolina Gold rice and made the Low Country rich through our ancestors' knowledge, sweat, and tears. Okra is a vegetable that is dear to many of us throughout the African diaspora. And, of course, there's shrimp, which is vital to our culture. This is a dish of pain, resilience, and celebration. It's the story of our existence in the so-called New World. If you were to give me one final meal to eat, it would be this.*

1 to 2 tablespoons vegetable oil

½ cup diced smoked sausage (optional)

½ cup finely diced yellow onions

2 tablespoons minced garlic

1 tablespoon minced ginger

2 tablespoons tomato paste

2 bay leaves

2 cups Carolina Gold rice

Salt and pepper to taste

2 cups okra, sliced ½ inch thick

4 cups chicken or veggie broth, warmed

2 cups peeled and deveined wild-caught American shrimp, 26- to 30-count (the smaller the better)

4 tablespoons butter

Preheat the oven to 350°F.

Add enough oil to coat the bottom of a Dutch oven and heat over medium heat. Add the sausage, if using, and cook for 1 minute. Add the onion. (If not using sausage, start with the onion.) Cook for 1 minute. Add the garlic, ginger, tomato paste, and bay leaves. Cook for another minute; do not let the garlic brown. Add the rice and mix for 1 more minute. Make sure to season with salt and pepper throughout the process. Add the okra, stir, then add the broth.

Put on the lid and slide the pot into the oven. After 15 minutes, remove the pot from the oven, add the shrimp and fluff with a fork, mixing the shrimp into the rice. Cover and let sit for 5 to 10 minutes; the residual heat will cook the shrimp through. When the time is up, add the butter and stir thoroughly. Season with more salt and pepper and serve.

**NOTE:** If you can't find 26- to 30-count shrimp, larger shrimp will work but just cut them in thirds.

Okra & Shrimp Purloo (page 151)

# SWEET POTATO SNACK

## by Howard Conyers, PhD

MAKES ENOUGH FOR A WEEK'S WORTH OF DAILY SNACKING

**1 pound sweet potatoes (should be 3 or 4 cured potatoes)**

**Vegetable oil for rubbing on potato skins (optional)**

**Salt to taste (optional)**

*My father used the sweet potato to teach my brother and me a work ethic. More than thirty-five years before, an older church member had given my father our particular heirloom potato, variety unknown, for doing a good deed. My father had given the church member the tires from the car he was about to trade in. At the time, the man could neither afford to buy new tires nor was he able to pay my father, but about three or four months before he died, he gave my father a bushel of sweet potatoes for seed and a bushel of sweet potatoes to eat.*

*My father worked as a welder maintaining the family farm. But on the side, he has been growing these sweet potatoes every year since receiving them, and they are literally the sweetest potato I have ever eaten. While growing up, these sweet potatoes were more than a food to me, they were a cultural classroom. My father taught us how to cultivate and preserve the taters in the same way he had been taught, like many generations before him. From helping to set the potato bed to generate slips (plants), to digging with a mule plow behind a tractor, and storing in a sweet potato bank, growing this sweet potato was just part of life. After the annual sweet potato harvest and curing (drying them for about two weeks is critically important), my mom would make one of our favorite snacks—a whole tray of oven-baked sweet potatoes. Or my father would bake whole potatoes in the ashes on the barbecue pit or in the fireplace. To this day, one of my favorite ways to enjoy the potatoes is as a snack, just after they have been grilled, which I prefer to baking them in the oven. I generally cook 3 to 4 pounds at a time on the grill to eat over a week.*

Prepare an outdoor grill for high heat (the charcoal should be light gray in color). Set the grill rack about 3 inches above the hot coals.

Wash the sweet potatoes just prior to putting them on the grill, then toss them with oil and salt, if desired. (I generally cook them plain.)

Grill the sweet potatoes for 45 to 60 minutes, turning them about every 15 minutes. (Turning the potatoes prevents the skins from getting burnt, so you can then eat the skins, too.) The sweet potatoes are done when you can push your thumb in about ¼ inch on all sides.

**NOTE:** If you do not have a grill, bake on a baking sheet at 375°F for 1 hour.

# COLLARDS

## with Pot Likker, Cornbread Dumplings & Green Tomato Chowchow

# by Adrian Lipscombe

MAKES 6 TO 8 SERVINGS

*My great-grandmother James's hands were in everything, from putting seeds in the soil to bringing the plates to the table. When it came to collard greens, she would say, "Triple wash your greens, then read the greens. The greens will tell you everything you need to know about how the world is doing. Look at the sand and dirt from the greens; it can tell you how farmers cared for them. The damage and insects found in collards tell you about the health of the farm and the soil and how often they were tended to. The color and hardiness of the collards informs you how the greens were cared for." She always reminded us that we have to care just as much about the farm and farmers as we do about the ingredients.*

**COLLARDS WITH
POT LIKKER**

2 pounds collard greens, tough stems removed and leaves coarsely chopped

2 tablespoons plus
2 teaspoons olive oil

1 unpeeled large onion, chopped in half

2 large garlic cloves, minced

½-inch piece ginger, peeled and sliced

1 pound smoked turkey wing (about 1 wing)

10 cups water or enough water to submerge collard greens

1 tablespoon kosher salt

½ teaspoon black caraway seeds, or nigella seeds

¼ teaspoon crushed red pepper flakes

**CORNBREAD DUMPLINGS**
Makes about 24 dumplings

1½ cups all-purpose flour

¾ cup cornmeal

2½ teaspoons baking powder

½ teaspoon salt

1 tablespoon plus
1 teaspoon sugar

⅛ teaspoon ground nutmeg (optional)

1 tablespoon butter, chilled and cut into small pieces

1 egg

½ cup cold milk, plus more as needed

Canola oil for frying

**GREEN TOMATO
CHOWCHOW**

½ medium cabbage, chopped

1 onion, diced

8 ounces green tomatoes, diced, about 2 small

8 ounces red and green sweet peppers, diced, about 1½ peppers

4 ounces banana peppers, diced, about 1

2 stalks celery, diced

1 jalapeño, stemmed and diced (seeded optional)

½ cup chopped parsley leaves

4 green onions, trimmed and diced

1 teaspoon salt

½ cup granulated sugar

½ teaspoon celery seed

½ teaspoon ground mustard

1½ teaspoons mustard seeds

¼ teaspoon ground turmeric

¼ teaspoon ground ginger

½ teaspoon cinnamon

¼ teaspoon ground cloves

1 teaspoon crushed red pepper flakes

1 cup apple cider vinegar

CONTINUED

**TO MAKE THE COLLARDS WITH POT LIKKER:** Soak the collard greens in warm water and wash three times or until all of the sand and soil come off in the water. Drain.

In a large Dutch oven, heat the 2 teaspoons of oil over medium-high heat. Add the onion, flesh side down, to the pot. Cook until the onion gets some black bits and starts to soften, 6 to 8 minutes, turning in the skillet a few times. Remove the onion from the pot. Remove the onion skin and chop.

Add the remaining 2 tablespoons oil to the pot along with the onion, garlic, and ginger and lightly sauté until the onion is translucent and fragrant, 3 to 4 minutes.

Add the collard greens, turkey wing, water, and salt to the pot. Cover the pot and bring to a boil. Turn down the heat to a low simmer and cook, covered, for 1 hour. Transfer the turkey wing to a cutting board to cool, 5 to 10 minutes.

While the turkey is cooling, add the caraway seeds and red pepper flakes to the greens. Simmer for 45 to 60 minutes until the greens are very tender.

When the turkey wing is cool enough to handle, pick the meat from the wing and discard the skin. Return the bones and turkey meat to the pot and finish simmering the collards.

**TO MAKE THE DUMPLINGS:** In a large bowl, sift together the flour, cornmeal, baking powder, salt, sugar, and nutmeg, if using.

Add the butter to the flour mixture and mix with your fingers or a fork until it has a sandy consistency.

In a separate bowl, mix the egg and milk.

Gradually add the egg mixture to the flour mixture. If the mixture looks too dry, add additional milk, 1 tablespoon at a time, kneading until the dough is soft and elastic and the sides of the bowl are clean.

Pour an inch of oil into a skillet and heat it until small bubbles cover the bottom of the pan.

Use a small ice cream scoop to drop golf ball–sized rounds (about 2 tablespoons each) of batter into the oil, about five at a time. Make sure not to crowd the pot, since this will cause the oil temperature to drop. Fry until golden brown all over, turning frequently, about 4 minutes.

Drain the fried dumplings on paper towels.

**TO MAKE THE CHOWCHOW:** In a large nonreactive bowl, combine the cabbage, onion, tomatoes, sweet peppers, banana peppers, celery, jalapeño, parsley, green onion, salt, and sugar. Add all of the spices and vinegar and stir to thoroughly combine. Cover and let stand for 4 hours or refrigerate overnight. Once combined, it can be canned to be used throughout the season.

**TO SERVE:** Add the cornbread dumplings to the pot likker, if desired, and serve with the chowchow on the side.

# LACE HOECAKES

## (or Skillet Corn Cakes with Sorghum Butter)

## by Charles Hunter III

MAKES 10 TO 12 CAKES

*My grandmother and great-grandmother lived in a duplex not far from our house. They had a garden in the back-yard, along with a chicken coop that was attached to a curing shed. The garden was laden with rows of corn and whatever else the season had inspired them to sow into the earth. And one dish you were sure to find at any of our family gatherings was cornbread, lace hoecakes, or corn-bread muffins—some sweet and some savory. This recipe transports me to a time when gathering around the table was something of an Olympic sport.*

**SKILLET CAKES**

**4 ears of corn** (to yield about 2 cups of corn kernels)

**3 tablespoons neutral oil or butter**, plus more for cooking

**½ cup Vidalia onion, diced**

**½ cup chopped green onions**

**1 teaspoon kosher salt**

**1 teaspoon black pepper**

**2 garlic cloves, grated**

**1 cup yellow cornmeal**

**1 egg, lightly beaten**

**⅔ cup full-fat buttermilk**

**2 tablespoons melted butter**

**SORGHUM BUTTER**

**8 tablespoons (1 stick) unsalted butter**, at room temperature

**2 tablespoons sorghum**

**Smidge of kosher salt**

**Sliced green onions and smoked paprika for garnish**

**TO MAKE THE CAKES:** In a large bowl, shave the corn kernels, being careful not to scrape too close to the cob. Then, using the back of your knife, scrape the milk from the cob into the bowl.

In a sauté pan over medium heat, add 1 tablespoon of the oil or butter and both onions and sauté for 6 to 7 minutes until the onions are translucent. Add the corn kernels, salt, and pepper, and cook for 3 to 4 more minutes. Add the garlic and cook for another 2 minutes until fragrant and well-blended. Turn down the heat if you are starting to get color on the onions. Transfer the corn mixture from the pan into a sepa-rate bowl and set aside to allow the corn to come to room temperature.

Meanwhile, in a second large bowl, combine the corn-meal, egg, buttermilk, and melted butter. Blend with a rubber spatula. Then add the cooked corn to the bat-ter. Fold the corn into the batter until fully combined.

Heat a skillet over medium heat and add the remain-ing 2 tablespoons oil or butter. Using a 2-ounce scoop, place three scoops of the batter into the skillet and lightly pat them down to a ¼-inch thickness. Make sure to leave 1 inch of space between the cakes so you have space to flip them. Cook for 2 to 3 minutes on each side. Transfer the finished cakes onto a sheet pan with a baking rack and keep them warm in a 200°F oven while you finish cooking the remaining batter. Add another tablespoon of oil or butter to the skillet before the next batch.

**TO MAKE THE BUTTER:** In a bowl, blend the butter, sorghum, and salt until partially combined. (You want some striations of sorghum left in the butter.)

**TO SERVE:** Shingle the hoecakes clockwise on a plat-ter and serve the butter in the center. Garnish with sliced green onions or smoked paprika.

Lace Hoecakes with Sorghum Butter (page 159)

# BLACK-EYED PEA & CHARRED OCTOPUS SALAD

## by Jerome Grant

MAKES 4 TO 6 SERVINGS

*Some of my fondest memories from my travels revolve around dining tables overflowing with fresh and bountiful seafood, from freshly shucked oysters to live-caught fish. But nothing compares to a perfectly seasoned and tender bite of octopus. While most people are intimidated by preparing this eight-tentacled mollusk, my black-eyed pea and charred octopus salad is simple to prepare and sure to impress guests at your next gathering. Originating from North Africa, black-eyed peas are an Old World staple that made their way into Europe by way of Spanish explorers and enslaved Africans. The combination of octopus, a popular Portuguese ingredient, with black-eyed peas is an illustration of the foodways and migration of the African diaspora into the New World. This great base recipe can be jazzed up with additional seasonal vegetables like tomatoes, corn, or squash.*

**1 pound octopus, cleaned**

**2 bay leaves**

**4 sprigs of thyme**

**Salt for boiling and to taste**

**½ cup olive oil**

**4 garlic cloves, minced**

**Juice of 2 limes**

**Pepper to taste**

**2½ cups cooked black-eyed peas (canned or homemade), drained (If canned, allow to drain for at least 30 minutes.)**

**2 tablespoons sliced green onions**

**3 tablespoons coarsely chopped parsley leaves**

**3 tablespoons coarsely chopped cilantro leaves**

Place the octopus in a large pot and cover with water, enough to keep the octopus submerged but not swimming in water. Add the bay leaves, thyme, and salt, then bring the water to a boil. Continue to boil for 30 minutes or until the octopus is tender.

Once the octopus is tender, remove from the water and rinse under cold water.

Place the octopus in a medium-size bowl and add ¼ cup of the oil, garlic, and half of the lime juice. Season with salt and pepper and let marinate for 45 minutes.

Heat a medium-size cast-iron skillet over medium-high heat. Begin charring the octopus, turning every 3 to 5 minutes. Once the octopus is nicely charred, remove it from the pan and slice it into medium-size pieces.

In a separate bowl, toss together the peas, green onion, parsley, cilantro, octopus, the remaining ¼ cup oil, and the remaining lime juice. Season with salt and pepper. Serve immediately.

**NOTE:** If a cast-iron pan isn't available, you can also use a heavy sauté pan or charcoal grill.

# GREEN BANANA CHOWDER

## by Leeonney Bentick

MAKES 4 SERVINGS

*Growing up in the Caribbean—namely St. Vincent and the Grenadines—fall and winter were unfamiliar terms. Nonetheless, what we share with North America is the plethora of spices, root vegetables, and comforting dishes that are enjoyed during these seasons. The islands' fertile volcanic soil allows for easy cultivation of green banana, breadfruit, and cassava, introduced through the slave trade. These crops are drought resistant, with an abundant yield, and fed and nourished the workers. "Ground provisions," as they are affectionately called, are not only central to our Caribbean foodways but also to the islands' economy.*

*This recipe embodies the flavors of St. Vincent and is near and dear to my heart. It is the epitome of Vincentian cooking—sustainable and simple, yet bold in flavor, a velvety smooth and nutritious soup. When handling green bananas and eddoe, please use caution and oil both hands and your knife generously as they tend to "stain" or darken your fingertips. Cut the ends from the banana, then make a shallow slit down its length and proceed to peel. If you have trouble, use a knife and peel as if peeling a potato. Much like potatoes they will oxidize if left out after peeling, so be sure to soak them in cold water while you prepare the remaining ingredients.*

**3 star anise pods**

**1 cinnamon stick**

**3-inch piece ginger, peeled and smashed with the back of a knife**

**5 by 5-inch piece of cheesecloth**

**2 tablespoons coconut oil**

**½ teaspoon cumin seeds**

**1 shallot, finely diced**

**1 stalk celery, diced (¼ cup)**

**3 pimento peppers, finely chopped**

**Small piece of Scotch bonnet chile, stemmed, seeded, and finely minced**

**2 garlic cloves, finely minced**

**5 green bananas, peeled and chopped into bite-size pieces (3 cups)**

**3 or 4 eddoes (taro roots), peeled and chopped into bite-size pieces (1 cup)**

**2 carrots, chopped into bite-size pieces (1 cup)**

**1 (13.5-ounce) can unsweetened coconut milk**

**3½ cups vegetable stock, plus more as needed**

**Salt and pepper to taste**

Begin by wrapping the aromatics (star anise, cinnamon stick, and ginger) in the cheesecloth and tie with a piece of kitchen twine. (If you don't have cheesecloth, you can sauté the star anise, cinnamon stick, and ginger along with the cumin seeds, shallot, celery, and pimento peppers in the next step. Be sure to remove the aromatics before serving.)

In a pot, heat the oil over medium heat and sauté the cumin seeds, shallot, celery, pimento peppers, and chile for 1 minute or until the shallot is translucent. Add the garlic, green bananas, eddoes, and carrots and sauté for an additional 2 minutes.

Add the coconut milk and vegetable stock to the pot, then nestle in the wrapped aromatics. Stir to mix well, cover, bring to a boil, then let simmer for 45 to 50 minutes over medium heat or until the root vegetables are fork-tender and the broth has thickened. Be sure to check that the liquid doesn't boil out, and add more if needed.

Remove the aromatics (star anise, cinnamon stick, and ginger) and turn off the heat. Season with salt and pepper and serve.

CHAPTER 5

ART BY DEBORAH ROBERTS

# CALL TO ACTION

## It's About Your Greens, Not Your Genes

# by Tracye McQuirter, MPH

Sis, I want you to go vegan. I want you to go 100 percent, full on, joyfully vegan. Why? Because I want you to feel what I feel: freedom.

I've been vegan for thirty-five years—from my twenties to my fifties and counting—and it has absolutely made me feel free. I know that lots of folks think being vegan means feeling deprived, but in reality, the opposite is true. I get to eat good food that's good *for* me and gives me the best chance of living a long, healthy, and disease-free life. And, it is kindest to people, animals, and the planet. I find incredible fulfillment and freedom in that.

My journey started in 1986, when I was a sophomore at Amherst College. Our Black Student Union brought the civil rights movement icon and global human rights activist Dick Gregory to campus to talk about the state of Black America. Instead, he decided to talk about the *plate* of Black America—about the politics, economics, health, and culture of what we ate, and why we should become vegans.

Most of us didn't know that Gregory had become vegan in the mid-1960s, inspired by the practice of nonviolence during the civil rights movement, which he extended to the treatment of animals, and influenced by naturopath Dr. Alvenia Fulton, who had

established the first vegan health food center on the South Side of Chicago in 1958.

So, by the time Gregory came to speak on my campus in 1986, he had been a vegan for nearly twenty years. In his speech, he traced the path of a hamburger from a cow on a factory farm to the slaughterhouse to a hamburger to a clogged artery to a heart attack, and it completely rocked my world.

After Gregory's lecture, I immediately went vegetarian—and lasted for about a week. But I couldn't get what he said out of my mind. When I went home for the summer, a few months later, I got all the books from the library about vegetarianism I could find (this was years before the internet). My mother and one of my sisters, Marya, read them, too. By the end of the summer, we had decided to go vegan.

I also discovered there was a large Black vegan community in my hometown of Washington, DC, that had established the first all-vegan restaurants and health food stores—thirteen of them—in the nation's capital, starting in the mid-1970s. I immersed myself in this community, learning more about the politics of food and how to make vegan food delicious, affordable, and convenient.

During my first ten years of being vegan, I worked as a museum director by day and spent my evenings and weekends doing vegan cooking demos and talks throughout the Washington, DC, area. My sister and I also created the first vegan website for African Americans in 1997. I loved teaching people about veganism so much that I eventually decided to change professions. I went back to school to get a master's degree in public health nutrition and have been helping people go vegan for the past thirty years, including writing the first vegan diet book for Black women in 2010.

As Toni Morrison said, the function of freedom is to free someone else. And my passion is to help change the health paradigm of Black women so we can live longer, healthier lives. The fact is that the majority of Black women are in a crisis when it comes to our health. We experience the highest rates of chronic diseases, like heart disease, stroke, diabetes, and certain cancers. And while systemic white supremacy is the root cause of these conditions, we have the power to take back control of our health.

So, sis, just because your mother, sister, or aunt had a chronic disease doesn't mean you will. It's about your greens, not your genes. Eating whole plant-based foods, along with exercising at least thirty minutes a day, being smoke-free, and maintaining a healthy weight can reduce the risk of developing chronic diseases by up to 80 percent. And of these lifestyle factors, eating healthy foods is most important.

That's why I created the 10,000 Black Vegan Women movement. As of this writing, nearly 12,000 women joined our first 21-Day Vegan Fresh Start and have begun to change their lives. And they're not alone. African Americans are the fastest-growing vegan demographic in the country. According to a 2016 Pew Research Center survey, 8 percent of African Americans are vegan and vegetarian, nearly three times higher than Americans overall. And Black women are leading the way. I want you to join us.

What's the next step? Start with your mind and your mouth will follow. Get crystal-clear on why *you* want to be vegan. Is it for your health, the animals, the environment, reducing world hunger, social justice, faith, a combination of these or something else? Educate yourself on the issues.

Watch vegan documentaries, read vegan books, join vegan communities for support, and find and follow your favorite vegan influencers. This will be the foundation for your healthy vegan journey.

And give yourself grace. Don't give up when you slip up. Just start again the next day. Know that all the things you're doing will be working together to help you mentally and physically transition. And if it takes you a month, six months or a year, it's okay. It's not a race or a competition. It's your journey. Enjoy it and embrace it and know that you can do it. Your freedom is worth it.

# BLACK WOMEN, FOOD & POWER

## by Psyche Williams-Forson, PhD

*i only want to*
*be there to kiss you*
*as you want to be kissed*
*when you need to be kissed*
*where i want to kiss you*
*cause it's my house*
*and i plan to live in it*

When I was in high school, I was on both the debate and forensics teams. I liked the latter more than the former because I could "perform." When I performed Nikki Giovanni's poem "My House," I knew I was cooking; I was doing a thing. It was Ms. Giovanni's insistence that she was going to create her own space, even as she gave of herself, that held my attention. She owns her space in ways that were unapologetic, and I learned to do the same.

As I think about the countless Black women descendants of the African diaspora who sought to "own their spaces" using food, my heart is filled with joy and sadness. In my work on issues around Black women, food, and power, I have come across so many of them in so many places. Some are fully named, while others are unknown or identified only by an aimless, random name, thrust upon them by the brutalities of enslavement. Some are fictional composites who come alive through poetry, literature, and on film, while others are found in our lyrics and on our tapestries and in our textiles. We have all encountered these women, but have we really seen them,

especially when they do not look like what we thought, or we do not find them where we expected?

*i really need to hug you*
*when i want to hug you*
*as you like to hug me*
*does this sound like a silly poem*

I think, for example, of the unnamed African women I met while working on the virtual exhibition *Fire and Freedom: Food and Enslavement in Early America*: African women, who were forced and carted like other provisions from the Continent, onto slave ships sailing the Atlantic and brought along for sale to satisfy horrific pleasures and "to dress the victuals," of rice and corn, as one slave captain indicated in his diary. Some of these women survived by complying, while many others resisted and perished. Though we do not know their names, we can imagine that some probably played significant roles in mutinies because they were the most familiar with the eating and sleeping habits and cycles of the ship's officers and captains. Along with the knowledge of how to cook many of the foods brought over from the Motherland, such as yams, okra, black-eyed peas, plantains, pigeon peas, rice, watermelon, peanuts, sesame seeds, and *melegueta* or red peppers, they also knew about spices and herbs used "to disguise spoiled meats and to enhance flavors." They were aware, (according to culinary historians like Jessica Harris, Robert Hall, and Michael Twitty), of various cooking techniques such as boiling, frying, and grilling, roasting cabbage instead of banana leaves, as well as how to use different grasses and herbs for medicinal and non-medicinal purposes.

These mothers, grandmothers, daughters, nieces, sisters, and friends carried their individual and collective power through care and feeding. Because of my work, I often think of them, holding their traumas as they cooked stockfish and beef or used flour to make bread, like the cook at George Washington's Mount Vernon, who used to rise at 4:00 a.m. to get the food started for the day. I think of the aged mother named Old Doll, who could be summoned by Washington at any hour to relieve someone's indigestion with her recipe for mint water. I am glad that Giovanni repeats "cause it's my house and i plan to live in it," because so many Black women and girls had no "house" to call their own.

> i mean it's my house
> and i want to fry pork chops
> and bake sweet potatoes
> and call them yams
> cause i run the kitchen
> and i can stand the heat

I also think of Priscilla, the enslaved young girl-child, who was one of six children (none over the age of ten) purchased at an auction in South Carolina by rice planter Elias Ball. She arrived at the South Carolina rice plantation in 1756, alone, afraid, and without family. Despite the poor conditions and high death rate of the other girls purchased by Ball, Priscilla survived. She overcame kidnapping, repeated rape (she had ten children), treacherous, snake-infested rice fields, and so much more. Hers is a story of generational survival and perseverance during some of the cruelest moments in history, on the contested cultural landscapes of the South Carolina Low Country. It is a story of race, gender, age, body, colonization, and creolization . . . and food. Priscilla's is a story that seven-generations later is still

being told and is a story of what geographer Judith Carney calls "Black rice." How many meals did Priscilla cook? Using what foods? And, for whom? And, how was her mental health after all that suffering? Priscilla could "stand the heat," because she had to, until she died at age sixty-five.

> i spent all winter in
> carpet stores gathering
> patches so i could make
> a quilt
> does this really sound
> like a silly poem
> i mean i want to keep you
> warm

> and my windows might be dirty
> but it's my house
> and if i can't see out sometimes
> they can't see in either

These stanzas from Giovanni's poem remind me of so many Black women, like those in Gordonsville, Virginia, and the ones who worked in urban city train depots and rural countryside whistle stops like Julia Brown, selling cut-up chickens so they could make a dollar out of 15 cents to feed their families and communities, start businesses, build houses, support local churches, and buy their own or someone else's freedom. In this respect, these women were no different from those like Ms. Eliza Johnson or Ms. Serena Gardiner whose windows were probably never dirty because it was their business to provide immaculate boarding and lodging houses, caring, then, for delegates and general attendees of the Colored Conventions, the state and national meetings held from the 1830 until the 1890s "to strategize about how they might achieve educational, labor, and legal justice."

Whether providing chilled Champagne, raw or baked oysters, ice creams, a range of confections, or the southern opossum Pauline Hopkins writes about in her 1900 novel *Contending*

*Forces,* neither was any less important than Giovanni's fried pork chops and baked sweet potatoes. This work was social action hidden by food provision and conviviality. These women influenced the political conversations of the day, even if they could not speak on the convention floor. They were precursors to Ms. Georgia Gilmore, who, during the Montgomery bus boycott, helped to fund the movement by selling food. Or the many Black women listed in the *Negro Motorist Green Book,* who, by working the underground, provided food, shelter, and drink to the weary traveler affected by the nastiness of Jim Crow.

These Black women showed us how to speak love through food long before Jill Scott told us, "It's Love" and asked, "Do you want it on your collard greens? Do you want it on your candy sweets?" Pickled beets? Rice and gravy? Biscuits or black-eyed peas?

*english isn't a good language*
*to express emotion through*
*mostly i imagine because people*
*try to speak english instead*
*of trying to speak through it*
*i don't know maybe it is*
*a silly poem*

Ms. Giovanni disrupts her beautiful narrative to tell us "english isn't a good language, to express emotion through, mostly i imagine because people try to speak english instead of trying to speak through it," to remind us of the power and control inherent in the written language. This is why we must remember the innumerable Black women domestics from enslavement to freedom, living in or commuting to and from white folks' homes and kitchens and who had their recipes stolen and published under someone else's name. This is why we must keep in mind the wise instruction of Nigerian novelist Chimimanda Ngozi Adichie, who admonishes us to remember that there is danger in a single story, stories that only make us feel good or cause us to want

to celebrate without acknowledging traumas, horrors, violence, in the face of hate and even because of love.

I am talking here about the stories that beg us to find resilience, when all we want to do is cook the pie and taste its sweetness. Pecola Breedlove, in Toni Morrison's *The Bluest Eye,* warns us of the dangers of seeing sweetness as the most important element. Morrison shows us how self-loathing and anger, among other emotions, are intertwined with food when she has Mrs. Pauline Breedlove slap her daughter, Pecola, for ruining the newly mopped kitchen floor in the white people's home after Pecola accidentally spills the blueberry cobbler. No sooner does Pauline throw her own child out of the house than she consoles the little white girl (who incidentally calls Mrs. Breedlove Polly), as she cries because the pie is ruined. We must remember Pecola's resilience and Mrs. Breedlove's decision making, chillingly ugly or not.

*i'm saying it's my house*
*and i'll make fudge and call*
*it love and touch my lips*
*to the chocolate warmth*
*and smile at old men and call*
*that revolution cause what's real*
*is really real*
*and i still like men in tight*
*pants cause everybody has some*
*thing to give and more*
*important needs something to take*

There are many stories of how Black women— of means and poor, lesbian, gay, bisexual, transgendered, heterosexual, on Monday through Sunday, from sunup and sundown, Muslim, Christian, Wiccan, atheist, vegan, vegetarian, meat-loving—exercised and continue to exhibit influence using food and/ or drink. We should take time to hear as many of these stories as we can and not just those with which we are familiar. From the tavern owners of yesteryear to the Black male army cooks of Craig Field to the James Beard award-winning culinarians of today, Black people have stories to tell about food. These stories are our influence. They are our power. They are the narratives I pass down to my daughter from my mother, who got it from her mother, and hers before her. Sometimes these stories are the fudge that we call love; sometimes they are in our song lyrics; sometimes they are in our recipes that we will never tell; or they are in the historical record buried under the terms "worker," "snack vendor," or "help." It is up to us to uncover them and learn to read beyond what we see. This is where you will find the narratives of Black women, food, and power. These are our "revolutions!"

*and this is my house and you make me happy*
*so this is your poem*

# CREATING SACRED SPACE
## as Part of the Black Food Ritual

# by Jocelyn Jackson

*"The Ritual"*

*Looking into each other's eyes, sort of like a nonverbal pitch pipe, slowly and powerfully my family began to sing:*

*Be present at our table, Lord*

*Be here and everywhere I go*

*These blessings bless and grant that we*

*May live in paradise with thee.*

*Amen*

I looked around the circle at my parents and siblings, aunts, uncles, cousins, and grandparents. Each of us knew the song by heart, creating layers of harmonies as the verse turned to chorus. My twelve-year-old self was finally coming to realize how special and purposeful this tradition of singing to bless the meal is to our legacy as a family and as a people. How this spiritual practice acknowledges the sacredness of our food and ourselves and honors the survival of our ancestors.

As I grew and experienced more of the world, I was able to add more context to the tradition and purpose of this blessing. Among these experiences was a return to West Africa. I was able to see peanuts and black-eyed peas and other diasporic soul foods of my childhood cultivated in the land of my ancestors. From my host families, I learned to cook tiga diga na and accara and so much more, using these ingredients and hearing the stories, which passed down their meaning and flavors. As my host family sat in a circle sharing our meals, we gave thanks for these blessings.

A few times a year, in my host village outside of Kaye in western Mali, after all the families had finished their supper, we gathered in the open space at the center of the thatch roof and adobe homes. During the day, this was the place where the women came together to *susu* the dried corn: a huge task made easier with three or four women rhythmically pounding their four-foot-long pestles into each vessel. But on these dark, star-filled nights, the young men of the village gathered chaff from the fields into a large pile and set fire to it. They continued to feed the flames throughout the night as a griot sang, drums beat, and people— young, old, and in between—danced with their whole bodies. As I watched and participated, my own body felt at home, and I was reminded of my own family's traditions.

## THE CALL

I didn't answer my calling to be of service through food until I was thirty-eight. In retrospect, I can see that I was collecting the experiences necessary to relearn the spiritual practice of food. My travels and research and formal study of art, law, ecology, and education were stepping-stones toward reanimating my instincts. All my life when I cooked, I felt the importance of this sensuous and elemental experience. That cooking was also a conduit for gathering together beloved community was no mistake. During my thirty-eighth birthday celebration, my community gathered in a circle and blessed me with stories of how my cooking was central to our connection, how food is the reason and requisite for this ritual we call life. That blessing circle released a resounding yes from my heart.

Almost immediately, I began my first food business. One of the people in that birthday blessing circle was my first client. As I'd often dreamed, I served "rice and sauce" dishes that I had learned to make during my travels and at my momma's side. JUSTUS Kitchen, my present solo food project, and the People's

Kitchen Collective, which I co-founded with Saqib Keval and Sita Kuratomi Bhaumik, directly flow from those first instincts to be of service to my community. Cultivating cultural food experiences that are centered around the survival and joy of people of color is at each project's core.

As an activist cook, my intentions and responsibilities are clear: I honor food from the seed to the soil to the soul. My actions are choreographed to guide us on a sacred journey that began ages ago and is manifested each time we plant food, eat food, and gather together to partake of that food. The griot tells us that we sing as we sow seeds and sing again when we enjoy the harvest. These blessings are explicit gratitude and a tangible way for us to create a sacred space for gratitude to unfold.

## THE ALTAR

A constant at the meals I co-create is an altar, a space dedicated to the ancestral, aesthetic, and liberated foundation of our foodways. Through the following process, I invite you into this spiritual practice of creating sacred space to express gratitude for life through food.

Begin by thinking about your family's food traditions. What did your grandparents cook for you? Did the recipe or ingredients have special significance? What did the table look like? How did you feel when you ate it? Who was at the table? Was the dish made in a specific season when the ingredient was available? Take time to reflect on what these guiding questions help you learn or feel more clearly.

Now find a surface in your home where you can create a small gratitude altar that connects you to your family's food traditions. It can be a bookcase, a curio cabinet, or a plant stand. Be creative. Clear the space with the smudging element of your choice. Place a picture of the ancestor that resonated most when you were thinking about your traditions. (For me, that's my great-grandma Lovey.) Place a small candle beside the picture. Perhaps add a piece of wax cloth or bogolan material, seeds of relevant ingredients, a plant, or a quote. A small dish where you can offer libations is also welcome. All of these items will act as focal points for your gratitude.

This altar is a sacred space where you can ignite the power of food to inhabit your heart, your home, and your lineage. Before making one of the dishes visualized during the reflection above, take a few moments at this altar to express your gratitude to your ancestors, Earth, and the source of spirit that makes it possible.

## THE FOOD

Now decide on the dish you'd like to make or use as a foundation for improv. (One of my favorites is my grandma's collard greens with turnips.) Write out the recipe so that it can be saved and collected into a family recipe book, smears of butter and all. If you have a victory garden or access to a community garden, take the time to harvest the ingredients that are available. When possible, source ingredients as close to the ground they came from, from farmers' markets and local farm stands. When those sources aren't accessible, honor whatever way you can get ingredients as just as sacred and beautiful. Never put judgment on survival.

Making food is a dance. Put on your Ella or Angélique or Erykah and your favorite apron. Show up for the experience with joy and purpose in your heart. Feel the flesh of the vegetables, smell the spices, taste the blending and building of flavors. Enjoy the activation of your senses at every step. Remind yourself of everyone who cooked these recipes and handled these ingredients before you. Give thanks.

While you're cooking, you will also be cleaning. The sacred always includes the mundane to keep us focused on the gifts that the entire experience has to offer. Cleaning is an opportunity to reflect on both completeness and continuity.

When you're done cooking, put some attention toward the platters and plates and cups that you use. Were they passed down from earlier generations? Are they lovingly mismatched and encompass the stories of shared community? What the food is served on holds importance as well.

As the vessels are placed on the table (perhaps with handpicked flowers and a colorful tablecloth or placemat) and folks begin to gather around, will you have a prepared blessing, or will you sing a song or have a moment of silence? It is up to you. Creating the sacred space of appreciation for these food traditions is intention plus instinct and often created collectively. Return to the reflection process and the images and memories it conjured to inspire your choices.

Eat with purpose. Share the story of the meal. Express the emotional vulnerability of its creation. Enjoy the power that every bite provides. Wrap a plate and take it to your neighbor or an elder. Pass the recipe on to other family members. Return to the altar you created. Express your gratitude for all that you learned through this experience.

## THE BLESSING

Black food isn't just ingredients and recipes and stories. It is also the spiritual practices and sacred spaces created when cooking and gathering together around these foods. It is the permission and invitation to feel welcome. It is the opportunity to honor our ancestors and our Afro futures. For me, food is a prayer. It is a sacred practice inherited from all my peoples. The stories of our food inspire empathy and connection. Food is about relationships and survival and creating the world we wish to see. Bless you on this powerful and liberatory journey.

# WHISKEY SOUR

## by Toni Tipton-Martin

MAKES 1 COCKTAIL

When entrepreneur, author, and historian Fawn Weaver discovered the rarely-told story of the formerly enslaved man behind Jack Daniels Whiskey, she sprang into action. She moved temporarily from her home in Los Angeles to Lynchburg, Tennessee, studied archives, and interviewed townsfolk to learn more about Nathan "Uncle Nearest" Green, the first known African American master distiller. Then, armed with more than ten thousand original documents and artifacts, she began sharing the story of Nearest Green's remarkable journey from enslavement to professional excellence with his family and the world.

It was Green who taught Jack Daniels the charcoal-mellowing technique for filtering whiskey, a ". . . unique and time-consuming craft, known as the Lincoln County Process (named after the county in which Nearest lived and worked)." According to the Nearest Green Foundation, the process is required in order for a whiskey to be considered Tennessee Whiskey.

Weaver dedicated her career to preserving and celebrating this inspirational legacy, establishing the Nearest Green Distillery in Shelbyville, Tennessee, that oversees the production of Uncle Nearest Whiskey, and founding a 501c3 nonprofit foundation.

This whiskey sour cocktail honors Weaver, Green, and the African American mixologists whose stories have yet to be told. It is adapted from my forthcoming cookbook, Juke Joints, Jazz Clubs, and Juice: Cocktails from Two Centuries of African American Mixology.

To spark my creativity, I consulted an African American cookbook by an author who pursued a "credit where credit is due" philosophy similar to Weaver's. In 1940, Rebecca West included a few recipes for classic cocktails in her collection Rebecca's Cookbook, memorializing two of her chef friends, George and Alonzo.

For her sweet-sour base, West mixed sugar and lemon juice in a large ice-filled glass, then topped off the beverage with seltzer. I adapted her cocktail with extra inspiration from Helen Mahammitt, another early twentieth century cookbook author and cooking school teacher. Here, freshly squeezed orange juice and homemade simple syrup replace granulated sugar. The citrus adds a natural sweetness that brightens the cocktail. Garnish with a cherry and a thin slice of orange.

**ORANGE-FLAVORED SIMPLE SYRUP**
Makes about ¾ cup

1 cup water

1 tablespoon grated orange zest

1 cup granulated sugar

2 ounces whiskey

2 ounces freshly squeezed orange juice

1½ ounces freshly squeezed lemon juice

1 cup ice

1 maraschino cherry

1 orange slice

**TO MAKE THE SYRUP:** In a heavy saucepan, combine the water, orange zest, and sugar. Stir over low heat until dissolved. Bring to a boil over medium-high heat, then turn down the heat to simmer until reduced by half and the syrup is thick, about 5 minutes. The syrup can be kept in a tightly covered container in the refrigerator for up to a month.

**TO MAKE THE COCKTAIL:** In a large cocktail shaker, combine the whiskey, orange juice, lemon juice, ½ ounce of the orange-flavored simple syrup, and ice. Cover and shake vigorously until the ingredients are well mixed and very cold. Pour into a tall glass. Garnish with the cherry and orange slice.

# SALTFISH FRITTERS

## by Kalisa Marie Martin

MAKES ABOUT 36 FRITTERS

*Saltfish fritters, also known as "stamp and go," are said to be one of Jamaica's first fast foods. They're crispy on the outside, tender on the inside, and full of well-seasoned salted codfish. Though traditionally served at breakfast, they're delicious any time of day.*

*Like many first-generation Americans, food is one of the main ways I've stayed connected to my roots. My maternal grandmother, the oldest of twelve children, has always loved cooking for her family and is the best cook I know. My mother, on the other hand, has never enjoyed or excelled at the culinary arts. Despite this, it's her recipe for saltfish fritters the whole family loves and the one I've happily inherited. While some fritters are pan-fried, giving them a flattened shape, we use baking powder and deep-fry ours, resulting in a puffy, rounded fritter with an almost cakelike center.*

*When I moved to Jamaica a few years ago, to host guests at my B&B there, I made these fritters weekly. It made me curious to look into the origins of saltfish and other Jamaican staples. I learned that saltfish—one of Jamaica's most celebrated foods—was actually introduced to the island by its colonizers in the eighteenth century as a cheap, long-lasting protein to feed enslaved people.*

*This complicated history is not unique. Oftentimes, the "fusion" cuisines we know and love have racist origins rooted in oppression. But we don't have to divorce that history in order to continue to enjoy them. Our ancestors adapted ingredients that were forced on them to make new dishes. This is not a celebration of colonial influence but a testament to our creativity, resilience, and self-reliance. It reminds me of the strength of my people and makes me love saltfish fritters even more.*

3 cups shredded, soaked, and deboned/skinned saltfish (from 1½ pounds saltfish)

¼ cup raw coconut oil (or other cooking oil of your choice)

1 cup chopped onions

1 cup chopped scallions

5 plum tomatoes, chopped

6 garlic cloves, minced

1 tablespoon fresh thyme leaves

½ Scotch bonnet chile, stem removed and minced (remove the seeds to make it less spicy or omit all together)

3 cups all-purpose flour (or gluten-free flour)

4 teaspoons baking powder

1 to 2 teaspoons salt

1 to 2 cups water

Oil for deep frying

**TO PREPARE THE SALTFISH (OVERNIGHT METHOD):** Rinse the saltfish of excess salt and place in a pot of cold water. Bring to a boil, remove from the heat, and let stand overnight in the fridge. The next day, taste a piece from the meatiest part. It should be flavorful but not overly salty. If it's still very salty, add it back to the pot with fresh water, bring it to a boil, and drain. Remove the skin and bones (if any) and flake into pieces.

**TO PREPARE THE SALTFISH (SAME-DAY METHOD):** Rinse the saltfish of excess salt and place in a pot of cold water. Bring to a boil and then discard the hot water. Add fresh cold water to the pot of saltfish, bring to a boil again, and drain again. Taste and repeat a third time, if necessary. Drain, remove the skin and bones (if any), and flake into pieces.

CONTINUED

## Saltfish Fritters, continued

**TO SAUTÉ THE SEASONINGS:** Heat the coconut oil in a large saucepan over medium-high heat. Add the onion, scallions, tomatoes, garlic, thyme, and chile and cook, stirring, until the onions are translucent and the water that the tomatoes release is mostly evaporated, about 15 minutes. Add the saltfish, stir, and allow to cook for another minute or two for the flavors to combine. Taste! Set aside to cool.

**TO PREPARE THE BATTER:** In a large bowl, mix together the flour, baking powder, and salt (the amount will depend on how seasoned your saltfish mixture tastes to you). Add the saltfish mixture to your flour mixture and stir to combine. Add the water, about ½ cup at a time, stirring between additions. You want to add just enough water to form a very thick batter.

**TO FRY THE FRITTERS:** Heat the oil in a deep, wide pot over medium heat. If you have a frying thermometer, use it! The target is 350°F. If not, after 10 minutes, stick a wooden spoon in the oil and if small steady bubbles form around it immediately, it's ready to go. (If bubbles do not form quickly, it's not hot enough; if they bubble vigorously, it's too hot.) Use two large spoons to drop the batter into the fryer and fry for 5 to 6 minutes until golden brown. Adjust the heat as necessary to maintain the temperature. Remove the fritters with a slotted spoon to a rack or paper towel–lined plate to cool. Enjoy!

**NOTES:** If you can't find saltfish (aka bacalao) at your usual grocery store, try a local Caribbean or Latin American market.

A habanero chile can be substituted for the Scotch bonnet.

If you're gluten free like me, swap in gluten-free, all-purpose flour.

# VEGAN BLACK-EYED PEA BEIGNETS

## with Warm Spiced Sugar & Green Tomato Jam

## by Elle Simone Scott

MAKES 20 TO 24 BEIGNETS

*Black-eyed peas are one of the most well-traveled legumes. They've made appearances in Brazil and Africa, but their most storied landing was in the southern part of America. I imagine that it was in some church basement in Mound Bayou, Mississippi, where my foremother first encountered them. I came to love them at seven years old, when my grandmother braised them with smoked turkey and onion, then poured them, piping hot, over some sweet cornbread. Since then, I've been fascinated with the ways that people of the diaspora have transformed the black-eyed pea. One of the most popular applications is in the black-eyed pea fritter, also known as accara or accarajé, which are Yoruba in origin but enjoyed worldwide.*

*This recipe is my adaptation of the accara, passed down to me with the southern influence from my ancestors. It's my way of reconciliation on a plate; although I may never know by name my African ancestors, their stories live on through me and in my cooking.*

**BLACK-EYED PEA MIXTURE**

¾ cup black-eyed peas, soaked overnight or follow "quick-soak" method on page 185

2 tablespoons vegetable oil

1 small to medium onion, thinly sliced

2 garlic cloves, thinly sliced

1 bay leaf

½ teaspoon garlic powder

¼ teaspoon cayenne pepper

1 teaspoon smoked paprika

1 teaspoon liquid smoke (optional)

2 teaspoons salt

2½ cups low-sodium vegetable broth

Black pepper to taste

**GREEN TOMATO JAM**
Makes about 16 ounces

3 pounds green tomatoes, unpeeled, chopped

1¾ cups granulated sugar

6 tablespoons fresh lemon juice (from 2 lemons), plus more as needed

¼ teaspoon cinnamon (optional)

Pinch of cayenne pepper, ground cardamom, or pimento (optional)

**WARM SPICED SUGAR**

¼ cup confectioners' sugar

1 tablespoon cinnamon

½ teaspoon ground nutmeg

½ teaspoon salt

½ teaspoon ground cardamom (black cardamom, if you can find it)

**DOUGH**

¾ cup nondairy milk (I use barista blend oat milk, which is richer)

1½ teaspoons active dry yeast

½ teaspoon sugar

2 tablespoons vegetable oil plus 4 quarts for frying

2¾ cups bread flour

1½ teaspoons salt

CONTINUED

## Vegan Black-Eyed Pea Beignets, continued

**TO MAKE THE BLACK-EYED PEA MIXTURE:** Soak the peas overnight or quickly soak them by bringing water to a boil, then shutting off the heat and soaking them for 2 hours (this results in about 2 cups of soaked peas).

In a small saucepan, heat the oil over medium heat, then add the onion and garlic and sauté until translucent. Add the soaked peas, bay leaf, spices, salt, broth, and pepper and bring to a boil. Turn down the heat to low and simmer, covered, for 2½ hours, until the peas are tender. Remove the cover for the remaining 30 minutes to reduce the broth.

While still hot, remove ½ cup of the peas and pulse in a food processor or use an immersion blender or the back of a fork in a bowl to mix until smooth. Add ¼ cup of the cooking liquid to the bowl and strain in the remaining 1½ cups whole peas. Set aside to cool.

**TO MAKE THE JAM:** In a large, wide pot, combine the tomatoes, sugar, lemon juice, and spices, if using, and bring to a rolling boil over medium-high heat, stirring often, until the sugar melts, about 10 minutes. The mixture will begin to foam; stir as needed to avoid burning while still allowing the mixture to reduce and thicken for about another 15 minutes. Stir occasionally and taste for tartness, adding more lemon juice, if desired. The mixture will begin to look glossy and gel as it reduces. Turn down the heat to low and use a spoon to test the texture by letting it cool on a spoon like a nape. If it doesn't thicken on the spoon, stir and let it cook for another 5 minutes and try again.

Push the mixture through a fine-mesh sieve or leave the tomato skins/seeds for a more textured jam. Cool and use immediately or can the jam. Jam can also be stored in the fridge for up to 14 days in an airtight container.

**TO MAKE THE SPICED SUGAR:** In a small bowl, combine all of the ingredients and set aside.

**TO MAKE THE DOUGH:** In a microwave, warm the milk to body temperature in a large microwave-safe bowl (30 to 60 seconds), then add the yeast, sugar, and

2 tablespoons oil and whisk for 30 seconds; let rest for 10 minutes. In a large bowl, mix the flour and salt.

Whisk or stir half of the flour into the yeast. Add half of the cooled black-eyed pea mixture and blend. Add the remaining flour and stir until it is combined and you can no longer use the spoon or whisk. Add the remaining black-eyed pea mixture.

Knead the mixture with your hands until the flour is absorbed. The mixture should be tacky and moist but not sticky. It should absorb all the flour in the bowl and form a smooth ball.

Lightly grease a bowl and the dough with oil, cover with plastic wrap, and let rest overnight in the fridge.

The next morning, remove the dough from the fridge, punch down, and knead for 5 minutes with lightly floured hands. The dough shouldn't dry out in the process but should retain its moist, springy texture. Let rest again for 30 minutes. (I like to knead for 5 minutes, press it into a rectangle, then a trifold, and finally press down to seal. This creates some folds in the final product and gives a headstart to the rectangle shape.)

Once the dough has rested, roll it out on a lightly floured surface into a ¼-inch-thick rectangle. Cut into 2½-inch squares. While giving the dough its final rest (10 to 15 minutes), heat the oil to 350°F in a Dutch oven or heavy-bottomed pot. You'll need a candy thermometer to check the temperature.

Gently drop the squares into the hot oil and cook for 1 to 2 minutes per side or until golden brown. (They will not get as dark as nonvegan beignets.)

Remove the beignets from the oil onto paper towels.

**TO SERVE:** While the beignets are still warm, sprinkle with the spiced sugar and serve with a dollop of jam. Eat (almost) immediately.

# LENTIL, OKRA & COCONUT STEW

## by Nina Compton

MAKES 4 TO 6 SERVINGS

*The inspiration behind this dish is cow foot soup, a rich and hearty lentil soup made with various ground provisions like yam, cassava, and okra, stewed together with cow's feet. You'll find versions of this dish throughout the Caribbean. It's a humble soup that uses humble ingredients and is served in food stalls and local markets all over the islands. This recipe is a simplified version but is just as tasty. I make it without the meat but with the addition of coconut milk, which adds a silky, almost velvety feel. You'll want more and more of this soul-satisfying soup, especially on a chilly night.*

3 tablespoons extra-virgin olive oil

1 large onion, finely chopped

4 garlic cloves, finely chopped

1 stalk lemongrass, smashed and very finely chopped

3-inch piece ginger, peeled and very finely chopped

6 teaspoons curry powder

1 (15-ounce) can crushed tomatoes

1 habanero chile, torn in half, stemmed and seeded (use only half if you like less spice)

1 (13.5-ounce) can unsweetened coconut milk

1 cup split lentils

2 teaspoons kosher salt, plus more as needed

6 cups water

1 cup okra, cut into ¼-inch rounds

1 small bunch cilantro, leaves picked

3 scallions, finely sliced

Heat the oil in a large Dutch oven over medium heat. Add the onion and cook, stirring often, just until translucent, 6 to 8 minutes.

Add the garlic, lemongrass, and ginger and cook, stirring often, until the garlic is starting to turn golden, about 5 minutes.

Lower the heat and add 5 teaspoons of the curry powder, tomatoes, and chile and cook, stirring constantly, until the spices are aromatic and starting to stick to the bottom of the pot, about 2 minutes.

Add the coconut milk and stir to loosen the spices, then stir in the lentils, salt, and water. Bring to a boil over medium-high heat, then lower the heat to medium-low to keep the soup at a gentle simmer. Cook until the lentils are broken down and the soup has thickened, 25 to 30 minutes, stirring occasionally.

Puree half, making sure you puree the chile, then add the puree back to the pot. Add the okra and remaining curry powder and simmer just to let the flavors come together on low heat. Taste and season again with more salt. Top with the cilantro and scallions and serve.

# JERK CHICKEN RAMEN

## by Suzanne Barr

MAKES 4 SERVINGS

*Jamaican food will always connect me to my parents. This dish is a dream for me: it represents who I am as a chef and celebrates my mother and father's birthplace, Jamaica, as well as the history of my ancestors, the Maroons, the Taino, and the Arawak people. An early form of food preservation used in the foothills of the Blue Mountains in Jamaica was smoking spiced and marinated food over pimento wood; this is jerk.*

*I learned the ritual of eating from my mother. I also went to cooking school because of her. When she was diagnosed with pancreatic cancer, I decided to move home to Plantation, Florida, to take care of her. The hardest part of that experience was the fact that I didn't know how to cook for her. She had spent so much of her life in the kitchen lovingly preparing food for me, my siblings, and my father, and I didn't even know where to begin. My journey in becoming a chef started because of her. She believed in the saying, "full the belly."*

*The recipe I developed is in honor of my mother's strength and her influence on me. I wanted to acknowledge the challenges she faced as a young woman leaving Jamaica and moving to London. The decision to fuse these two incredible dishes, jerk chicken and ramen, reflects my love for travel and influences that inspired my journey as a Black female chef. I respect and honor the ritual of making ramen, with its origins in China and now a mainstay in Japanese cuisine.*

**JERK CHICKEN MARINADE**

2 bunches scallions, white and light-green parts only, trimmed, greens reserved

3 carrots, cut into coins

2 Scotch bonnet chiles, stems removed

1 to 2 tablespoons canola oil

2 tablespoons peeled and thinly sliced fresh ginger

3 tablespoons thyme leaves

2 garlic cloves, minced

¼ cup ground allspice

½ cup orange juice

2 tablespoons white vinegar

1½ tablespoons packed brown sugar

¼ cup lime juice

1 teaspoon cinnamon

1 teaspoon ground cloves

2 tablespoons salt

**CHICKEN**

2 pounds chicken thighs, bones removed and reserved for broth

**CHICKEN BROTH**

1 pound reserved chicken bones from thighs

1 pound chicken necks and chicken backs

1 carrot, cut into 1-inch pieces

1 onion, quartered

½ bunch thyme

3 scallions, root ends trimmed

1 knob ginger, peeled

2 garlic cloves

1 tablespoon whole allspice

2 bay leaves

4 quarts water

¾ cup pineapple juice

**NOODLES**

4 (3-ounce) packages dried ramen noodles

**TARE**

¼ cup reserved jerk chicken liquid

¼ cup pineapple juice

¼ cup soy sauce

**GARNISHES**

2 soft-boiled eggs

Reserved scallion greens, sliced

1 cup steamed cabbage

CONTINUED

## Jerk Chicken Ramen, continued

**TO MAKE THE MARINADE:** Turn the oven to 375°F. Line a sheet pan with parchment paper.

In a bowl, place the scallions, carrots, and chiles. Drizzle with the oil, coating well.

Spread the scallion, carrots, and chiles evenly on the prepared pan. Roast in the oven until the ingredients are charred but not burnt, 12 to 17 minutes. Remove the pan from the oven and allow the ingredients to cool before coarsely chopping and placing them in a food processor with the remaining marinade ingredients. Puree until you have a thick pastelike consistency. Reserve ¼ cup of the marinade to be used later in the tare recipe.

**TO MARINATE THE CHICKEN:** Place the chicken thighs in a large bowl and massage with the jerk marinade, allowing to sit overnight in the fridge or for a minimum of 2 hours before cooking.

**TO MAKE THE BROTH:** In a large pot, bring water to a boil. Add the reserved chicken bones and chicken necks and backs, and boil for 10 minutes. A lot of scum will surface. Drain and wash the bones under running cold water, one by one, removing coagulated blood along the spine of the chicken and any other brown bits.

Add the cleaned bones and the rest of the broth ingredients to the cleaned pot along with the water and pineapple juice, then bring to a boil. When scum surfaces, occasionally scoop it off gently using a ladle. Do not mix the broth with the ladle when removing the scum, since it will cause the broth to become cloudy. After removing the scum four or five times, turn down the heat to simmer gently. Simmer for 2 hours with a lid on but slightly ajar, allowing for ventilation. Turn off the heat. Put the broth through a fine-mesh sieve and collect only the liquid; discard the solids.

**TO ROAST THE CHICKEN:** Remove the chicken from the fridge and allow it to come to room temperature before roasting. Turn the broiler on. Place the chicken thighs in a roasting pan in an even layer; do not stack directly on top of each other. Allow the chicken to caramelize, 15 to 20 minutes, to give the thighs a nice charred flavor. Turn down the oven to 350°F and remove the pan from the oven. Add 2 cups of water to the roasting pan and cover with tinfoil. Return the pan to the oven for another 20 to 25 minutes until the chicken is cooked through and the meat is tender and juicy. Remove the pan from the oven and allow to cool before placing the chicken thighs on a cooling rack. Once cool, slice the chicken thighs into strips. Strain the jerk chicken liquid and reserve for later.

**TO PREPARE THE RAMEN:** Bring water to a boil in a medium pot, according to package instructions, add the noodles, and cook for 3 to 4 minutes until tender, then drain.

**TO MAKE THE TARE AND SERVE:** Place 1 teaspoon of the reserved jerk chicken liquid, 1 tablespoon of pineapple juice, and 2 teaspoons of soy sauce into each bowl.

**TO SERVE:** Ladle the broth into four bowls and adjust the seasoning if necessary. Add the noodles to the bowls and then top with the sliced chicken. Garnish each bowl with ½ soft-boiled egg, sliced scallions, and ¼ cup steamed cabbage.

# THE BEST POTATO SALAD EVER . . .

## Yeah, I Said It!

## by Monifa Dayo

MAKES 6 TO 8 SERVINGS

*I know what every Black person is thinking right now: who does she think she is talking about—her potato salad is the best ever? I get it. We as Black people take potato salad very seriously. That's why we stay side eyeing Becky with her raisins. This recipe ain't your grandmother's or your favorite auntie's version. No disrespect, none at all, but this potato salad gives you life in a way that deviates from the traditional heavy mayonnaise, mustard, and sweet relish styles. It's not a summer potato salad nor some stuck-up French-style either. This potato salad is the code switch that never feels spirit breaking. It's the dish that would sell out instantly at my supper club in Oakland. Inevitably, it became the treasured birthday gift or the über-favored contribution to Sunday gatherings with friends.*

*The Yukon gold potatoes introduce a rich texture, while the aioli is a more tasty and velvety expression of a creaminess than mayonnaise would render. The tanginess of the yogurt paired with the vinegar gives it the umami that makes it so addictive. The delicate poaching of the eggs brings a sophistication and lends reverence to the outstanding flavor of farm-fresh eggs. My people thought I was crazy to contribute this recipe to this project. They felt that this potato salad is so unique and honestly so ridiculously good that it should rest solely between the pages of my own cookbook. So, let this recipe be my gift to you, family: something for us, a new expression of what Black Food is and can be. Bon appétit!*

**4 shallots**

**½ cup apple cider vinegar**

**kosher salt**

**4 pounds medium Yukon gold potatoes, quartered**

**EVOO for drizzling**

**Freshly ground black pepper to taste**

**1 pint full-fat yogurt (Straus is best)**

**1 cup aioli (classic recipe will do, or store-bought)**

**1 cup capers**

**1 bunch parsley leaves, coarsely chopped**

**1 bunch cilantro leaves, coarsely chopped**

**8 farm eggs**

**Fleur de sel to taste**

**1 bunch tarragon, leaves picked but not chopped, for garnish**

**1 bunch dill, leaves picked but not chopped, for garnish**

**Fresh coriander seeds for sprinkling (optional)**

Finely dice the shallots, place in a small bowl and cover with the vinegar and 1½ tablespoons salt.

Place the potatoes in a pot filled with super-salty water. Boil gently until the water is cloudy and the potatoes are fork-tender. Strain the potatoes in a colander, drain off the water, then let cool on a sheet pan.

When the potatoes are cool enough to touch, peel and discard the skins. Once peeled, use your hands to break the potatoes into smaller pieces.

CONTINUED

## The Best Potato Salad Ever, continued

Drain the vinegar from the shallots over the potatoes and drizzle generously with the oil. Add the drained shallots. Gently mix with your hands. Sprinkle heavily with the pepper and add more oil. Spoon large dollops of yogurt and aioli in each corner. Add the capers. Sprinkle the parsley and cilantro on top.

Gently mix with your hands or a large spoon, being careful to leave each element intact and distinct.

In the meantime, bring water to boil in a small Dutch oven. Just before the water boils, crack a few eggs in the water, making sure to ever so gently swirl the water. Poach the eggs until the yolks are set but soft, keeping the water below a simmer. Retrieve the eggs from the water and lightly dry on a towel. Season each egg with fleur de sel and oil. Let cool.

Place the eggs atop the potato salad. Using a spoon, cut a few into halves and some into quarters. Ever so gently, with your hands, incorporate the eggs into the salad. You want to show off the yokes, but you also want some of the eggs nestled in the potatoes.

Spoon the salad onto a serving dish, drizzle with additional oil, and season with more black pepper and the fleur de sel. Garnish with the tarragon and dill. If in season, sprinkle fresh coriander seeds on top as well. Enjoy!

**TIPS:** Use Straus's maple-flavored yogurt if you are a sweet potato salad kind of person.

Add some butter lettuce hearts (keep them whole) in with the chopped herbs. This aids in stretching the salad and reduces the guilt of eating copious amounts of potato and dairy!

# COCOA-ORANGE FISH

## by Nicole Taylor

*Cocoa powder transforms both savory and sweet dishes. Its luxurious earthiness adds depth to proteins, like the fish in this recipe. Be sure to use unsweetened cocoa powder; swapping out the benne seeds with sesame seeds and maple sugar with light brown sugar is fine. Any variety of hot chile flakes works here, too. Other fish fillets, such as wild Alaskan salmon or snapper, can be substituted for catfish.*

**COCOA RUB**

2 tablespoons kosher salt

2 teaspoons benne seeds

¼ teaspoon dried bird's eye chile flakes

1 tablespoon unsweetened cocoa powder

2 teaspoons maple sugar

½ teaspoon caraway seeds

**FISH**

1 pound oranges (about 2 medium)

2 pounds US-raised catfish fillets

5 tablespoons olive oil

**TO MAKE THE RUB:** In a large bowl, combine all of the rub ingredients and mix well. This seasoning can be made in advance and stored in an airtight container.

**TO PREPARE THE FISH:** Slice the oranges into 12 slices and set aside.

Adjust the oven rack to the top position and preheat the oven to 400°F.

Carefully rinse the fish and pat dry with a clean kitchen towel or paper towel. Place the fish on a large sheet pan and liberally sprinkle both sides with the rub. Drizzle with the oil, then place the orange slices on top of the catfish fillets.

Place the sheet pan on the top rack and roast until the catfish is moist and gently flakes, about 8 minutes. (If using a thicker variety of fish such as salmon, the cooking time will be about 12 minutes.)

# SMOKED COLLARD GREENS

## with Pepper Vinegar & Braised with an Onion Trinity

## by Mashama Bailey

MAKES 4 TO 6 SERVINGS

*Growing up, I hated collard greens. I found them to be bit-ter, chewy, and strong in flavor. The funniest thing, though, is that braised collards was the dish my family would often ask my mother to make. My family loved them, so why didn't I? It wasn't until we visited my grandmother in Georgia one winter when my opinion on collards changed. It was the first time that I had my grandmother's stewed collard greens with pig tails. The pot filled with greens, pork, and spices bubbled and boiled all day long! When they were done, I ate them because that's what you do when your grandmother cooks for you—you eat, no matter what it is. So I did. To my surprise, those greens were different. They were spicy, tender, slippery, and sweet—I even went in for seconds and thirds. When we returned to New York City, my mom and I found ourselves in our own kitchen trying to replicate that delicious combination.*

*This recipe isn't my grandmother's version, but she inspired it. I hope to invoke those same feelings about these greens that her greens invoked in me: patience and deliciousness.*

1 pound pecan wood chips

7 pounds collard greens, stemmed and washed

1½ cups chopped red onions

1½ cups chopped white onions

1½ cups thinly sliced leeks, white and light green parts

1 large shallot, sliced

1 quart olive oil

Salt

8 cups water

**PEPPER VINEGAR**

1 cup apple cider vinegar

¼ cup sugar

¼ cup thinly sliced serrano chiles

**SMOKE THE COLLARDS IN 2 BATCHES:** Preheat the oven to 200°F. To create a smoker, use two large aluminum pans. First, heat the wood chips in a cast-iron pan over hight heat, until they begin to smoke. Remove the cast-iron pan from the heat and place the hot wood chips in one of the aluminum pans. Then, using a small but sharp knife, punch holes in the bot-tom of the second pan and place it on top of the first pan with the wood chips inside. Add the collards to the top pan, place in the oven, and smoke for 15 minutes. Remove from the oven and set aside.

In a Dutch oven, sweat the red and white onions, leeks, and shallot with 2 cups of the olive oil and a nice pinch of salt. Add the smoked collards in increments until they cook down, then add more. Once all of the collards are in the pot, add the remaining oil and 8 cups of water. Cook, covered, on low heat, until done, about 1½ to 2 hours.

**TO MAKE THE PEPPER VINEGAR:** Bring the vinegar and sugar to a boil and stir to dissolve. Add the chiles and cool in the fridge for at least 2 hours to overnight.

**TO SERVE:** Dress the collard greens with the pepper vinegar to taste.

# PEACH HAND PIES

## by Cheryl Day

MAKES 8 SERVINGS

*Eating a perfectly ripe peach is an experience that evokes childhood memories for me. With every bite, I'm transported to my grandmother's porch in Alabama all over again. Every summer, from a young age, my family and I packed up the station wagon and traveled down South for the adventure of my childhood. On days when it could not possibly get any hotter, we would sit on the porch in hopes of catching a breeze. Somehow eating a perfectly ripe peach would cool you off (or distract you), as the juices dripped down your arm with every bite.*

*My parents were part of the Great Migration, along with millions of pioneering Black folks who left the American South for cities about which they'd heard whispers of equal opportunities for all. When I think of their courage to venture out into the unknown, it is not lost on me. I am grateful. They did it to make a better life for themselves— and for me.*

*My parents put down roots in Los Angeles, where I grew up. Southern food and culture were always a part of my upbringing. My mother was determined to teach me about what her life had been like growing up in Alabama. She shared our family history and recipes, and all of these conversations happened in the kitchen. My mother was a natural-born storyteller, and I wanted to hear them all. We baked biscuits, cakes, and pies together, and that time spent with her brings some of my most cherished memories.*

*Everyone loves pie. These hand pies are the perfect size for one. Rich, buttery, flaky dough, filled with those juicy peaches tossed with brown sugar, cinnamon, mace, and black pepper. I don't even peel the peaches in this recipe. The skins soften once baked and remind me of that perfect peach.*

### ALL-BUTTER PIE DOUGH
Makes two 9-inch piecrusts or 1 double crust

2½ cups unbleached all-purpose flour

1 tablespoon granulated sugar

1 teaspoon baking powder, preferably aluminum-free

1 teaspoon fine sea salt

½ cup ice water

1 tablespoon apple cider vinegar

½ pound (2 sticks) cold unsalted butter, cut into 1-inch cubes

### PEACH FILLING

2 cups sliced (¼ inch) fresh peaches (about 5 peaches); can substitute frozen

2 teaspoons grated lemon zest

1 tablespoon fresh lemon juice

½ cup packed light brown sugar

¼ teaspoon ground pepper

¼ teaspoon cinnamon

¼ teaspoon ground mace

2 tablespoons unbleached all-purpose flour

¼ teaspoon fine sea salt

1 large egg, lightly beaten with a pinch of fine sea salt, for egg wash

### VANILLA SUGAR GLAZE

1 cup confectioners' sugar

1 tablespoon plus 1 teaspoon milk

¼ teaspoon pure vanilla extract

**TO MAKE THE PIECRUST:** In a medium bowl, whisk together the flour, sugar, baking powder, and salt. Set aside.

In a measuring cup or a small bowl, combine the water and vinegar. Set aside.

CONTINUED

## Peach Hand Pies, continued

Toss the butter in the flour mixture to gently coat the cubes. Then use a pastry blender to cut the butter into the flour. You should have various-size pieces of butter, ranging from sandy patches to pea-size chunks, with some larger bits as well. Drizzle in about half of the water-vinegar mixture and stir lightly with a fork until the flour is evenly moistened and the dough starts to come together. If the dough seems dry, add a little more ice water, 1 to 2 tablespoons at a time. The dough will still look a bit shaggy at this point. If you grab a small piece of dough and press it slightly with your hand, it should mostly hold together.

Dump the dough out onto an unfloured work surface and gather it together into a tight mound. Using the heel of your hand, smear the dough a little at a time, pushing it away from you and working your way down the mass of dough to create flat layers of flour and butter. Then gather the dough back together with a bench scraper, layering the clumps of dough on top of one another. Repeat the process once or twice more; the dough should still have some big pieces of butter visible.

Cut the dough in half. Shape each piece into a disk and flatten it. Wrap the disks in plastic wrap and put them in the refrigerator for at least 2 hours, or overnight, to rest. The dough can be stored for 3 days in the refrigerator or up to 1 month in the freezer. If frozen, defrost in the refrigerator overnight before using.

**TO ROLL OUT THE PIECRUST:** If the dough has been chilled overnight, it will need to sit at room temperature for 10 to 15 minutes before rolling.

Line two baking sheets with parchment paper. On a floured surface, roll out each disk of dough into a 10-inch square, a scant ¼ inch thick. Cut each piece into four equal squares. Transfer the squares to the prepared baking sheets, four to a pan. Cover with plastic wrap and refrigerate while you make the filling.

**TO MAKE THE FILLING:** In a large bowl, combine the peaches, lemon zest and juice, brown sugar, pepper, cinnamon, mace, flour, and salt and toss to combine. Set aside.

**TO ASSEMBLE THE PIES:** Remove the dough from the refrigerator and lightly brush the edges of each square with egg wash. Divide the filling among the squares, using a scant ¼ cup for each, leaving a ½-inch border around the edges. Gently fold each square of dough over to make a triangle and press the edges with your fingers to seal; make sure the filling does not ooze out of the sides. Crimp the edges of each hand pie with your fingers or a fork to seal.

Lightly brush the tops of the pies with egg wash. Cut three small slits for steam vents in the top of each pie. Chill the pies, uncovered, for 30 minutes, or up to 2 hours, to set the crust.

Position a rack in the middle of the oven and preheat the oven to 400°F.

Bake the hand pies for 20 to 25 minutes, until deep golden brown, rotating the pans halfway for even cooking.

**WHILE THE HAND PIES ARE COOLING, MAKE THE GLAZE:** In a small bowl, mix the confectioners' sugar, milk, and vanilla. Set aside.

Glaze the hand pies with a generous amount of glaze coating the top.

# I LOVE NY PINK + GOLD COOKIES

## by Lani Halliday

MAKES 12 3½-INCH COOKIES

*I loved developing this recipe; it's my take on the iconic New York City–baked good, the black and white cookie. My twist has a fabulous pink and gold colorway, with sweet potato in both the cookie and the glaze that is a nod to my family's southern roots. The sweet potato's importance in the diet and history of Black folks in the region cannot be overstated. This recipe is gluten-, egg-, soy-, and nut-free.*

**COOKIES**

2 cups Bob's Red Mill 1-to-1 Gluten-Free Flour

1 teaspoon baking powder

½ teaspoon kosher salt

¼ teaspoon baking soda

½ cup full-fat sour cream

¼ cup water

1 tablespoon vanilla extract

8 tablespoons (1 stick) butter, at room temperature

¾ cup sugar

⅓ cup sweet potato puree (you can use canned; homemade may require a little additional water)

**SWEET POTATO GLAZE**

2 cups sifted confectioners' sugar (it's important to sift first, then measure; otherwise, you'll end up with too much sugar)

¼ cup sweet potato puree (thin with 2 to 4 tablespoons of water if using homemade)

3 drops red gel food coloring, plus more if needed to achieve desired shade

**GOLD FINISH PAINT**

1 tablespoon gold powder

3 tablespoons vodka

**TO MAKE THE COOKIES:** Adjust the oven rack to the middle position and preheat the oven to 375°F. Line a baking sheet with parchment paper.

Measure and sift the flour, baking powder, salt, and baking soda in a medium-size bowl and set aside.

Whisk together the sour cream, water, and vanilla and set aside.

In the bowl of a stand mixer fitted with a paddle attachment or with a hand mixer and large bowl, add the butter and sugar. Beat for 5 to 7 minutes or until light and fluffy, stopping to scrape two or three times. Add the sweet potato and beat until mixed. Add the sifted dry ingredients, beat until combined, then add the wet ingredients until thoroughly mixed and even. Because it's gluten-free, don't worry about overmixing; the batter will be thick but not so stiff that it holds its shape.

Using a cookie scoop, scoop the batter onto the prepared sheet pan and bake for 5 minutes. Rotate and bake for an additional 4 to 5 minutes, depending on the size of your scoop. The cookies are done when they spring back slightly in the center and are slightly golden around the edges. Remove the sheet pan from the oven and allow to cool completely while you make the glaze.

**TO GLAZE:** Combine all of the ingredients in a small bowl and whisk until smooth.

CONTINUED

## I LOVE NY Pink + Gold Cookies, continued

Flip the cookies over and glaze the bottom sides, which will be a more even surface. Glaze them, either by spreading in a circle atop each cookie or carefully dipping the cooled cookie into the fresh glaze. Allow to dry completely, 10 to 15 minutes.

**TO ADD THE GOLD FINISH PAINT:** In a small container, combine the gold powder and vodka and mix thoroughly. You may need to adjust the amount of powder to vodka because the vodka evaporates over time.

Using a clean, small paintbrush, brush the gold paint over one-half of the pink circle glaze atop the cookies. Allow to dry completely. If there is any gold paint left over, it can be covered with plastic wrap and stored for 3 or 4 days without adding additional vodka.

Voilà! These cookies are best enjoyed the same day. They can be stored overnight in an airtight container. Do not stack without using parchment or wax paper. Over time, the cookies absorb moisture and develop a gummy texture. Cookies can be made a day ahead and glazed the next day.

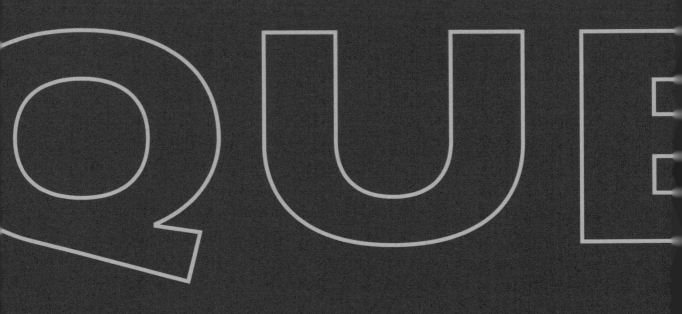

CHAPTER 6

ART BY DEVONN FRANCIS

# NECTARINES FOR DINNER

## The Politics of Black Queer Taste

## by Savannah Shange, PhD

No one needs a nectarine.

It isn't a protein or a starch. It won't fill you up at the end of your second shift or count as a dark, leafy green superfood. A nectarine won't balance a baby on one hip while you chop scallions and use your white voice on the phone with the doctor's office. It doesn't even have the plump symbolism of the peach that punctuates late-night text exchanges and adorns regional memorabilia. Nectarines are not useful food—they don't cook or preserve particularly well, and they tend to be impudently bland when you try to make them into a sauce or syrup.

They don't *do* much, which is exactly why I love them.

As a Black person in the Americas, every bone in my body knows how to *do*. Work has been extracted from ten generations of my flesh. Yes, cutting cane and harvesting rice and rolling biscuits. But also spreading thighs, opening mouths, and pushing children into the world. The forced culinary, sexual, and care labor of Black women is tied into a knot at the center of the world, and its unraveling is the work of generations to come. This means that every time we encounter food or sex, we also catch a glimpse of the ghost in the mirror, the one that equates our value with external measures of strength and productivity.

For Black folks of all genders, our ancestors' literal value was determined by the value of what we could produce, less the cost to keep us alive or at least not dead. What, then, would it mean for me as a Black woman to *make* nothing at all, to be willfully unproductive?

**What would it feel like to enter both the kitchen and the bedroom with no one's appetite but my own?**

A nectarine is there for eating, for splitting open its taut, tart skin, its namesake nectar unavoidably spilling down your chin. Olfactory overwhelm—the nectarine's scent comes first, filling the conjoined cavities of nose, mouth, and gullet. Yes, its namesake nectar even coats that little dangly thing in the back of your throat, citric acid comingling with saliva and triggering the gut to get ready for more.

In a divine coincidence, nectarines have the same pH as a vulva, sour and sweet like an invitation to good things to come. After a phase of being an, *ahem*, omnivore, I am about twenty years deep off in the game of being both gay and vegan. At this point, these practices are so ingrained in the shape of me that I just fry my tofu, kiss my boo, and go on about my day. For many of us, queerness has become an unremarkable fact of everyday life.

For me, queerness is not a "sexual prefer-ence." It's a political practice steeped in diasporic joy and care. When some folks hear the word vegan, it sounds like one big NO—no chicken, no eggs, no fish, no cheese! As I was taught in Black ital traditions, plant-based eating is actually a practice of saying *yes* to hundreds of ingredients and dishes we may have overlooked before. There are more than a thousand types of vegetables cultivated across the globe that we welcome onto our plates when we shift toward a plant-based diet that makes room for the diversity of grains, legumes, leaves, fruits, and herbs that can sustain us.

Likewise, my commitment to Black queer love is an invitation to intimacy, with the thousand genders of Black being that exceed the inher-ited script of manhood.

Tops and bottoms, studs and femmes, gods for gods, earths for earths, t4t and all enby errythang we who recognize each other as "family" have a taste for one another. Black queer practice is the consummation of love for self. It is a site of delicious refusal—each juicy kiss hushes the lie that you are unlovable, uncherishable, and only as valuable as what you can make, earn, cook, marry, or produce. This is not to say that we don't *also* earn, cook, marry, and produce—queerness is not an escape from respectability politics, just an exuberant asterisk on its terms.

To be black and queer is to sit at the table of the self and gorge.

**What might it mean to savor Black being-ness, to encounter ourselves and each other as delectable?**

The Black queer palate should not be confused with the vampiric thirst of empire that seeks to literally *consume* Blackness in all of its forms. I ask, "How does Black queer *taste*? What flavor notes predominate on a Black queer palate?

How *do* we tell a nectarine from a peach, and are we going to grill it or eat it raw? Black queer practice is a tasting, not an *eating* that disappears the other, but a savoring that culti-vates a taste for an other-wise world. It's here that swearing off the D (at least the built-in kind) connects to swearing off of animal products. Both these commitments get misper-ceived as *limitations* instead of as *invitations*.

Veganness and queerness are disciplines of Black joy that provide me opportunities to practice liberation in everyday life. But the thing is, they are not special or precious or sanctified. I have made a lovely life with a tender country queer who puts bacon on their Beyond Burger. We are the heirs to a whole constellation of Black joy technologies that can guide our compass toward an *other*-wise world, and each star has a light to offer on that path. Some of our comrades are committed to eating locally, maintaining zero waste house-holds, or ensuring that every dollar they spend goes to someone who makes a fair wage. Other folks are developing mutual-aid projects and community-based safety protocols to keep the police off our blocks. Maybe you are working toward moving off-grid and healing your relationship with the land by cultivating your own food and medicine. Whichever freedom star catches your eye, I invite you to orient yourself by its light and commit to building an infrastructure of Black joy in the here and now.

Or you could just bite into this here nectarine and savor until you are satisfied.

# BLACK. QUEER.

## by Lazarus Lynch

Boyhood. I grew up in New York City in the mid-'90s in the Black Apostolic Pentecostal church. From early childhood, I loved playing dress-up in my mama's Sunday best. I'd put on her high heels and long dress and pretend I was the gospel singer Shirley Caesar. I was obsessed with Shirley Caesar as a child. I could imitate her voice, her mannerisms when she would jerk full of the Holy Ghost, her shouting and speaking in tongues. Watching and pretending to be her was trancelike. For a moment, as a tender child in my mother's closet, I felt free.

Black. Queer. Male. Labels I did not ask for at birth. My Black self was treated as wealth in my family and community. Being Black meant having rhythm, clapping on the two and the four, smothering your skin in Vaseline, and getting your ass whooped for getting smart with adults. Being queer was taboo, strange, abominable. In church, my queer identity was chastised, preached against, and punished. It did not matter if a church leader was privately queer; as long as they pretended to be happily married and did not disclose their sex life in public, that was enough to have church as usual. This act of denial seemed to be the order of the day.

I remember my first time being interested in a boy. Let's call him Jason. He was my classmate in preschool. One day at recess, we showed each other our penises. Feeling nothing intrinsically sexual between us, just a curiosity of what we had down there. We got caught and reprimanded by our teacher. For the remainder of that day, Jason and I were separated, patrolled by the teacher's watchful eyes that were filled with disgust.

I tell that story because it was the first time I remember feeling shame in connection with my queerness. As children, we knew the repercussions of our inappropriate actions. But instead of acknowledging innate erotic impulses and discussing them openly and lovingly, I learned to suppress—an action dangerous for Black queer boys.

I have vivid memories of adult figures in my life telling me to stand up straight and take my hand off my waist because those postures made me look like a girl. I once had a Black woman, a teacher, tell me to untie my hoodie from around my waist because I looked like a faggot. I could not have been any older than ten at the time. I had peers on the school bus argue precisely this subject: "how to know if a boy is gay," presenting ridiculous postulations like the way he holds out his hand when checking the length of his fingernails or whether the permanent creases in the corners of his lips were shaped a certain way; these were positive indications of dick-sucking activity. We were kids, yet so many ideas about sexual identity and sexual practice had already been formed. Such impressions followed me into early adulthood.

I remain fascinated with Black boyhood and specifically Black queer boyhood. Young Black boys are taught the implications of race at an early age. By their teen years, most are given "the talk"; that is, how to conduct themselves with the police, how their Black bodies can be targets of brutality and exploitation. But what happens when a young Black boy's queerness is a threat to those whose skin is black like his? What happens when his Black queer body is under the surveillance of homophobic tyranny, when he feels unsafe among his own? I think about the times I would adjust the way I stood or change up my voice with the boys from my neighborhood to cloak my queerness in order to feel safe. Imagine that heavy burden for a young Black queer boy.

In the Black community, conversations of safety tend to focus on external forces: white people, police, strangers. Rarely do we prepare our young Black queers for the acts of violence and brutality committed against them by their own. Black queer youth need the welfare and support of a loving community to thrive. Black queer youth need spaces to be themselves and feel safe in their Black queer bodies.

I read a lot about Black queer struggle, and so often, joy is absent from its testimony. Black queer identity is intersectional, and pain often underscores our experience. Black queer individuals learn how to navigate in a heteronormative world in order to survive. Claiming joy is an act of resistance and revolution—an opportunity for transformation.

Homophobia from Black people against Black queer folk is a unique hurt; it is a form of internalized oppression. In George M. Johnson's memoir *All Boys Aren't Blue,* he writes, "Homophobia denies queer people happiness." Black queer people want to be happy! We are often celebrated for our contributions to culture—our art, our food, our intellect, our kookiness, our athleticism—yet penalized for being who we are. I am often astounded by the hypocrisy in Black culture toward Black queer people. For example, it is seemingly acceptable that a Black queer person can design a product we all love and consume or write a hit song so long as whom they date, fuck, and love stay out of the narrative. Capitalist consumerism teaches Black queer people to deny who they are if they want to play the game. I cannot hide my queerness or my Blackness. To hide is to deny. To deny is death.

There is no greater fear to overcome than the fear to be yourself.

In the Black family, gender roles still carry an invisible but heavy weight. Cisgendered Black men are expected to perform gender roles: men take out the trash, men are tough, men don't cry, men play sports. As Black queer people, we tend to internalize these messages. In the Black community, for Black men, how we dap, how we walk, whether or not we nod, wave, smile, or hug our fellow Black brothers and sisters upon greeting them, all these interactions get scanned through invisible heteronormative detectors, a process familiar to Black queer folk. To not comply with certain behavioral codes and ways of being is to transgress and consequently, bear rejection.

Black queer images in mainstream media and culture have the power to shift paradigms. Within my Christian upbringing, images of men in drag were publicly despised yet privately fetishized. All too often, these images perpetuate wrongful generalizations about all gay men in the psyche of heteronormative-patriarchal society. They become the monetized tropes.

Identity in itself does not tell us the whole story of another. Rather, identity is a portal to discovering more intimately the deeper parts of another. And, in its most rigid interpretations, identity is fraught with constructs we must undo. Here's one: that manhood and womanhood are defined by gender expression and sexual practice. Here's another: to acknowledge the beauty of individuals of the same sex makes one queer. While acknowledging identity is important, binaries can do harm. Carefully resisting the urge to assign an individual's characteristics to all members of a group (all Black queer men aren't femmes, for example) is a step toward decolonizing our minds and imaginations around identity until we are fully radicalized.

Black queer people have spiritual needs, too. So often removed from our stories is the part of us that seeks and desires intimacy with God. Who is God unto the Black queer? Who is God unto the weary? In the biblical book of Matthew, Jesus appeals, "Come to me, all you who are weary and burdened, and I will give you rest." The invitation by the Spirit for repose and renewal offers a kind of strength and healing to anyone—the operative word is "all"—who may find themselves in a weakened state. We, as Black queer folk, can access internal liberation and freedom through spiritual pursuit and spiritual awakening. We can find a space to be sustained, a place to be whole.

Black people are resilient. The plate is where we discover who we are, where we're going, and where we've been. Like a bridge over troubled waters, so is our food and laughter in troubled times. Our feasts are roads to happiness and self-care. It's in the greasing of our hair, scalp, skin, and skillets that we preserve who we are. And who we are is not an apology.

The future of Black Queer is a path of sweet glory—a road to triumphant victory. The future of Black Queer is a colorful array of LGBTQIAP+ superheroes and toy figures. The future of Black Queer is unlimited joy and the affirmation of childhood fantasy. The future of Black Queer is political leadership and government. The future of Black Queer is here and now!

*I be Black queer.*

*I be Black queer when I rise out of bed each morning, my feet firmly planted on the ground.*

*I be Black queer in the mirror, the reflection of my radiant brown skin beaming in all its majesty, telling me I am worthy.*

*I be Black queer in the shower, singing along with Marvin Gaye; making psalms, hymns, and spiritual songs.*

*I be Black queer in my underwear, in passionate intimacy, in rapture.*

*I be Black queer, gathering family recipes; lyrics from the songbooks of our ancestors, seeking to nourish my soul and body.*

*I be Black queer, creating art, laughing out loud, dreaming up, conjuring, in my Black queer glory.*

*I be Black queer, making greens and cornbread, steeping sorrel tea, reading, writing, listening, elevating my mind.*

*I be Black queer, affirming my Black life matters, and taking up space.*

*I be Black queer, loving myself as religion, forgiving myself, permitting myself, being myself.*

*I be Black queer, running shit, owning shit, building shit, erecting shit, feeding the planet; mothering Her children.*

*I be Black queer, reaching my highest potential, opening my heart to the universe, being a vessel, expanding my consciousness, reframing the story I once told myself.*

*I be Black queer in inner silence, in prayer and meditation, requesting Divine guidance and traveling mercies.*

*I be Black queer joy. Dancing. Smiling. Alive in my own skin.*

*I be Black, queer, and proud. In style, in speech, in dress, in drag, in liberation.*

*I be Black queer 'cause Black queer is dignity. Black queer is power. Black queer is revolution. Black queer is healing unto the world. Black queer is me.*

# CREATING SPACE

## by Ebony Derr

If community is essential to thrive, what happens to those actively deprived of it?

Food has long been a foundational element to establishing community, especially for Black people. To feed one's own body is an act of pure compassion and support. Feeding those we care for is nourishment for the soul.

For most Black folks in the United States, Thanksgiving and Christmas are easily two of the most important holidays of the year—feast days where we appreciate and nurture the bonds with those we're closest to. Our connections to one another are ancestral—deep and potent. With so much of our Black identity rooted in collective struggle and ceremony, the moments we can experience true belonging, acceptance, and praise often come when we are among ourselves.

However, for many, such spaces for acceptance, nurturing, and love simply do not exist. Black folks routinely exclude queer, and especially transgender Black people, from these ritual celebrations. Family, friendship, and community are elements of life that Black trans folks often have to sacrifice in order to find their path to living authentically. Being Black and trans becomes synonymous with being an outcast, forced to exist at the margins of society. As a result, Black transgender folks are disproportionately likely to be impacted by poverty, unemployment, homelessness, abuse, and addiction. Black trans women have an average life expectancy of thirty-two years and are targeted with extreme violence from within the Black community.

The holiday season can exacerbate feelings of loneliness for our Black trans siblings. Beyond being denied an invite to a Thanksgiving dinner or being side eyed by that one God-fearing relative (because we all have at least one)—when almost everyone else that looks like you and shares the same ancestral bonds—determines that you aren't welcome to sit at their table, where else do you go? For many Black trans folks, these observances are clear reminders that they are not welcome in their families and communities.

During the holiday season of 2018, Ianne Fields Stewart heard the call of immeasurable loneliness from her fellow black transgender siblings. Many of them struggled with feeling ostracized—absent any family or community to gather, celebrate, and eat with. She responded by creating a space where they could create and share meals with each other, a space where they could always be connected. By founding The Okra Project, Stewart addressed the sense of exclusion and alienation suffered by Black trans people by feeding them home-cooked meals made by Black trans chefs and sharing resources to uplift them in other areas of need.

There is no doubting the power of culture to construct our understanding of ourselves, our place in the world, and our overall collective identity. At its best, culture can be a unifying and uplifting aspect of life that gives a sense of love, purpose, belonging, support and understanding to its participants. But at its worst, culture can be limiting, regressive, and dehumanizing. It can impose unhealthy standards, suppress autonomy, and distort one's sense of self. In the globalized "post-colonization" era, most cultures have been manipulated and appropriated to fit into a mold of whiteness. Black culture is a prime example. Many Black people, in order to avoid disparagement and brutal criminalization, have had to disrupt their traditions, abandon their languages, and tuck away their values. To this day, our collective identity continues to be reshaped for congruency with white culture.

Much of the "Blackness" consumed in contemporary American culture has been carefully filtered through a lens of whiteness and presented back to Black people with clear delineations between what is and is not acceptable. The more easily packaged our Blackness is for the cisgender, heterosexual, capitalist white men and women of the world, the more agreeably it's presented. And Black folks often join in with the rest of the world in sorting ourselves into categories of acceptable and not acceptable. It's understandable: with your very personhood placed under such scrutiny, who wouldn't do whatever it takes to be considered acceptable? So what if it requires perpetuating a certain disparagement onto others? Rather than attacking negative perceptions of Blackness to begin with, it can feel easier to just attribute them to even less desirable Black folks. Black trans people, then, are forced to hold the weight of a thousand negative perceptions of Blackness.

However, Black trans people are also the *epitome* of nonconforming, which makes them a threat to the world as it currently exists, even and especially to Black culture. This is why it has been critical to create spaces specifically for nurturing and empowering Black trans people. We may have been pushed to exist on the margins of this society, but when we are among one another, we live in an entirely different world of our own. In a world that consistently seeks to devalue Black trans lives, it is more important than ever that we protect and expand spaces that reaffirm their value.

# TO ACT BEYOND CIRCUMSTANCE

## by Leigh Gaymon-Jones

*What practices are we cultivating to prepare for life inside liberation?*

This is today's question, born out of my beliefs in possibility and a future beyond.

This is the question that tugs at me and pulls my attention and intention and stumps me and worries me and drives me.

*Who is we? We Black folks. We queer folks. We human folks. We earth-based life forms. We cosmic beings. We, you, me, us. We all.*

*What is life? To breathe. To interconnect. To grow. To thrive. To live.*

*What is liberation? What indeed! And when! And where! But for now, how.*

How is where I begin. I turn to the collective, to two of my co-conspirators: Moretta Browne and Jas Wade. With these two, I have planted seeds, weeded paths, harvested fruits, prepared meals, broken bread, sweat, cried, and howled with laughter. In 2016, we three entered a farm apprenticeship, alongside some thirty other food-cultivating enthusiasts. Together, we learned to grow fruits, vegetables, herbs, and seeds, navigate community, discover more about ourselves.

Moretta—spell caster, plant whisperer, master of joyous disguise, beloved sibling. My first memory of Mo Browne, as I often call them—is wearing a floppy garden hat, farm-dusted Doc Marten boots, a smile only out-beamed by the sun itself, and flowers—in their hands, or in their hat. I'm not sure. But I remember flowers with Mo Browne.

Jas—path companion, righteous healer, conjurer, light-filled fam friend. The fondest time I shared with Jas was on the dance floor. Well, it was a greenhouse, turned dance floor, and Jas's moves and commitment dragged my spirit off the wall and out of the corner. They compelled me to work it all out and leave it in a pile of sweat on the greenhouse dance floor.

They are to whom I turn today, to share my questions about a liberated future, to share my deep and nagging and ugly fear that in our fierce commitment to rightly fighting for a collective liberation, that we may be neglecting to prepare to live and thrive once we realize our dreams. And what if the only practices we have built are how to righteously struggle, persevere through suffering, resist oppression and fight? If we truly arrive at, discover, reveal, build, birth a liberated future, but without practices and muscle memory for how to really live there, what then?

This is what is on my mind these days, and most days.

Here, I share a collage of a conversation among Jas, Mo, and I, held one Saturday afternoon in October 2020 via online video call, each of us in our respective homes along the California coast. I came to them with my questions and curiosity and anxiety. And I asked for their listening, space holding, wisdom, love, and hope.

## IDENTITY AND LOCATION

*Moretta: Sometimes it's easier for me to put myself in a box than explain the depth of what I'm feeling or how I want to show up in that moment, but it does a disservice to myself and to the person who then perceives me in a way that is not full.*

Jas: I often think that as Black folks, we speak in poetry, but I don't have the indigenous language of my ancestors.

In a chapter entitled "Black, Queer, Food," there is an invitation or request to identify. And yet, identifications are frequently so limiting and misleading and incomplete. While I welcome the opportunity to queer the linear format and solo nature of this essay, I am aware of the slipperiness of queer as an identity marker. Identifications falsely generate a sense of knowing about something that is often so personal, unique, and even evolving; that false sense of knowing impedes possibility and imagination. So, when I was invited to participate in the "Black, Queer, Food" chapter, and then decided to extend that invitation to two loved ones, I felt we had to begin our conversation there.

So, I ask, casually, how do you identify?

JW: Multiple. Multiple identities, multiple roles, not singular. I would say that I've been in a practice of identifying myself *for* myself, or in my relationship to community—rather than the conditioned limitations and the boxes that we usually have to check.

MB: *My perception of Blackness and queerness always comes with struggle and oppression, which come from internalized capitalism.*

And racism and homophobia, I add. But yes, definitely rooted in capitalism, which has served as a driving force to erect borders between groups and justify the exploitation of the many.

While we recognize the complication of the labels we claim or that are thrust upon us, we also acknowledge language serves as a tool we can use to move closer to one another, closer to community. The emptiness and misrepresentation of language can all but render language meaningless, and yet somehow, self-location offers a thread of useful connection. Location implies relationship. And self-location speaks to agency, sovereignty.

JW: Identity is something I relate to in terms of how I locate myself in the world and informs how I build and sustain relationships.

If I were to use language, I identify as African, as Black, as an African descendant. I identify as queer. I identify as trans, nonbinary. I identify as an abolitionist.

MB: *There are multiple Morettas living inside of me. I can say I am a binary queer grower of*

*plants, who is unapologetically and enthusiastically Black. And that's never gonna change.*

JW: And these are who I know myself to be, versus what I'm told.

MB: *What does it look like for the Black future, at the intersection of all of these terms?*

It seems, then, that the utility of naming, of self-locating, is twofold:

1. Embedded in the act of self-location is the practice of self-inquiry and discovery;

2. Self-identification serves as a siren to comrades to connect and build collectively.

*The Black elder on the train sounds her siren with a head nod when I board, telling me . . . "If it goes down, girl, I got you."*

Today, we three claim Black, we claim queer, we claim deep relationship to the land. We hold these identities clearly and loosely as we ground our experience and set wild our imaginations.

## PRACTICES

MB: *These identities shouldn't feel like a burden. What would it look like to identify as a Black queer person and be on the other side of that? The possibilities feel infinite.*

JW: Whatever I'm practicing, I'm either perpetuating something that is in opposition and agitation to my values or I'm doing some real cell differentiation shit.

We are dreaming a circumstance of infinite possibility and abundance, while living in a reality of restriction and lack. How do we reconcile that? And what if we don't? What if we don't cultivate new practices intentionally designed to sustain a thriving life in a liberated world? Will we re-create the conditions for suffering and the practices of oppression?

**Mo's grounding practice pulls me from paralysis . . .**

MB: *I watch the monarchs. As a Black queer person, I find so much inspiration in nature right outside my door. Blanketed in smoke and hearing the sirens from the fire trucks—there's a tension that is living right above the surface of everyone's skin—everyone's experiencing the shift, and folks are on edge, but I walk out my door and I see the tithonia that we planted for the monarchs.*

*I think about our plant-cestors. They were here before us, and there's been all this time and trauma, and they're still here. How can I do that? What can I learn from the monarch butterfly?*

*I want Black people to be able to do that. Sit and be still and reground.*

**My grandmother on my father's side kept a garden in her backyard for as long as I can recall, for as long as my father can recall. The last time I saw my grandmother, while she lay in a hospice bed in her living room, she told me her father was a farmer and talked about her collard greens in the backyard. We had never before discussed farming. I resisted the impulse to share all I knew about growing collards. I sat still and listened.**

JW: The practices that we are doing now is the foundation for our liberated future, which is now.

Stillness. Removing myself from the expectation to perform or be on. Always externalizing can be so exhausting. To be up against how my body is violated by people outside me telling me "no, this is who you are" creates disassociation and the feeling of not being aligned. Nature, the natural world, the elementals have gifted me such deep healing and wholeness in just being mirrors for me. As far as how we get there, it's spending time in our interior. That

practice sustains my integrity, and by integrity, I mean that what I feel and believe matches, mirrors my action.

MB: *Food is care.*

JW: In the beginnings of my own healing and radical self-love was food. Cooking became such a ritual of the radical self-love and self-care that I really needed. Food and cooking and the kitchen also became a temple of sorts, where I could hear and commune with ancestors. So, while I'm cooking, I'm like "this is the energy I'm putting into the food," while I'm cooking. I would say affirmations because I was going to ingest all of that. I would think about ancestors who sowed the seeds of grain in their hair to make sure sustenance came with them into the unknown.

My healing journey has really guided me back toward home and a sense of belonging that I am a part of the ecosystem. Connection to nature is our birthright and what we inherit, as Black queer people.

**Medicine. Where else do you find medicine?**

JW: Find it wherever you can

MB: *Laugh; Have a cackle fest*

JW: Take your own medicine. Honor your own medicine

Water

MB: *Prioritize happiness*

JW: Move through your own wilderness of feelings and emotions and desires

Pleasure—pleasure that includes, but is not limited to, the sexual self—thoroughly enjoy a bowl of chili

Take refuge in sitting and sipping tea

MB: *Writing. Reading.*

Jas and Mo encourage me to believe, inspire me to believe, the future is now.

Embedded in this winding conversation among friends, maybe we tapped into a well of resources that not only holds practices to cultivate in preparation for a liberated future but perhaps also something about the nature of liberation itself.

## LIBERATION IS BEYOND

**What is liberation?**

JW: I'll tell you what it's not!

But that's the question . . . how do we define ourselves and our futures and our dreams not as resistance or response? How do we just articulate, describe, map a liberatory future for ourselves?

**Liberation is collective.**

JW: For me, liberation is a collective experience. It's divested from the individual. In queer/trans communities, we have examples, that are imperfect, for liberation—sharing resources, collectivizing liberation, whether that's money for a gender-affirming surgery, housing, clothing, medicine. Liberation doesn't only mean what I want, but it's global.

MB: *Do the work of liberating ourselves individually to play into the collective.*

**Liberation is in the details.**

JW: Liberation is in the details of things . . . building relationships with my neighbors. What are ways to equip ourselves to deal with crises, so we don't have to rely on the State; where can we cut our reliance on this violent system, cultivate community resources *right now*?

Liberation is how we're relating to one another and communicating with one another.

**Liberation is truth.**

JW: It is a liberated tongue; I speak my truth; I call it like I see it, and I disagree and find comfort in the discomfort, because that is what it's going to take.

MB: *Being able to show up as my full self without worrying about how others are perceiving me.*

**Liberation is happening.**

MB: *Liberation is unlocking the infinite within you, which is already happening because we're here having this conversation. And it takes time.*

*I obsess over Afro futurism because I don't think it's that far away. I want liberation to happen now, and it is happening.*

*Liberation is multiple, multiple, multiple. Liberation is happening right now.*

MB: *When people take things away from us, we find a way to grow out of nothing. Imagine if we had everything, what we could do.*

**Imagine. And remember. Remember that so many Black people, queer people, women people, so many people have walked this Earth in the midst of limited possibilities greater than we can truly fathom, and yet here we are. Alive.**

JW: Ancestors. I can't say what they envisioned, but they got us here. If I were to really honor survivorship, can you imagine? If I can go through the list of ancestors, whether it's Marsha P., Toni Morrison, James Baldwin, Lorraine Hansberry—ancestors also at the intersection, in the extreme conditions—ancestors able to create enough space within the day-to-day to meditate and create music, organize and create Black cooperatives. There's a deep knowing in that. I can't name it.

There is a deep knowing to be able to act beyond circumstance. To believe beyond circumstance. And so much joy. There's joy. There's joy!

When I think about liberation, I think about all the different healing characteristics that we have and benefit from, those plants cultivated over years. I think about the class of herbs that are nervines—the nervous system tonic; I think about adaptogens—and that's the tonic that increases our ability to cope with mental/ physical/emotional stress. In this human body, what is medicine that I have cultivated in choosing to journey through and process personal and generational pain and trauma? We transmute pain, transmute trauma, and that's resilience. And on a personal level, liberation is in that transmuting.

Ancestors. Plant-cestors. What a resource we have.

**As a self-located Black queer woman in deep relationship with land and food, in the truth of experience that exists beyond the imperfection of identity and naming, is a possibility, a magic that can uniquely be accessed by me and those who inhabit that intersection. In my bloodline, along the path I walk because of the form I was born into and the choices I have made, and in the air we all breathe together are keys for life and living. From my particular vantage point, I have access to particular resources that will not only see me to a more liberated future, as they have for my ancestors and their ancestors, but also support my ability to thrive in the future that we are all co-creating in this very moment.**

JW: At the intersection of my Blackness, my queerness, my transness is having access to ancestors and spirit. Having the wisdom to listen. Having the innate ability to innovate and the ability to explore our interior. Having the ability to have conversations and commune with plants and one another in a way that transports me, us, to another space beyond the oppression that is in front of us and up against us. Cleverness, ingenuity, genius.

MB: *At the intersection of Blackness and queerness is Afrofuturism.*

*nature, stillness, care, food, healing, multiplicity, innovation, Afrofuturism, transmutation, joy*

**These resources are active practices, and there are many more, and they are continually revealing themselves.**

**We, we Black folks, know how to make delicacies of hog scraps. We, we queer folks, know how to make family of choice when our bloodlines fail us. I had hoped and imagined that the answer to my question was buried in the historical responses of Black queer people to our circumstances, but today's conversation hasn't delivered us to any singular path forward. Yet perhaps the practices of those lineages will guide us to a liberatory future nevertheless. Perhaps Black queer folks are not only visionary culture keepers of today but also the holders of the tools, technologies, resources and practices needed to map, construct, divine that expansive tomorrow. Perhaps the traditions and instincts that have been passed through soil and blood and story across time are akin to the seeds passed through braids across oceans—**

JW: The seeds of sustenance to take into the unknown.

**When I struggle to find the next step on that path, I am grateful to turn to my homies, my ancestors, my plant-cestors, my people, my crew, my beloveds. I turn to the collective.**

**Today, perhaps the need is simply to, as Jas said, "act beyond circumstance."**

# QUEER INTELLIGENCE
## We Mobilize Through Food

## by Zoe Adjonyoh

Hi, I'm Zoe Adjonyoh, and I'm a culinary queer.

There you go—it's out of the bag.

It was never in *the bag*—let's be real.

Like many queer folk, I was born into a family I didn't quite get and who didn't quite get me back. So, over the past thirty or so years, I have made additional emotional resources available to myself through "chosen" families of queer people. Since childhood, I have moved in otherness across academia and in my career. All the time I have been hiding in plain sight.

I wear my differences openly—you can see my melanin, you can hear my opinions (I am not shy about sharing them) and the sloppy *souf* east accent that accompanies them. My ambition is open and fired up by my "othered" experience. I'm out and proud, though not necessarily shouting about it (anymore). It's just part of who I am.

I signpost my queerness every time I mention my wife or I reference *Ru Paul's Drag Race* in a parody Instagram post. Could you tell by the way I flourished that salt over your plate with a cheeky smile and twinkle in my eye—*"Salt, Bae? You mean Salt,* Gay, right?"

I lean on camp—sure—it's fun, it's irreverent, it's silly and yet it's political at the same time.

With camp, we get to poke fun at heteronormative, cis, patriarchal society without anyone even noticing. That is both a defense and a coping mechanism—for me anyway—it's the translation of my interior experience into a way of being in the world.

It's impossible for me to separate my intersectional identity and therefore my politics and identity from my food.

My menus and style of food are inherently "different" because I am the sum of my otherness.

For context, I am a queer Black woman with mixed-race heritage, born to two immigrants. My mum is Irish and my dad Ghanaian. That makes me a third-culture child. Both my parents emigrated to the UK as teenagers, at a time when posters shouting No Blacks, No Irish, and No Dogs were plastered on the entrances of many shops, bars, restaurants and letting agents.

As a child myself, six years after their arrival, it was not uncommon to be sneered at, taunted, or chased by skinheads—the object of racism from both Black and white people on a daily basis. I grew up watching my father, an intelligent, agile-minded man, destroy his life under the pressure to be something and send all the rewards home and yet be blocked at every turn by the institutions, laws, and principles of white supremacy. Instead, he turned to alternative modes of survival that were often not legal or healthy. I watched my mum suffer the consequences of financial hardship and single parenting as the result of his choices.

With a life centered on being "othered," I have always had a keen sense of injustice—even as a child. Fighting for the underdog and beating up bullies. Social justice, then, has perhaps always been a part of my DNA. My very existence is mired in politics.

After studying law and journalism and after finishing an MA in creative writing, the universe pulled me to work in food—leaving behind years of practice, with my identity scoffed at or poked and prodded to satisfy someone else's curiosity.

And in the ten years I've been a professional chef, my queerness has never been brought up. No journalist has ever asked what is like to be queer working in hospitality. Plenty have asked me about being a woman. No one has ever asked me what it is like to be working class in this industry. Few have asked me about being a Black woman, until recent global events shifted consciousness around the basic notion that Black lives matter.

Here's the deal. Plenty of restaurants run by gay chefs are not necessarily queer. Neither does there need to be anything explicitly queer about the menu or the space for it to be queer. Queer people hail from every region, every state, every city; we exist across religion, race, and class. We are not a monolith.

We have lived parallel to the mainstream, passing off dishes, recipes, and words on food as normal, when they are, in fact, queer AF.

My queerness can be seen in the way I social engineer a dinner party or supper club—there's no rainbow flag across the table—there are no

glitter bombs (maybe later) or sparkles—but I am there hosting—loudly and proudly a lesbian woman who will readily drop a double entendre to make the room smile or laugh—slip in a saucy joke to make a guest blush—I'll talk about my wife, I'll arrange the table and guest list to make sure loud and quiet are balanced—nobody wants to host a dull dinner! Sensuality creeps into my food and the way I talk about it—I suggest a soupçon in an elaborate French accent when I mean a dollop. I talk about sexy spice when I describe heat—I talk about the way heat moves through and down my palette in sensual terms—caress, slip, slide, open up, and I have been known to claim a dish will stimulate orgasm.

My sides come served sprinkled with a heavy dose of flirtation. I serve herbal bitters that are West African liquid Viagra—as an aperitif (Alamo Bitters) to get everyone's libido up and running for the after-party. These are amalgamations of lived experience in the queer community that I cannot help but give a playful nod to in my food and dining. It's how I live, how I speak, how I breathe, and how I cook, and they are a huge part of the joyfulness that comes from being queer.

And the experience of the queer community is full of joy and celebration of ourselves, and everybody on the outside loves to bathe in that liberation and lightness of being!

Can we attribute my stellar hosting skills to my queerness? Yes. Yes, we can, though not in isolation. We must also consider my access to easy Irish charm and an inherited gift of the gab—the tradition of storytelling from Africa going back thousands of years. *Did I mention that I was Black?*

Our differences are uniquely unifying in queer spaces. We actually embrace all—not just virtue signal that shit.

For me and many of my queer friends, to fully exist in our identities is to embrace a wide spectrum of radical ideas, including "alternative" eating and diets. This is part of our "queer intelligence" (a phrase coined by Lani Sol). Veganism was shorthand for lesbianism when I was growing up and has long been associated with queer women (and, increasingly nonbinary and trans folks).

We tend to absorb radical ideas like activated probiotics. We inherently care about the environment, sustainability, social justice, equal access in all areas of life—we know abundance through our adversity. We recognize faith when we see it because we have had to practice it deeply. We demand authenticity in every available interaction and can cut through bullshit with a shade-casting eye roll. This is more than Gaydar. This is *Queer Intelligence.*

When there are so many aspects to my identity, I have often had to choose which part of me is the identity the world needs to know or understand. This priority has transformed according to where I was in the world, in time, in mindset, in heart set and in purpose. This presents something of a philosophical dilemma. I was gay before I was comfortable with being a lesbian. I was a lesbian before I was comfortable being queer. I am queer and a chef, yet would I be comfortable with a category of "queer food" appearing as a category in food delivery apps?

The friction lies in the requirement of a patriarchal colonialist society for clear labels, categories by which we "other" in order to somehow "include" more pointedly. The burgeoning queer food movement is more than just the presence of queer people at the table. It includes explicitly queer restaurants, dinner parties, supper clubs, pop-ups, soup kitchens, food writing, and food media (Mei Meis, Queer Soup, Adas' Supper Club, Hamburger Marys, Nik Sharma, Lukas Volga, Michael Twitty).

While queer culture has become a currency for capitalism best illustrated by bank-sponsored Pride carnivals around the world and cafés serving us rainbow cupcakes and lattes—our queer-owned businesses have activism already built in. Every plate at our queer restaurants and bars serves the cause, and our fundraising and campaigning are perennial, not just one day a year. We look after our own with the same autonomic reflexes as when our nervous system chooses fight or flight without asking.

Food has become a vehicle through which the queer community has found commonality, sought visibility, championed diversity, and encouraged activism. Look at how communities like Queer Soup, Food Plus People, and Kia Cares came together during the height of Covid to look after each other. My own Zoe's Ghana Kitchen Community Kitchen set up for three months, fundraising for others' teetering businesses and going to the front lines to feed vulnerable people of all castes, including our own.

We mobilize through food.

# COCONUT-CURRY HARVEST SOUP

## by Fresh Roberson

MAKES 4 TO 6 SERVINGS

When my community eats my food, I want them to feel as if they are sitting down to a meal cooked for them by someone who loves and cares for them. I want them to feel held and nourished. A pot of soup will often do that for me, especially when paired with some crackers or a simple quick bread.

I first created this soup while at a Healers of Color Retreat off the grid on a Black farm/eco-campus in Pembroke, Illinois. By the time we got to one of the final lunches of the weekend, there were two butternut squash, a handful of sweet potatoes, a bag of apples, and more than twenty-five people staring at me excitedly. Luckily, I had also come equipped with several cans of coconut milk and a couple of bags of Trader Joe's Thai Lime & Chili Cashews that I used as the protein to carry on the energy of my people. Those few items, along with my desire to create something nourishing for people who always pour out themselves for the healing of others, was what birthed this recipe.

Since that weekend, this impromptu soup has become a community favorite, and its creation seems emblematic for how I feed my queer community. I want to create accessible, pleasurable food and make even the spaces that seem to lack resources feel abundant and delicious. I prioritize feeding LGBTQIA folx in my cooking, and the queer street-based young people who solidified my name as Chef Fresh. I hope you enjoy, and I hope you take this base and make it your own.

**2 tablespoons coconut oil, or neutral cooking oil**

**1 large sweet potato, diced large**

**2 apples, cored and diced medium**

**1 butternut squash, diced large**

**Salt to taste**

**2 tablespoons curry powder**

**1 or 2 (13.5-ounce) cans unsweetened coconut milk**

**1 to 2 tablespoons brown sugar**

**Juice of ½ lemon, plus more to taste**

**Splash of fish sauce to taste (optional)**

**1 cup Trader Joe's Thai Lime & Chile Cashews, or plain roasted cashews**

Add the oil to a 4-quart heavy-bottomed pot, turn the heat to medium, and add the sweet potatoes, apples, and squash. Sauté for 10 minutes. Add a sprinkle of salt and the curry powder and cook for an additional 5 minutes.

Add 1 can of the coconut milk and simmer until the ingredients are completely tender, about 10 minutes. Depending on your preference, you can add the second can of coconut milk or add a can full of water if a thinner soup is desired. Using 2 cans of coconut milk will make a very creamy soup that is calorically dense.

Let the soup simmer, uncovered, for 10 minutes, stirring frequently to prevent sticking. Season with the brown sugar, starting with 1 tablespoon, then add the lemon juice, and fish sauce, if using. If upon tasting, you find you would like a slightly sweeter soup, add the additional tablespoon of brown sugar and more lemon juice. Finally, add the cashews. Enjoy.

**NOTE:** I love a fragrant very yellow curry powder for this soup that doesn't have spicy heat, but feel free to use a curry powder that works with your tastes.

# FARRO & RED BEAN-STUFFED COLLARD GREENS

## by LaLa Harrison

MAKES 4 SERVINGS

*I don't think of myself as a "queer" chef. Personally, I don't put myself in a category based on my sexuality. I honestly don't think my sexuality affects my career as much as being a Black woman does. Being a strong Black woman has had, and continues to have, a much greater impact on my career in this industry than being a queer woman. Today, my kitchen provides a supportive place for young people from the Black/African American community. Someone helped me as a young person, and now it's my turn to help someone else.*

2 cups dried red beans

2 bay leaves

½ cup olive oil, plus 1 tablespoon

2 cups farro

1 jumbo garnet yam, or sweet potato, diced

Salt to taste

½ teaspoon ground allspice

½ cup sliced scallions

1 tablespoon chopped garlic

1 teaspoon smoked paprika

1 tablespoon chile powder

1 bunch collard greens, stems and tough parts removed

BRAISING LIQUID

½ cup brandy

¼ cup apple cider vinegar

3 garlic cloves, smashed

2 bay leaves

3 sprigs of thyme

Salt to taste

8 cups vegetable stock, plus more as needed

Finely sliced scallions for garnish

Soak the beans overnight. The next day, drain the beans and put them in a medium pot with enough water to cover by 1 inch. Add the bay leaves. Bring the beans to a boil, turn down the heat to a simmer, and cook until the beans are tender. Drain, discard the bay leaves, transfer to a bowl, and cover with the ½ cup of oil. Let stand for 30 minutes.

Preheat the oven to 350°F.

Cook the farro like pasta in boiling salted water until tender. Drain and mix with the beans.

In a medium bowl, toss the yams with the tablespoon of oil. Add the salt and allspice. Place on a sheet pan and roast until tender, 10 to 15 minutes. Set aside to cool. Reduce the oven temperature to 300°F. Mix the scallions and garlic with the farro and beans. Add the paprika, chile powder, and the cooled yams. Mash lightly to combine, put on the sheet tray, and set aside.

Boil a pot of water and prepare an ice bath. Put a pinch of salt in the boiling water and blanch the greens (about 30 to 60 seconds), then shock them in the ice bath. Lay out the greens on a cutting board, pat dry with a towel, and cool.

PREPARE THE BRAISING LIQUID: Pour the brandy into a large saucepan and cook over medium heat, letting the alcohol burn off. Add the vinegar, garlic, bay leaves, thyme sprigs, and salt. Add the vegetable stock, bring to a boil, then lower the heat and let simmer for 10 to 15 minutes.

**TO PREPARE THE STUFFED COLLARDS:** Place a collard leaf with the stem toward you. Spoon ¼ cup of the farro-bean mixture into the center of the leaf. Fold the sides in and roll up away from you. Place the bundles, folded side down, in a casserole dish. Pour the braising liquid over the bundles; the liquid should cover them half way up; add additional vegetable stock if not. Cover the dish with tinfoil and bake in the oven for 45 minutes, or until the greens are tender. The liquid should always remain about half full and not evaporate too much; if it does, add more vegetable stock. Pull out of the oven and serve on your favorite platter or dish of choice. Garnish with the sliced scallions.

# SWEET POTATO GRITS

## by Kia Damon

MAKES 4 TO 6 SERVINGS

*For as long as I can remember, my grandmother always had a pot of grits on the back of her stove. Sometimes they were fresh, ready to be paired with scrambled eggs and a piece of sausage. Other times, they were from a previous day with the weird film that formed a tint over the now clumpy and dry cornmeal. I've never known a day without grits while I was living with her, especially for breakfast and lunch.*

*It is a known fact that proper grits need only milk, salt, and a pat of butter. The late Edna Lewis said, "People should really leave grits alone," but I see good grits as a beautiful creamy vehicle that, if handled responsibly, can result in some tempting combinations. The roasted sweet potato adds a sweet and earthy element to these grits and only ups the creamy, custardy mouthfeel.*

*I would definitely eat these grits with shrimp smothered in a bacon gravy, fried catfish, or mushrooms simmered in a red curry. You can also enjoy them as our ancestors intended, with just a simple pat of butter.*

**1 sweet potato (about 1 pound)**

**3 cups unsalted chicken stock**

**1½ cups whole milk**

**1 cup white stone-ground grits**

**4 tablespoons unsalted butter**

**Kosher salt to taste**

**Black pepper to taste**

Preheat the oven to 400°F.

Once the oven is hot, wrap the sweet potato in tinfoil and place it on the middle rack. Cook for about 40 minutes until the sweet potato is completely soft and mushy to the touch. Set aside to cool.

In a large pot, slowly heat the stock and milk until the liquid begins to simmer.

Add the grits to a medium bowl and cover with cool water. Use your hands to stir around the grits so the chaff separates and rises to the top. Skim the chaff off the top, strain the grits through a fine-mesh strainer, and repeat this process two more times. Drain and discard the water.

Stir the grits into the milk mixture and use a whisk to make sure there aren't any clumps. It'll look like too much liquid at first, but the grits will expand into creamy goodness. Cook the grits, whisking them until they begin to thicken. It should take about 30 minutes. They should be thick and creamy with a little bite.

At this point, you want to add in your sweet potato. Remove the sweet potato from the skin and place the flesh in a bowl; you should have about 2 cups. I find that an immersion blender for this next part works best. Add the sweet potato to the grits and use the immersion blender to incorporate it all. The blender also yields creamier grits because it breaks up the grains even further.

Mix in the butter and season with salt and pepper.

# BRAISED GOAT

## with Preserved Citrus & Cassava Crepes

## by DeVonn Francis

MAKES 4 SERVINGS

*The influence of root vegetables like cassava (or manioc) has spread as far and wide as the diaspora. This dish has its origins in southern Brazil as well as with Caribbean dishes like bammy. In addition to telling a rich global food history, this dish also makes a case for alternative flours—beyond their uses for dietary restrictions. Incidentally, cassava flour is great as an alternative to wheat flour for those with gluten sensitivity. The toothiness of the dough is akin to masa, though slightly denser in feel. The finished product is half crepe, half flatbread, perfect to serve with stewed meat like this braised goat.*

**QUICK "PRESERVE" KUMQUATS**

12 to 14 kumquats

1 bay leaf

2 lime leaves

1 tablespoon kosher salt

2 tablespoons sugar

**PULLED GOAT**

1 tablespoon kosher salt, plus more to taste

3 tablespoons chaat, or garam masala

1 tablespoon toasted and coarsely ground cumin seeds

4 sprigs of thyme, leaves picked

1 teaspoon crushed chile de arbol

3 pounds bone-in goat shoulder, or any bone-in parts available

Oil for coating the bottom of pan

1 white onion, coarsely chopped

6 garlic cloves

6 cups chicken stock

1 cup apple juice

4 bay leaves

**CREPES**

1 cup cassava flour

2 large eggs

1 cup full-fat coconut milk, plus more as needed

1 cup yogurt

1½ tablespoons olive oil

Pinch of salt

Mint, parsley, watercress, yogurt for garnish

**TO PRESERVE THE KUMQUATS:** Slice the kumquats into thin, coinlike rounds. Put the kumquats, bay and lime leaves into a bowl and sprinkle with the salt and sugar. Gently massage the kumquats with your hands or shake in the bowl. Transfer to a glass jar.

Let the mixture sit for at least 3 hours at room temperature, shaking the jar periodically. Serve immediately or if you want to preserve longer, turn the jar upside down every week or so.

**TO PREPARE THE GOAT:** Combine the salt, chaat, cumin, thyme, and chile de arbol in a large bowl. Rub the spice mixture over the goat.

Heat a large Dutch oven over medium-high heat and add enough oil to coat the bottom of the pan. Add the goat and brown on all sides. You may need to do this in batches. Once the goat is browned, remove and set aside.

To the same pot, add the onion and cook for 15 to 20 minutes on medium-low heat, until golden and caramelized. Add salt to taste. Add the browned goat. Add the garlic, chicken stock, apple juice, and bay leaves and an additional generous pinch of salt on top of the caramelized onions. The meat should be completely covered with liquid. Bring to a boil and then turn down to a simmer and cover with a lid.

Braise the meat for 3 to 4 hours, until it is easily separated from the bone. Remove the bones from the meat. You can discard the onions and broth or reserve for another use.

**TO MAKE THE CREPES:** Combine the flour, eggs, coconut milk, yogurt, oil, and salt in a bowl and mix for 30 to 60 seconds. The batter should be very thin; add more coconut milk if not.

Heat a 10-inch nonstick skillet over medium heat. Pour ¼ cup of the batter into the center of the pan, quickly swirl the pan to coat the bottom, and cook for 2 to 3 minutes. Flip once the top skims over. Place the crepe on a paper towel and repeat. The crepes may be fragile.

**TO SERVE:** Place some of the goat pieces on top of each crepe and top with preserved kumquats. Garnish with the herbs and some yogurt.

# BAOBAB PANKO SALMON

## with Wild Rice & Asparagus

## by Zoe Adjonyoh

MAKES 4 SERVINGS

*I shared this recipe on Nigella Lawson's Instagram account during the #sharethemicfoodandbev campaign, and it did very well. It was just a picture of the ingredients for my dinner—without a recipe, a mere suggestion of what to do. Given that interest, I have created a proper recipe here for you. This is one of the myriad ways in which I sneak baobab into my diet. I say sneak, because healthy ingredients seem like they deserve consideration only at breakfast or brunch—especially when they are immune boosting ones such as baobab. We think of smoothies, shakes, and granola bars—well, we can be more expansive than that, can't we? Baobab's bright, fresh, tangy, and zesty flavor works well with any fish or vegetable marinade, so get sneaking with it.*

### BAOBAB FISH RUB

1 tablespoon baobab powder (see Note)

1 teaspoon salt

½ teaspoon garlic powder

½ teaspoon onion powder

½ teaspoon dried basil

½ teaspoon dried oregano

½ teaspoon cayenne pepper

½ teaspoon smoked paprika (Hungarian)

1 teaspoon dark brown sugar

### BAOBAB BUTTER

1 teaspoon baobab powder (see Note)

1 teaspoon cayenne pepper

3 tablespoons unsalted butter, softened

Sea salt to taste

Pinch of crushed toasted alligator pepper (or coarsely ground tropical peppercorns)

### SALMON

1 tablespoon reserved baobab fish rub

⅓ cup panko bread crumbs

1½ tablespoons flaxseed oil, or olive oil

Two 9- to 10-ounce salmon fillets, skin on

Sea salt to taste

2 garlic cloves, thinly sliced

Sprig of thyme or oregano

¾ cup wild rice

¾ cup coconut milk (about half of a 13.5-ounce can)

½ pound asparagus or other seasonal vegetable, trimmed

Juice of ½ lemon

½ cup of your favorite pesto with ¼ to ½ teaspoon moringa powder (see Note), mixed in

**TO MAKE THE FISH RUB:** Combine all of the spices and grind using a mortar and pestle or spice grinder. Add the sugar and mix to combine. Reserve 1 tablespoon for use in the recipe and store the remaining quantity in an airtight container for another day.

**TO MAKE THE BAOBAB BUTTER:** In a small bowl, mix the ingredients together evenly with a fork. Set aside.

**TO PREPARE THE SALMON:** Heat the oven to 350°F.

Carefully combine 1 tablespoon of the reserved baobab fish rub with the panko crumbs, being careful not to crush the panko too much. Gently stir in half of the oil. Use a kitchen towel to absorb the moisture from each side of the salmon. Lightly sprinkle the skin with salt.

Heat a skillet on medium-high heat. Add the remaining oil to the pan and sauté the garlic with the thyme. Sauté the garlic until it's well done and crispy and brown. Remove the garlic and thyme and reserve for garnish.

Apply the panko mixture to the flesh side of the salmon, compacting it down evenly. Carefully transfer the fish to the heated pan to sear the skin for 2 to 3 minutes.

Remove the pan from the heat and transfer the salmon to an ovenproof dish or baking tray, ready to transfer to the oven. Wipe out the pan with a paper towel.

Wash the rice two or three times. In a medium saucepan, add enough water to just cover the rice. Add salt to season, then add the coconut milk and stir once.

Bring to a boil over medium-high heat, then turn down the heat to medium, cover, and cook for 20 minutes until the rice is tender. Remove the pan from the heat and allow the rice to finish in its own steam for another 5 to 8 minutes with the lid firmly on (you may want to line the lid with tinfoil, beeswax liners, or something similar to contain the steam if the lid doesn't sit tightly).

Transfer the salmon to the oven and bake for 8 to 10 minutes, or as long as 15 minutes for a thick fillet, until the panko crumbs are golden.

Heat the cleaned skillet. Melt half of the baobab butter, then add the asparagus and the remaining butter and grill or pan-fry until al dente. Toss frequently to ensure the asparagus is well coated. Remove the asparagus from the pan and squeeze the lemon juice into the pan to deglaze. Remove the pan from the heat.

**TO SERVE:** Smear a spoonful of pesto across a serving plate. Place the salmon, asparagus, and rice on the pesto. Use 1 or 2 tablespoons of the pan juices from the asparagus to dress the dish. Serve immediately.

**NOTE:** Baobab fish rub, baobab powder, and moringa powder are available online at *zoesghanakitchen.com*.

# RUM RAISIN PLANTAINS FOSTER

## with Vegan Coco Mango Ice Cream

## by Lazarus Lynch

MAKES 6 SERVINGS

*Fried sweet plantains were one of my favorite snack foods as a child. (The rum came later!) I borrow the idea from the traditional bananas foster recipe, adding my own Caribbean spin. I typically like to serve this with rum raisin ice cream, but here's a really easy, fun vegan replacement that is equally addictive.*

**COCO MANGO ICE CREAM**

2 (10-ounce) bags frozen mangoes, about 4 cups

2 cups chopped overripe frozen bananas

1 (15-ounce) can of Coco Lopez-Real Cream of Coconut

½ teaspoon kosher salt

**PLANTAINS FOSTER**

1 tablespoon coconut butter or coconut oil

½ cup packed brown sugar

¼ teaspoon cinnamon

2 ripe sweet plantains, sliced on an angle into ½-inch-thick pieces

¼ cup raisins

¼ cup dark rum

½ cup sweetened coconut flakes, toasted, for garnish

Sea salt for sprinkling

**TO MAKE THE ICE CREAM:** First, prep your ice cream maker insert by placing in the freezer for several hours. Add mangoes, bananas, cream of coconut, and salt to a blender or food processor and pulse until smooth. Transfer the mixture to the cold ice cream maker insert. Cover and return to the freezer for 2 hours. Remove the ice cream from the freezer and let it thaw on the counter for 10 minutes for serving.

**TO MAKE THE PLANTAINS FOSTER:** Melt the coconut butter in a large nonstick skillet over medium heat. Add the brown sugar and cinnamon and cook, stirring, until the sugar has dissolved, about 2 minutes.

Add the plantains and move them around in the pan to evenly coat them with the coconut butter and sugar. Add the raisins.

Remove the skillet from the heat briefly and add in the rum. Return the pan to medium heat and cook until the alcohol has evaporated, 5 to 7 minutes. (The alcohol may catch on fire; don't fret! Just step back and let the fire cook out the alcohol.)

**TO SERVE:** Scoop some of the ice cream into each of four bowls. Spoon the pan sauce, plantains, and raisins over the ice cream. Garnish with the coconut flakes. Sprinkle with sea salt and serve.

# INTERLUDE

ART BY SARINA MANTLE

# CARING FOR THE WHOLE THROUGH THIS BLACK BODY

## by adrienne maree brown

As a Black body, I have a responsibility to attend to myself, by which I mean to attend to my whole self. It is a responsibility I inherited; I was gifted this precious Black body, which holds a material and spiritual lineage to Black bodies that were not held as precious, lovable, safe, and trustworthy. Held as deserving of care.

I inherited the bricks of tenderness needed and not received, the tension of long-term longing, of stolen belonging, the rigid heft of trauma, the water weight of grief. I didn't know, when I was young, why I felt such a drag on my magic. It got heavier each year away from the womb, each year of understanding that some aspect of my inherent self was offensive. To strangers. And as the why got unveiled, I slowly began to understand that my inheritance—a Black body, alive and wired for pleasure and connection in spite of every violence and injustice and shrinking of long-suffering history—was mine to care for, and that to care for this body, to claim it as worthy of my own and others' care, was radical.

Thank Audre Lorde for making it plain that caring for myself was political warfare. Thank Octavia Butler for showing us Anyanwu, a shape-shifting healer protagonist, who invites us to listen within for what needs healing and learn from every other species how to return to wholeness. Thank Tricia Hersey for daily reminders that I, we, can rest. Thank Sonya Renee Taylor for declaring that the body, my body, is not an apology.

Because the next realization, after understanding I have to care for myself, is that I am not a solo Black body, but a cell of *the* Black body. As Alexis Pauline Gumbs teaches, "We are not individuals," we are part of interdependent ecosystems, where our survival and quality of life depend on the health of the other parts, human and earth and animal and air. It helps me to understand that I am a fractal of the Black body. And from that perspective, I know that the whole body of Blackness is not an apology, it is a blessing; it is a unique hydra of experiences that tie together at the root.

And I do not at all mean the root of suffering in the United States, though that is omnipresent and shared. I speak here of the root that takes us back to our indigeneity, to our home dirt, to the places we were given instructions for, to the radical care we once grew up immersed in giving and receiving. We are a body in desperate need of care, care that we remember, care that we were made to forget, care that we rediscovered in the margins of white supremacy's story, care that is bringing us back to the center of our own stories.

The wisdom of fractals is that certain patterns in nature repeat at scale: if I extrapolate from the curvature of fiddleheads, the clusters of broccoli, I see the blood veins of deltas on a southern map; I see the snapshots of galaxies on my fingertips; I see the flocking nature of Black people uprising on city streets where we are tired of grieving our children, neighbors, and beloveds.

The behaviors we have been trained in at the smallest scale are shaped by the trauma of plantation life. Work until you bend, break, bleed. Work while disrespected, work for the bare minimum needed to survive, work while being injured again and again. And then disappear, because you are replaceable. This is how colonization shaped us. This is the slick spill of white supremacy through the sieve of capitalism—what matters is profit, what matters is dominance, what matters is holding power over everyone.

To truly heal ourselves from the legacies of slavery, Jim Crow, genocide, and this era of police brutality, we must decenter whiteness and decolonize our lives. Radical self-care is an assertion at the smallest scale on which we can act, our own bodies, our own cluster of cells and stardust, an assertion that we are our own center. The harm that was done to us is not the beginning of our story. Our Black bodies are the beginning and the miracle and the protagonist and the essence of our stories. We are not free if we are looking at whiteness in admiration or in horror. We are not free if we are running away. We are not free if we are coping with white sugar and white flour and white cigarettes and white powder. We are not free so long as whiteness holds the center of our behaviors and our lives.

And something powerful is available to us now. We are remembering, awakening, to Blackness. Black as beauty, yes. Black as power, yes. And Blackness as a fertile ground, an epic soil, a creative wonderland. Black that is not trying to aspire to anyone else's standards but is reckoning with our own wisdom, generating our own excellence, looking toward the North Star we can only see in communion with other Black bodies.

We are becoming more creative about how we care for ourselves and for each other. For centuries, our care has had to be quiet, secret, done after harm, done in the dark so we wouldn't get punished for loving and tending to each other. Now, we are broadcasting everything we remember and are learning about care for each other.

We are cooking from scratch, we are growing our food. Our herbs sit in our windows. We are oiling our hair and nourishing our skin and teaching our babies how to meditate. We are learning yoga and qi gong and letting them activate the practices of body motion and strength that were lost at sea. We are shouting at each other to rest, to pace ourselves, to stop cold any attempts to hook us back into centering our oppressors over our freedom.

We are giving ourselves permission to finally grieve. To grieve what is happening still, now, every day, and to grieve for Tulsa, to grieve for all the lynching, to grieve for the Middle Passage and the violence before and the violence after. We are giving ourselves permission to express that grief as rage, as wailing, as organizing, as boundaries, as closure. We are giving ourselves permission to feel a wider range of emotion: we are not just grief; we are not just suffering. We are done hiding our genius in the realm of joy, our capacity for love, our wild and brilliant ways of celebrating our miraculous lives.

The more we re-center the collective Black body, the less we have to guard and defend our hearts. Radical self-care is a way of inviting the heart forward, letting the heart point us toward the lives we most long to live, the worlds we are dreaming up for our grandchildren, the futures that will shrink our suffering to the smallest part of the Black story.

What you are going to read in this chapter are the myriad ways that Black people are filling our cups. We are filling ourselves up with a radical root-based practice of caring for ourselves out loud, intentionally shifting the culture from colonial scarcity to liberated abundance. Each page will offer you a way to practice your own daily, practical, radical re-centering of your life. Bring your attention to the care needed in your community. Bring your attention to the care needed in the Black body. Bring your attention to the care needed in *your* precious Black body.

Read this chapter as many times as you need to. Every time you need to remember who you are and what you need to be up to. This is a continuous political project for the rest of your life: care yourself into freedom.

# RADICAL PRACTICES OF CARE
## A Blueprint

## by Zahra Alabanza

i am a Black, queer, multicultural, care-free, and worrisome person raised poor and working class in Hawaii and California, at different points by my mother, a sister, the foster care system, and my paternal grandmother. i'm a wandering, overloving adventurer, creator, and cultural organizer, who works hard for simplicity and leisure. Dreams have been deferred, i've become a parent in an unconventional way, the outdoors and the elements have saved me, and sometimes i think i know what i'm doing, but often i have no idea. i'm out here experimenting with my life, and my children's lives in search of a path that does them justice, doesn't fuck them up, and aligns with how i want to be in the world. It has not come easy; it has come with struggle, but i kinda trust the journey.

The later part of my mother's earthy existence has served as a blueprint for how i exist. After raising seven children, she needed to reinvent herself in a way that would soothe, allowing for rest and simplicity. With no formal education or employment, she somehow picked up and created a new way to be her fullest self in Hawaii. The fruit doesn't fall far from the tree, because twenty-six years after Nina Dear transitioned, I followed in her footsteps. With two children in tow, i left behind all i knew and turned toward the unknown, believing it to be better than where i was, and that it was part of the journey to get back to who i wanted to be. Leaving all i knew behind became my effort to relearn the ways of life robbed from us when we are plugged into the grind. This reminded me of what's important, what i work hard for, and how to sustain my sanity when i'm confronted with the noise and the problems life continues to serve us.

My radical self-care is a practice that embodies my deepest desires, the ones i tuck away and slowly and privately plan for as i work hard for this money and tend to the responsibilities of life. My radical self-care practice is the answer to my whys. It is why i work and love so hard, why i dream off the beaten path, why i have the strength to keep on. When i am radically caring for myself, i am living my wildest adventures and more aligned with my values. This practice is the reward, the pleasure, the joy that comes from being a Black woman whose soul was exhausted from outpouring and just existing in this world.

My radical self-care practice:

Is likely to exist because the prepackaged self-care doesn't satisfy me

Is full of pauses i must take when i'm too close to the edge of losing my sanity. These pauses remind me i can live exactly the way i want

Is the reward i give myself after i've over-poured long and thoughtfully into life

Is a spell that evokes an audacious spirit and grand ideas

Is principled. It is centered on living simply; being easy on the earth; the nonnuclear family; the deep, deep development of tribe; and community care

Is a reflection of possibilities for all the things we want for ourselves but don't have a blueprint for.

i'm an independent parent raising two Black boy children in Atlanta. i'm a business owner, project-starting multipotentialist, and community member. i've been known to do the most—even when trying not to. Unfortunately, i'm hustling to not be broke, to have enough financial gains for generational wealth so that i can rest in this lifetime and my children in theirs. i know this is a setup, yet here i am caught in the grind. Since ima be on this uncompromising grind, i must do so on my own terms to the best of my ability. So sometimes, especially when i'm on the brink of losing my sanity, i undo my whole life for a more ideal version of it.

These pauses save me. They used to happen by force when my body would become ill for months from doing the most, and ridiculous stress levels had me unable to tend to much else other than my wellness. This kind of pause didn't come about for the best reason but provided me with the space to recalibrate and move forward in ways that better serve me. Now i plan for the pauses. Ideally, once a year i pause long enough to remind myself how i actually want to be in the world and i go live that way for a moment or two.

My first intentional pause didn't come until i was drowning and literally needed to escape the abundance i had created for myself. Yup, you read correct. i've lived in moments where i had everything i asked for, worked for, and manifested, yet i was blinded by despair. i was doing the work i wanted to do, had the tribe i committed to, was growing food, playing like i was thirteen years old again, was healthy and, and, and—but miserable. i had temporarily sacrificed ways i wanted to be—adventuring the world, for one—because i couldn't figure out how to live them with children. How could i work abroad in ways i enjoyed and make ends meet? i didn't have the answers, but when i finally started believing that if i fucked up, i could recover just fine, i found the courage, time, and energy to give up our home, packed up three backpacks and a fun bag, and we were out. For six months, we adventured through the USA (including Hawaii), Canada, and all of Central America (except Belize). During our two and a half months living in Central America, i finally unwound and detoxed enough to identify this was exactly how i wanted to live. The boys were technically unschooled; the world was their classroom. We thrived on and had more abundance on the same monthly income with more pleasure, satisfaction, and quality than we could have had in the States. We were living unplugged in paradise, filled by the Earth's offerings. i was flourishing.

The idea that we couldn't keep moving around was tugging at me; the longing for my community and the need for something a bit more stagnant brought that pause to an end. We returned to the States, and i picked up the rhythm of project starting and hustling—but with a new resolve. Like fuck what you heard, ima take bold risks to thrive in an extraordinary existence by any means necessary. The pause taught me to value the journey more than the destination.

In 2008, i met a woman, Nora Dye, who rode her bicycle across the country. i'd never heard of such a thing, like who does this? (A: White people do it. Their privilege allows them to be audacious without a second thought. They do things so many of us don't have the space to even dream up, as we are too often just trying to survive the grind.) My encounter with Nora demonstrated that i had become just another rat in a race i could never win. Knowing what she did bloomed a life design that made me uncomfortable to start but thrilled to begin executing. She affirmed that i needed to be more imaginative and dream bigger, so i did. Who was i *not to* do this? Couldn't i embody audacity, too? A year and a half after meeting Nora, eight women, including myself, designed and completed my first bike tour. It took us

fifteen days, with everything we needed on our bikes to propel ourselves from Eugene, Oregon, to San Francisco. i've since completed multiple three-hundred-plus-mile bike tours (one with a five-year-old), hiked sections of the Appalachian trail, and co-founded Black Freedom Outfitters, a company that curates one-of-a-kind experiences and supports Black people to dare in their outdoor exploration pursuits. i did all of this while raising Black boy children to know they can be anything they have ever seen and deserve to exist in ways that remind them they are alive.

The willingness to take surprising and uncharted risks, ones without a compass are hard AF but necessary for me to feel fulfilled and alive. This audacious spirit contributes to the courage i have to leave everything behind and start anew; it's what encourages me to go bigger than i can even imagine for myself. This spirit helps me help others who don't know where or how to start. It has ignited me into being a creator of space and experiences that fuel other people, that nurture and prepare them to take bold risks and free themselves up from the grind, even if just for the moment.

"Live simply so that others can simply live." These profound words by Mother bell hooks have guided my life since i put eyes on them. When i'm radically caring for myself, i'm reminded to remain aligned with this spell. So, when i'm centering my care by pausing and being audacious, i'm still considering the impact of my actions on the broader world.

This principled practice soothes me in a world that asks too much of anyone, especially a person like me who holds multiple identities that are always under attack. Radical self-care, pauses as a way of being, an audacious spirit, living simply—these all illuminate my path and guide me along my journey. For me, this kind of practice—and the sanity and health it enables—cannot be compromised.

# NOURISHING OURSELVES, AND EACH OTHER, IS NOT AN INDULGENCE

## by Charlene Carruthers

I've spent the past ten years on the road, traveling across the United States, and the globe, working with people organizing to build a radically different world. I always make it back home, Chicago, exhausted, hungry, and in need of a recharge. So, what do I do? I spend any remaining brain space figuring out what I'm going to eat. I have two options: to order take-out or cook something for myself. More often than not, I choose the latter and make a trip to the local grocery store. Feeling unrushed, I take my time wandering through the aisles. The simple act of going from aisle to aisle, doubling back to grab something I forgot to add to my cart brings me back to myself. The sight of produce in its multi-textured, naturally rainbow state, imperfect or shiny, clears my mind. The sweet, yeasty aroma of the bakery section wakes up my heart.

As a Black queer woman living in a patriarchal, capitalist, and imperialist country, sensory satisfaction and the process of preparing a meal for myself is central to my personal resilience practice. I've cooked the same dish dozens of times with the goal of mastery. Other times, when I'm attempting something new, I move with greater anarchy. I learned from a young age how to improvise. My mama taught me how to drain pasta with a plate on top of a pot. Who needed a colander when a plate was available? I know how to make do with one knife and a big spoon. I can do almost anything with just a few seasonings. I did not know what a cutting board was until much later in life—I used a well-cleaned counter or a plate. The kitchen is where I practiced resilience before I ever heard of the term. It is where I care for myself. As poet, intellectual, and activist Audre Lorde teaches, this act of care "is not self-indulgence. It is self-preservation, and . . . an act of political warfare."

I care for other people through food. Feeding and nourishing people is one of my life's callings. I enjoy selecting menus for meetings and conferences. Give me a list of dietary needs—I don't think of them as restrictions—I will work with anyone to make it happen. Many of the people I've worked with over the past fifteen years have been mistreated and undervalued. They are often the same people who hold great responsibilities for their families and in their communities. Because of this, I find it important to do what I can, knowing that even if some people leave unsatisfied, I have done whatever was within my power to do.

Whether you are a descendant of enslaved Africans or someone whose lands were colonized, food, and our relationship to it, is inherently political. Growing, cooking, and sharing food do not exist in a vacuum; they are crucial parts of what historian Cedric Robinson called the Black Radical Tradition. The Black Radical Tradition disrupts (and re-creates) social, political, economic, and cultural norms. There is a role for everyone in this tradition. There are activists for single causes, campaign strategists, strategic communicators, intellectuals, healing justice practitioners, artists, childcare workers, those who manage the physical labor of setting up and breaking down events, and then, there are those who do the work of feeding people: the farmers, the chefs, the prep cooks, the people doing the shopping, and the people cleaning up after everyone has eaten; each have essential roles.

Feeding people across communities has always been central to this tradition. I learned early on that people were more likely to, and more able to, attend a meeting or event if (good) food was provided.

There is a Black culinary tradition of resistance and resilience, often with Black women at its center. Demands and visions for access to quality food, the transformation of food systems and land stewardship all exist within this tradition. Black folks have used and continue to use food as a means to care for each other,

fund community organizing, and as protest. We care for ourselves while caring for others. One of the best-known examples of this was the Black Panther Party for Self-Defense Free Breakfast program, which was a direct action against the state, aimed at meeting the needs of Black families and illustrating how access to quality food was essential to Black liberation.

Lesser-known, yet essential to understanding the civil rights movement (also known as the southern freedom movement) is Chef Georgia Gilmore and the Club from Nowhere. The Club from Nowhere was a city-wide network of Black women chefs who sold meals to protestors in order to fund the Montgomery bus boycott. Doing the work was a risk each chef took on, not only to provide financial resources to support the movement's infrastructure but also to provide consistent nourishment for those participating in the 381-day direct action protest. This culinary protest work served as a primary organ in the body of a historical collective action. (See Thérèse Nelson's article in *Southern Living*, "The Story of Georgia Gilmore: This Montgomery, Alabama, Cook Helped Fund the Civil Rights Movement" for more on this extraordinary woman.)

So why is there not a collective understanding of the people, very often Black women, queer and trans folks, who apply their skills to feed and make our movements possible? How can we better understand this incomplete story of protests? We can start by recognizing the work of feeding people in movement spaces as care work. Care work is often under-recognized—when even recognized at all. Ranging from childcare to eldercare, care work is often understood as a "woman's" job or as feminized labor. This is a product of a global system of patriarchy that sorts individuals into roles along binaries and hierarchies that reinforce capitalism, anti-Blackness, and white supremacy.

What would be possible if we viewed the labor of caring for ourselves and for others—be it through food or other means—as the collective responsibility of every person? What would be possible if our storytellers, historians, and educators were committed to telling a complete story about Black liberation movements, including the cooks and the caregivers? My assessment is that we would all be better positioned to break down the blockades between dignity and suffering. We would develop more complete solutions. We would be better positioned to truly value all Black lives.

Just as we know that children cannot learn well on empty stomachs, we must also understand that movements cannot flourish without the nourishment of those who dedicate their time and energy to our collective liberation. That labor should be appreciated, valued, and treated as core to the movement.

Let us all extend appreciation to the cooks, chefs, and cocinerxs, who make sure folks marching, driving, and moving for miles at protests are well fed. Let us all show grace to those who take care to consider various dietary needs and work to meet them with as much passion as they do for people who can eat everything. Let us all take the time to build movements focused on creating the best conditions for the people who plant and cultivate the food that crosses our individual palates— especially those who are un/underpaid and those working in unsafe conditions.

There is no Black liberation without meeting basic human needs for care and nourishment. But our work can and must go beyond survival—we must do the work so that we can all thrive. Now is the time for us to embrace the history and future of care as essential work. In doing so, not only will we deliver well-deserved recognition but we will fortify our path toward collective liberation.

# QUESTIONS
## We're All Just Figuring It Out

## by Glenn Lutz

As human beings, one of the ways we can all relate to each other is through a shared experience of hurt, of pain. We understand sadness and that feeling of being burdened by the weight life places upon us. This year has been difficult for us all and for many, the toughest year of our lives. I've experienced paralyzing grief, uncertainty, self-doubt, and loneliness, all jam-packed into a gumbo called 2020. I've spent the year in reflection and meditation, and yet, in the toughest moments, I struggled to make it through the day.

In many ways, writing about self-care feels hypocritical. It often feels as if I'm being pinned beneath my stresses, but the first step in self-care is to accept myself where I am, with my flaws and the goodness that shape me in any given moment. I know all too well that I'll never fully arrive; it's a process. Mental wellness is a lifestyle that requires presence, honesty, and a willingness to ask myself the hard questions. If I want to be the best version of myself, it's important to be humble and honest about my flaws.

When I don't know what to do, I strive to look deeper within. I've designed a list of questions that I am able to ask myself over the course of a year. Some of them address my daily routines, while others examine the existential. In sharing them, I hope they can assist you on your journey and in your quest to be the best you—today and in the future.

---

What does self-care mean to me? Do I practice that self-care on a daily basis?

What routines in my life am I proud of? What do they add to my life, and when did I start doing them?

How do I find peace after a stressful day? What's stressing me out, and is there a way to look at those stressors differently?

Am I getting eight hours of sleep every night, and do I feel rested when I wake up? If not, what can I do to have a more restful sleep?

Am I cultivating healthy relationships in my life?

Do I listen to others deeply when they're confiding in me?

What makes me laugh, and how important is laughter in my life?

How much water am I drinking a day?

When I need a snack, what do I grab? Is it something that promotes healthful living? If not, what might be better?

How many hours a day am I on my phone? How do I feel when I put it down?

Are the films and shows I'm watching, and the music I'm listening to, aiding me in being a better person?

What does the perfect day look like?

What is something I can do for a loved one in my life that would brighten their day?

If I had more time in the day, what would I do with it?

Is there a way to adjust my schedule to ensure that I can spend thirty minutes doing something that I love?

Who are ten people who have made a positive impact in my life? Am I able to tell them today how grateful I am for what they've done for me? If not, is there something I can do today that honors their legacy?

Where in my body do I feel the things that stress me out? Am I able to stretch or relieve that tension in that part of my body?

When something angers me, do I attempt to ignore it, or am I able to express that frustration constructively in the moment?

Do I find myself thinking the most about the past, the present or the future?

How many hours a day am I in direct contact with nature and the outside world? When I'm there, do I notice the world around me or am I trapped in my mind?

What social issues are important to me, and am I able to give back or volunteer for that cause?

What is something that I've always wanted to learn but it seemed "too difficult" to pick up?

Am I able to give five, ten, or fifteen minutes a day to practicing that thing?

How many days a week do I exercise, and how could I improve my fitness routine?

Do I feel anxious throughout the day? If so, what are the things that trigger it? What do I do when those feelings come up?

Am I speaking to anyone about the things that bother me? Do I have someone to talk to about my fears and self-doubts?

Am I able to create a gratitude journal and list five things every day that I'm grateful for?

Do I feel that I'm living up to my full potential?

Where do I want to be in five years?

Am I creating goals, for the short-term and long-term? Am I holding myself accountable to meet them?

Do I enjoy the work I do? If not, how can I create a new reality, one that I enjoy, one that has purpose, and one that makes me feel whole?

Am I afraid of my dreams and aspirations?

Do I feel as if I'm failing those who rely on me and look up to me? Why?

Am I being too hard on myself about who I am now and how I'm doing?

Do I forgive myself when I slip up?

Am I wasting my time, doing things that dull my feelings, rather than taking actions to be the person I want to become?

Am I scared to be the real me when I walk in a room? Am I embarrassed of my story?

Am I holding onto grudges aimed at people who've hurt me?

Am I living in an "us versus them" mentality? If so, is it solving anything?

Am I angry at the world, blaming my life on external circumstances?

Do I believe that being vulnerable is being weak? What does healthy vulnerability look like in my life?

How many hours a day am I spending on social media, and is that the amount of time I want to be spending?

Do I run from those who love me when I need them the most?

Is it easy to pretend that I'm fine when I'm not?

Am I real with myself and where I'm at in my life?

Do I like what I see when I look in the mirror?

Do I forgive myself when I make mistakes?

Do I feel like I'm a failure?

If I died tomorrow, would I be happy with how I lived my life?

Can I remind myself of my achievements big and small?

---

At the end of this examination, I find it useful to repeat this reminder: as difficult as life can be, I've never encountered something I can't overcome. I have hope, and I have the power to design the life I want to live.

# A BLESSING FROM MY ANCESTORS

## by Krystal C. Mack

i learned about the use of okra as a tool for spiritual cleansing in 2018 as i was conducting research for my dinner series "Clearing the Field," which explores my personal healing and the healing of trauma within my family. In developing the menu for the dinner series, i wanted to incorporate ingredients that were memorable parts of my personal food history with my family and use foods that were known to have not only healing nutritional properties but also aid in cleansing the spirit. i learned about the use of okra in the spiritual practice of Ifá, originating from the Yoruba tribe of Nigeria. In many spiritual practices of the diaspora, okra is used in baths to aid in the removal of negativity and toxic energy.

This past summer, i developed a two-part bath ritual incorporating okra and i found it really helped calm my anxiety when the stress and overwhelm of 2020 began to weigh me down. In this ritual, i call on my ancestor's wisdom and guidance, asking them to bring joy and positivity into the bath. i aim to be intentional, with as many steps as possible when conjuring this bath.

For my first bath, i used okra grown in my backyard with seeds gifted to me from a colleague's family farm in North Carolina. When i was low on okra from my own garden, i'd buy from Black farmers in Baltimore. If that wasn't possible, i'd go to the grocery store. Buying your okra from the grocery store for this bath is fine; i just prefer to know the growers of the okra and its growing conditions. i want as much positivity on them as i can get, especially when it's being used in energy work!

This is my personal adaptation, drawn from multiple rituals i have come across these past few years, all shared over many generations. Sometimes i incorporate the rose bath soak into my ritual and at other times i do not. This is a personal ritual that works well for me. As with any offering, please take what works for you and leave what does not.

# HEALING ROSE BATH SOAK & VIBRATIONAL OKRA BATH

MAKES ABOUT 1¼ CUPS OF HEALING SOAK, ENOUGH FOR 10 SOAKS

*i came up with this bath soak when i wanted to open up my life to more loving energy, and this bath helped to do just that. i often soak in the rose bath the night before i do my okra bath.*

### ROSE BATH SOAK

½ cup pink mineral salt

1 teaspoon almond oil

4 drops of rose essential oil

¼ cup rose petals

¼ cup rolled oats

Rose quartz crystal (optional)

2 white candles

### VIBRATIONAL OKRA BATH

3 white candles

Frankincense incense

2 large bowls

Warm water

Agua de Florida

35 pods okra, rinsed clean

Rose quartz crystal, charged

Strainer

Ylang-ylang essential oil

White or pastel clothing

White or pastel fabric (for wrapping your head)

**TO MAKE THE BATH SOAK:** Combine the pink salt, almond oil, and rose essential oil in a large bowl and whisk together until the salt is well combined. Add the rose petals and rolled oats and whisk again to fully combine. Store the bath soak in an airtight container.

When ready to use: Scoop 2 tablespoons of the bath soak into a muslin tea bag or cheesecloth; tie closed. Draw a hot bath and place the tea bag and rose quartz, if using, into the water. Light two white candles and place one at each end of the bathtub. Soak and relax.

Empty the tea bag and rinse and clean the bag for future use.

**TO PREPARE THE OKRA BATH:** Light one of the candles and burn some of the incense. Place both the candle and the lit incense on your ancestral altar. My altar has photos of ancestors, crystals, and objects with sacred meaning to me, like wood carvings or family heirlooms and occasionally a food offering. (You can slice and fry five of the okra pods for the offering.)

Fill one of the bowls halfway with warm water and add the Florida water. Cutting two okra pods at a time and with the blade of your knife facing away from you, slice rings of okra into the bowl of water. As you cut the okra, speak intention into the bowl. This can be a prayer to your ancestors. It is critically important to speak with conviction as you prepare the bath. Doing so will feed intention into the water.

Once you've finished cutting the okra, massage the sliced pods to encourage the release of the okra film. While massaging the okra, visualize the liquid capturing all of the negative energy. The liquid will continue to get more viscous as you massage the okra and will become more like a loose gel. It is this gel that is trapping the negative and stale energy. As you continue to massage, visualize prosperity, protection, a release from pain, and the removal of toxicity from your life. Again, these are usually my requests but speak to what you yourself are in need of.

Place the rose quartz crystal in the bowl and place the bowl on your altar for about 40 minutes and rest.

CONTINUED

## Healing Rose Bath Soak & Vibrational Okra Bath, continued

After 40 minutes, pour the liquid through the strainer, allowing the liquid to collect in your second bowl. Set aside the sliced okra. The viscous liquid that remains is your bath. Add a bit more warm water to the bowl to bring the bath closer to a comfortable body temperature. Light the remaining two candles and place them at each end of the bathtub or shower entrance. These candles symbolize a light-embodied entryway to the cleansing that is about to take place. Keep these candles lit during the ritual.

Take your bath bowl into the bathtub or shower and pour the mixture over the top of your head and all over your body. You want your hair and the entirety of your body completely covered in the bath. Visualize the bath capturing all of the negativity that you wish to do away with. Rinse your head and body with cool water, ensuring that all of the okra bath and the trapped bad energy is washed away. Make sure that you also rinse all of the okra bath out of the tub and down the drain. Exit the bathtub or shower, passing again between the lit candles.

Apply the ylang-ylang and Florida water to all chakra points and put on white or pastel clothing to attract light and positive energy, then wrap your head in the white or light-colored fabric. Move the two candles from in front of the bathtub or shower onto your altar. Dispose of the okra by composting it or burying it in the backyard.

Spend the next twenty-four hours in a rested state, protective of your energy, and avoid any emotionally exhaustive activities or interactions.

# POTION: WHISKEY AS RITUAL

## by Jamey Hatley

*pōSH(ə)n| noun: a liquid with healing, magical, or poisonous properties*

### TO KNOW WHAT LOVE IS:

**1 teaspoon whiskey**

- A bit of black tea

- Sugar

- Hot water

- The prettiest tiny china teacup ringed with pink roses and edged with gold

- Listen to the parents standing over the harvest gold stove, the blue gas flame spitting under the pot. "What's wrong with the baby?" the daddy asks. You can't hear the next bit, so it must be Mama. She knows you are listening, so she says the next bit louder, "It will all be fine."

- Hold the pretty cup between your little hands and try to smile.

### TO BECOME A FILMMAKER:

**2 mini-bottles of whiskey***

- Go pour a libation of a tiny bottle of whiskey at the magnolia tree on Mulberry Street. The day has been still until then, but the wind answers.

- Drive down Highway 61 to your parents' home.

- Do not say what you are looking for but search for a blue suitcase that you are not sure still exists or has been destroyed in a house fire.

- Give up looking for said suitcase. Confess to your mother what you were looking for.

- Your mother, who is into her eighties, insists that she go up into the attic to get the suitcase because she knows just where it is.

- You beg her not to.

- She ignores you.

- You hold the rickety pull-down ladder, as the woman twice your age goes horizontal, reaching, reaching, reaching for something. Grabs hold.

- She pulls the prize out and hands the small blue suitcase to you, gently, gently.

- You click the latches, and the scent of your grandmother flies out, a haunting. You gasp. It is not the suitcase you were thinking of. In it are her last things: tiny cream slips, starched hankies, sticks of chewing gum, a coin purse that snaps open and closed. A tiny bottle of Black Draught and a tiny bottle of whiskey, the same brand that you used for your ceremony.

- "Is that what you were looking for?" your mother asks. You start to sob.

- In the pocket of the suitcase is your grandfather's obituary. You have never seen it. Your mother was pregnant with you when he died. Like the whiskey, he is also called Jack. Marvin "Jack" Harris. His is the only character with a full name in your film. He, too, is a wind that has answered you when you called.

*The two mini-bottles of whiskey must be bought at least twenty-five years apart.

# TO SURVIVE A HURRICANE (YEARS LATER):
**several jugs of whiskey**

- 1 punch bowl, big pickle jar, or any available vessel

- 1 case of slow-moving dread around the anniversary of the storm, which you will years later learn is depression

- 1 (550-square-foot) shotgun apartment off Tchoupitoulas Street, insides painted haint blue

- 1 flower bed full of mint because your sweet neighbor who will later have a nervous breakdown feels sorry that all of your flowers perished while his flourished

- Decide to do something with your sadness this year as everybody mourns, even if New Orleanians mourn better than most anybody.

- Learn that you have a blues heart that leans toward melancholy.

- Choose to celebrate your breath. Put up an invite on social media and do not look at the replies.

- Name this cocktail, in New Orleans there are always cocktails, the Jamey Julep.

- Do not record quantities, make everything by hand in your tiny kitchen. Be still making things as people arrive.

- Make lemonade from scratch.

- Make sweet tea from scratch.

- Mint simple syrup

- Pineapple juice

- Orange juice, maybe grapefruit, or lime or blood orange, too

- Put first batch in freezer so that base gets slushy.

- Start muddling mint in cups as people come in.

- Someone puts on music and you are tipsy and happy.

- Over fifty people come through your tiny house that day.

- The last batch of punch is mostly just bourbon. People adjust, someone goes for ice. Someone takes out the trash.

- You learn how to throw open your door and make family. You learn how to let yourself be loved.

# MEDICINAL PLANTS

## by Kanchan Dawn Hunter

Today we are going to engage with the plant realms. Plants are significant allies to all humans. Traditionally, our African ancestors relied on plants for their healing properties. In fact, our ancestors were pioneers in the field of medicine, and they brought much of that wisdom to this continent, albeit against their will.

### GROWING

We will be growing herbs for a soothing tea blend that includes peppermint, holy basil (tulsi), and lemon balm. As Black folx, we have had our fair share of trauma. Trauma affects every system in the body. These plants are well suited to heal trauma in the mind, body, and soul. They support digestion, heal anxiety, and promote healthy rest. These are plants that are easy to grow in most places. All of these plants have similar watering needs (once a week) and sun requirements, so they can share the same pot or ground area in your garden. Be sure to plant after the final winter frost has passed.

### YOU WILL NEED

If planting in the ground, plant each start, once sprouted, at least 1 foot apart. Once they are at least 1 foot tall or wide, harvest the aerial parts; that is, the leaves and flowers. Your plants should be ready to harvest after one year.

A (25-gallon) pot or the earth

Some dirt

Seeds or seedlings of peppermint, holy basil (tulsi), and lemon balm

A place to put the pot (preferably in a sunny spot)

Sun

Water

Air

Love

### CONNECTING TO PLANTS

When plants reach their harvest stage, it is a great time to sit with them, listen to their subtle voices, and inhale their fragrance. Growing our own plant medicine is a way to imprint our particular healing needs on the plant that we are bringing into our bodies. Plants feel our energy and are affected by our intentions. This is why it is so important that we spend time connecting with them as they grow.

### HARVESTING AND PREPARATION

The best herbal teas utilize dried plant material. In this blend, we are using plants that concentrate a significant amount of nourishing essential oils. To dry your plants, select a cool, indoor, dust-free area. You can use a paper bag or tray or hang them from a string, either on your wall or from your ceiling, whatever you can easily access. The plants are usually ready for use within three weeks. You can store dried herbs in a Mason jar in your cupboard for future use. Use approximately 2 tablespoons of plant material per boiling cup of water for best results.

Knowledge is power! I encourage everyone to research these wonderful plants and their properties. Also consider diving deeper into other medicinal plants that you feel might be supportive on your healing journey. In Joy!

# SEED WEAVING, ALTAR WORK & ANCESTRY

## by Latham Thomas

Medicinal foods provide us a tether to the land.

Our ancestry bound in the bounty of root systems.

A calling home unto the sacred land to guide us in healing.

Plants communicate with our cells and tap us into lineage.

Our connection to culinary plants and healing herbs has been a tool for liberation, an anchor to our traditions and a pathway to vital health.

### ALTAR WORK & ANCESTRAL FOODS

Altars are energetically charged, sacred spaces for ritual. You can turn any surface into an altar. It can be as simple as placing objects on a table or shelf that remind you of important people and events in your life. With thoughtfulness, you can transform any space into a sacred sanctuary.

I've gathered objects from around the world and used them to create altar spaces that hold the energy that I want to cultivate in my personal space and in my life. You can collect beautiful glass vases, flowers, sculptures, talismans, seashells, cowries, rocks, gemstones, or crystals and place them on your altar. Photographs of elders, leaders, figures from history, or from your lineage that inspire you should be placed upon the altar for tribute and to evoke the energy of encouragement and bestowment of blessing.

I recommend fortifying your altar with edible ancestral ingredients: fresh heirloom okra fingers, dried black-eyed peas, rice, cassava, yam, kidney and lima beans, millet, peanut, sorghum, licorice, plantain, watermelon, *Guinea pepper,* sesame, sassafras, pepper, ackee, pumpkin, castor bean, coconut, lime, hibiscus, and palm oil. You can use whatever form of the food you have at your disposal. Seed, fruit, flower, root, leaf or oil, fresh or dried—all are potent elements. Bring at least three ancestral foods into your altar space. Consider anchoring those foods in your meal planning for the day/week/season.

These are just some of the many plants that sustained our ancestors along their arduous journey as enslaved people, through the

Middle Passage and after they arrived in the Americas. Many of our maternal ancestors braided rice into their hair; some swallowed okra seeds to ensure seed dispersal when they arrived in the Americas. They had the foresight to bring these foods, not for themselves but for the future—for us.

These foods are part of the botanical legacy that weave all of us together. These foods make up our cells and blood, our thoughts and our actions. They provided the nourishment that supported their bodies during enslavement. These foods are part of rituals and rites constituting spiritual expression and these foods are rooted in various ways in our collective traditions.

## SEED-WEAVING CENTERING PRACTICE

Before sitting at the altar and grounding yourself, here are some things you should have:

- A cup of Overnight Ancestral Tonic (see recipe on page 260)

- Comfortable and quiet place to sit

- Candles

- Holy oils, woods, leaves, resins, or incense to burn

- Journal and pen to answer reflective prompts

## MEDITATION

Seated comfortably, connect with your breath.

Allow yourself to settle and give thanks.

Choose the seed(s) that you would like to hold and connect with, then repeat silently or aloud:

*I celebrate and weave seed into my altar. I honor the blessed seed, fruit, flower, leaf, root, and oil that sustained my ancestors. I give thanks for the abundant connection to foods and flavor that center me deep in my ancestry.*

Hold your tea in both hands, bring it to your nose to scent, then repeat silently or aloud:

*I celebrate and weave seed into my body. I honor the blessed seed, fruit, flower, leaf, root, and oil that sustained my ancestors. I give thanks for the abundant connection to foods and flavor that center me deep in my ancestry.*

And drink the tonic. Sit for as long as feels comfortable.

Seal your practice by placing your right hand over your heart and your left hand over your belly. And voicing a word through intention or reflection.

*Ashé.*

## REFLECTIVE PROMPTS (POST MEDITATION)

- Think about what ancestral foods sustained your people. Consider your lineage and what recipes they prepared for celebration.

- What did they pour and drink for libation?

- How did food bond them and anchor them in tradition?

- How important are these foods in your life?

- Who in your family carries the culinary signature through generations?

CONTINUED

- What healing plants have been used in your lineage?

- How can you deepen your healing practice with plants?

## PREPARING YOUR OVERNIGHT HERBAL INFUSION

Grounding in the energy of the seasons is what's most necessary for you right now. Preparations from the evening gather the potency and charge of the plants and release the power into the water—which is evident in the color and taste of the tonic. Plant medicine was a way of life and sustained our people when they had no access to medical care.

Herbalism was part of our radical ancestral self-care. During slavery, water infusions were the primary method used because it was the easiest way to prepare herbal preparations for enslaved people. Herbalism was a daily practice of empowerment and healing for Black people because there were very few other options and support for healing.

When connecting with the herbs, intuit what you need. A mix of dried and fresh herbs is welcome. Singular tonics are great; you can also blend. When working with healing plants, use your hands, touch, bring your hands to your face to smell the plant, taste, be present with the preparation.

# OVERNIGHT ANCESTRAL TONIC

**Handful of dried nettles**

**4 or 5 sprigs of basil**

**4 or 5 sprigs of mint**

**Half a handful dried hibiscus**

**1-inch piece ginger, peeled and sliced**

**1 tablespoon honey (optional)**

Place the herbs in a 32-ounce container, add the ginger and honey, then pour hot water over them to fill. Seal and let stand overnight. The following morning, use a fine-mesh sieve to strain the herbs. Serve at your altar during meditation.

**NOTE:** Nettles are blood builders and loaded with iron; they are known to be effective in treating hypertension and diabetes. Basil is known to reduce anxiety and stress, boost immunity, and soothe cold and flu symptoms. Mint helps relieve indigestion. Hibiscus contains cancer-fighting antioxidants and helps to lower cholesterol. Ginger curbs nausea, reduces painful periods, and helps lower blood sugar. Honey has antibacterial and antifungal properties; it's immune-boosting and has anti-cancer benefits.

# DICK GREGORY'S SELF-CARE JOURNEY

## by Frederick Douglass Opie, PhD

In the 1960s, Dick Gregory (1932–2017) became one of the country's leading nightclub comics and political satirists. In his 1964 book *Nigger: An Autobiography,* he said meeting Martin Luther King Jr. changed him from a comedian to a civil rights activist. Gregory also gradually changed his eating habits and self-care practice. He explained that during a civil rights march in the South, a sheriff had kicked his wife and he hadn't come to her defense. "I had to convince myself," says Gregory, "that the reason that I didn't do anything about it was because I was nonviolent." He adds, "Then I said, 'If thou shalt not kill,' that should mean animals, too. So, in 1963, I just decided I wasn't going to eat anything else that had to be killed," he explains. "I still drank a fifth of scotch a day and smoked four packs of cigarettes. So, my becoming a vegetarian didn't have anything to do with health reasons. And I didn't even know how to spell it; I didn't know what a vegetarian was." But, after about eighteen months of being a vegetarian, his sinus trouble was gone, and about six months after that, his ulcers healed. In an interview I did with Gregory in 2005, he told me, "That was the first time I realized that there was something about the food that

they didn't tell us about." Starting in 1967, even more enlightenment came, when Gregory met Dr. Alvenia Fulton.

A nutritionist and naturopath, Dr. Fulton founded Fultonia's Health Food and Fasting Center in Chicago's South Side in the late 1950s. Gregory met Fulton during his 1967 campaign for mayor of Chicago against the incumbent, Richard Daley. Fulton stopped by campaign headquarters and dropped off some salad for Gregory and his staff. "I went by one day to thank her, and it turned my whole life around," he said. They sat and talked, and Fulton heard that Gregory was going to go on a forty-day fast to protest the war in Vietnam. "And she thought I knew something about fasting, which I didn't! And she taught me from day one to day forty what was going to go on in my body."

In a May 1973 article published in the magazine *Sepia,* Gregory told journalist Alfred Duckett that during his fast, he went from 350 to 98 pounds and ran twenty-five miles a day. After the fast, his weight returned to 148 pounds; he was healthy, and he began to fast on a regular basis. Over the next several years, Gregory and Fulton became close friends, regularly sharing their knowledge about fasting, herbs, and nutrition with anybody who would listen.

Fulton collaborated with Gregory on their 1973 cookbook entitled *Dick Gregory's Natural Diet for Folks Who Eat: Cookin' with Mother Nature,* edited by James R. McGraw with Alvenia Fulton. The book is the most compelling evidence that Fulton's work was an important influence on Gregory. In the cookbook, Gregory, with assistance from Fulton, points to improper eating as the cause of bloating, baldness, varicose veins, swollen ankles, high blood pressure, heart trouble, and nervous tension. As he writes in the book, all these illnesses are the result of "heavy starch consumption, cooked food and greasy fried food consumption, and sugar and salt consumption." The same year he published the cookbook, Gregory also stopped doing his stand-up comedy routine at nightclubs. In 1973, he explained to reporter Vernon Jarrett of the *Chicago Tribune* that "he had a problem in doing anything that would encourage people to consume alcohol or do anything that might be damaging to one's personal health." Jarrett wrote, "Dick's near full-time commitment today is to the human body and what is done to it and with it. And there is nothing funny about this commitment."

# SUNSHINE & RAIN

## by Damon Brown

I get my personality from my mom, a South Jersey way of having direct conversations and addressing the elephant in the room. I get my intellectual prowess from my stepdad, who raised me, a southern-meets-Socratic way of sussing out the truth. And I get my public demeanor from my dad, a rural Jersey calm, almost taciturn exterior. Deeper in my paternal lineage, about three generations back, is New Orleans. My great-grandmother was an orphan there. My leaning toward pleasure and a penchant for extremely spicy food and easy comfort in the kitchen aren't really matched by other folks on any side of my family. I must have reached back for that shit.

So, I laugh as big as I cry. When I faced cancer a decade and a half ago, I told my partner I expected a second-line procession funeral. I beamed when I saw each of my children come out of my wife. I passionately share my opinion with strangers. I sob when I know I've written the last line to a book (I just published my twenty-fifth).

I saw my stepdad cry one time. I was around my eldest son's age—six or so—and I heard a commotion in my parents' bedroom. I saw my pop, his large, strong hands covering his face. He sat on the edge of the bed, away from the door. My mom explained that Great Grandma had died. I might have quietly left the room. Frankly, I can't remember anything after that.

Decades later, I saw my dad cry. My eldest son had just been born. Within weeks, my grandfather died. Sleep-deprived from all-night feedings, I took a red-eye to Jersey for his funeral. I had already cried several times during the service, when my dad broke down. I remember him whispering, "Sorry," when he did.

And on one nondescript winter's day, my mom called to tell me that my sick grandmother had died. I was in the middle of booking a flight to get to Jersey—a flight to see her. I would have been there the next night. I cried on the phone briefly with my mom, for my mom. Not too much, though; as the eldest, she had to shift to planning mode. I then sat with my kids.

It was February 2020. George Floyd was a stranger, still alive. A virus ravaging China only encouraged me to tell international friends to be careful. Daily death tolls were not on the front page of the *Las Vegas Review–Journal*. Death was rare. It felt sharper. It was not yet quantifiable.

I explain to my kids that Great-Nomma has passed. My six-year-old asks seemingly infinite questions, including concerns about zombies. I answer them all as well as I can. My three-year-old plays with his LEGOs, hugs me, then alternates between the two, hugging and playing. And all the while, my eyes well up, my voice cracks, my face falls. I would have moments like this for the next couple weeks, at breakfast, while the kids and I were playing, or as I pick them up from school. It's not about the funeral grandstanding, run-ning into the street screaming or jumping on caskets—we have plenty of that in our family. Nor is it the preplanned, designated times to be sad—emotions don't give a fuck about our Google Calendars. It is about the practice of allowing things to suck, when they suck, how

they suck, until they suck less. Especially for us. Being a Black man in America is hard, not only because of systemic issues that push against us but also because we are a projection of fantasies: self-hatred, political impotence, inferiority complexes masked as superior-ity beliefs, and, most notably, unconscious emotions. We are what Carl Jung would call the other, that dark side of the moon, where would-be repressors stuff all the undesirable traits that they actually possess but refuse to own.

We are constantly dealing with other people's emotional baggage. You'd better make sure yours are unpacked.

Frankly, I didn't see any major changes in my kids after they saw their dad cry. But perhaps, when they are strong Black-and-brown men in a moment of remarkable pleasure or emotional pain, they'll remember what they saw him proudly do when they were children. And then they'll cry as fiercely as they love.

# BREATH WORK

## by Christopher Pearson

We can go weeks without food, days without water, yet only moments without breath. Breath connects all living organisms. We move through our lives giving little thought to the quality of our breath until we are short of breath. It is only through conscious participation that we can learn to deepen and lengthen our breath. Take a moment. Breathe deeply. Did your chest rise? Chances are it did. Almost two-thirds of our breathing capacity is in the lower lobes of our lungs. We can only access the lower lobes with diaphragmatic breathing, also known as belly breathing. There are four simple ways to strengthen your routines and deepen your conscious-breathing practice. Self-care is about consistent discipline and regular habits for well-being. Become more aware of your breath and deepen your connection to a mindful state with these four exercises:

- Deepening our exhalations by extending them for 3 or 4 seconds.

- Pause between exhale and inhale; pause between inhale and exhale.

- Breathe into the lowest part of your belly first, then fill all parts of your lungs, breathing into the back and front of your ribs.

- Be easy and deliberate with your practice.

Here's an example of a daily breathing routine:

Find a comfortable space to lie flat on your back with your knees slightly elevated. Place a sacred object directly over your belly button. A sacred object can be a book, a stone, a shell, or anything that grounds you in your life's purpose. Be sure the object has a weight that is comfortable for you and holds meaning in your life. On each inhale, breathe life into the object and lift up through your belly button. Realizing your conscious intention gives life to your sacred object and the beliefs it supports. Pause at the peak of your inhale. Observe the stillness created by a moment of pause. Release the held breath and fill the world with your intention. Allow the weight of your sacred object to press down toward the spine. Once the lungs are empty and your purpose has filled the room, you are in pause. Observe the stillness created by a moment of pause. Remember to keep your routine simple and easy to repeat.

Over time, your awareness of the pause will become more apparent in real time, and breath will begin to flow effortlessly. Your increased awareness of where you are in a given moment will increase your sense of well-being. Mindful breathing is a cornerstone of self-care.

# A RECIPE FOR COMMUNITY CARE

## by Prentis Hemphill

Our progress in the pursuit of healing is measured through our relationship to ourselves. This relationship is foundational, but there is another way we can come to know ourselves. Healing is also measured in the quality and nature of our relationships with others and the world around us, how we are able to be with the ones we love and even with those we do not. It's measured in how we relate to the place where we are, the soil and environment and all of the other nonhuman organisms with whom we share an ecosystem. Healing on all levels is shown through these relationships.

What we know as self-care can often be an incomplete and isolating approach to what is actually a collective issue. It can reinforce the most self-reliant and individualistic inclinations in our culture. It can have us falsely equate care with commodity and make our distress a strictly private and personal matter. This version of self-care is not inherently wrong. I not only enjoy but need the solitude of retreat, the singular and concentrated attention of massage. It's only when it becomes the only pathway to care that it misleads and obscures. The depletion that results from the pressure of our lives is not a failure of individual bodies. Exhaustion and overwhelm are widespread, and often, in order to stay in our lives long-term, we build escape hatches that we call self-care. The exertion/depletion/escape cycle has been our best adaptation to the demands that require we leave our lives as often as possible. But the real issue is bigger than us. It lies in a social and economic architecture that doesn't relate to the humanity in us, the organic stuff we each are. Cultural expectations around how we work and how we build a home have little to do with what a body needs to naturally renew each day. The burden to address this imbalance can't only rest on each of us as individuals to carve out enough moments of escape. The charge lies with us as a collective: to rely on each other, to cultivate a replenishing intimacy in our lives, to circle up with the ones we love and lift burdens and allow our own burdens to be lifted. The call is for community care and for an ethic, made clearer in this moment of instability, for care to be central in the systems that we create. What can you offer? Where is your abundance? And where can you surrender into receptivity to become a beneficiary of another's abundance? It is giving and receiving and in that, creating more sustainable cycles in our lives.

Community care is the approach that tends to our exhaustion and overwhelm at scale, creating everyday pockets of respite that don't require money to access and don't rely on escape. The restoration of this cultural fabric of relationship is how we heal as individuals and communities. We look at these relationships as a way to measure where we are on our path to healing.

CONCLUSION

EDNA LEWIS PORTRAIT BY JOHN T. HILL

# A (FOOD) FUTURE IN DELIGHT

## by Ashanté Reese, PhD

I, like many who work in food justice, want some basic life-sustaining things for all Black people. I want no one to go hungry in a world where we produce (and waste) enough food to efficiently feed the whole planet several times over. I want no one to be deprived of choice. I want no corporation to have the power to determine or influence taste, need, availability, or wages. I want our biological, social, and cultural food needs to be met with care. These are not only about need but about what we deserve—what any human being deserves.

When I think about our food futures, I wander through and beyond these basics. Capitalist food production and the inequities it produces do more than maintain hierarchies of wealth and tastes. They also attempt to steal our imaginations and foreclose seeing and dreaming futures beyond restoring what is already rightfully ours. The work of Black people the world over has, in part, been a work of struggle: wrestling with the state and corporations

to—if not protect and feed us—at least not murder us. The work has also been to create and maintain lives through and beyond state and corporate neglect. That work of imagining is what I turn to. When all Black people's basic food needs are met, what then?

I think about how I want us to *feel*. I wonder: how do we take what already exists in fragments, bind them to the ancestral knowledge we carry in skills, stories, and our own bodies and create Black food futures steeped not in struggle but in delight? What would it look and feel like to harness the power in Black kitchens, in Black neighborhoods, at Black-ass family reunions, and wherever Black people gather for nourishment?

As I sit down to write this essay, at a tiny desk in my new home in Austin, Texas, my mind and heart wander to my grandmother's garden: a small, fenced-in plot of land behind her house in Porter Springs, Texas. I made a beeline for that garden many days, my feet carrying me through her front room, kitchen, and out the back door when she didn't respond to me calling her name. She would be outside, bent over rows of tomatoes, collards, or whatever else she was growing. Sometimes she sang. Most often she was quiet as she coaxed the vegetables from seed to table. My grandmother would be considered a recreational gardener,

> "THE PRESENT WAS AN EGG LAID BY THE PAST THAT HAD THE FUTURE INSIDE ITS SHELL."
>
> —Zora Neale Hurston

# "WHAT THE WORLD WILL BECOME ALREADY EXISTS IN FRAGMENTS AND PIECES, IN EXPERIMENTS AND POSSIBILITIES."

—Ruth Wilson Gilmore

I suppose. She didn't grow all of her own food, but what she grew she delighted in. She was of the generation that witnessed firsthand the ravages of tenant farming and sharecropping—her own kin fighting to keep control of their land, part of which my family still owns. She was under no illusions about what it meant to grow food or how—in the gendered division of labor—the responsibility for feeding the family was primarily hers; the consequences of not adequately doing so also resting on her shoulders. And yet she, like many others, held onto the promise that growing and preparing food was essential to crafting free lives.

For a long time, I lamented not spending more time with her in her garden. Had I done so, I thought, I'd have more skill, more passion to grow my own food. I know now that elder and ancestral knowledge are not linear in that way. They are passed along through skill but not unilaterally so. They exceed skills transmission. They elide one-dimensional time. Thus, when I sat down to write this essay, it wasn't the planting, the harvesting, or the consuming of what she grew that captured me this time. It was my grandmother's delight.

Delight
*noun:* (1) a high degree of gratification or pleasure; (2) something that gives great pleasure; (3) *archaic:* the power of affording pleasure

*verb:* (1) to take great pleasure; (2) to give keen enjoyment; (3) to give joy or satisfaction

Black people have always found delight in spite of persecution and struggle, sometimes even in the midst of it. I open this essay with a quote from Zora Neale Hurston's *Moses, Man of the Mountain.* Those words appear after the Egyptians are drowned, and the Israelites usher in their newfound liberation with song, dance, and glee. Moses, sitting on a boulder apart from the celebrations, reflects on how they had gotten there and how his previous crossings had enabled this joyous one. I think of this text in relation to my grandmother, the possibilities we now hold because of ancestors like her who forged space for delight. Food justice is nothing if not a future-making project: we take what we know, collectively grapple with what we don't, and try to create what does not yet exist in a sustainable way.

I believe that all Black people will have those necessities I outlined in the beginning of this essay. When we do, are we ready to create and hold down food spaces that build on the best of our lineages and practices rather than on the worst we inherit and reproduce through heteropatriarchal racial capitalism? What futures do the eggs produced by our ancestors hold? What past lessons and experiences have prepared us for food futures defined not by struggle but delight?

In the food futures I see, we draw on the creativity and ingenuity that have sustained Black lives through colonialism, enslavement, theft of land and body, and over policing. In the food futures I look forward to, our (food) lives are not measured by prescriptive outputs or constrained by and through policy or capitalist preservation. Instead, we build on the past and the present to give our food, our communities a future in which we have space and time to delight in feeding ourselves and each other, a future in which holistic nourishment is the goal to which we hold ourselves accountable. We are creating this already—in gardens, in farms, in meals. Let us tarry there and give our (food) lives a different future.

# MILLET SALAD

## How One Simple Dish Holds the Promise for the Future of Black Food

## by Selassie Atadika

My family moved to the United States when I was about six years old. Once the other children in school found out I was from Africa, the top questions they asked were:

1. Did you live in a hut?

2. Did you have a pet lion?

3. What did you eat?

I chose to ignore the first two questions but would happily answer the third. I'd tell them about the kelewele, tatale, and klaklo we used to make from plantain, the crispy on the outside and soft on the inside perfectly fried yam chips. And about the yakayake and the staple gari that we made from cassava.

Ours was a regional cuisine, based on the produce native to where our communities and towns developed. My mother grew up in Tamale, the regional capital of northern Ghana, where millet was plentiful. She would tell me about eating a spiced fermented millet porridge for breakfast with *tuo zaafi* (TZ), a dumpling, also made from millet, which accompanied rich soups and stews in the northern Ghanaian kitchen.

Fast forward thirty years and imagine my shock when I moved back to Ghana and realized our once-diverse national cuisine had become rice-ified. (This is my made-up word to describe the rice-based diet you now find in many urban centers in West Africa, often consisting of rice imported from Asia.) In the time I had been out of the country, lifestyles had changed, and like everywhere else in the world, people were looking to simplify their lives with more convenient options for food. When talking to people who grew up in the northern regions of Ghana, they will tell you millet porridge was once part of their morning routine and that throughout the rest of the day, they would eat TZ. They will also tell you about *pito*, a beer, and *fura*, a dairy-based drink, both made with millet. In Accra today, young people whose families came from these same regions have never made or had TZ made from millet, because it's now being made with corn and cassava flour. This substitution is partly due to convenience, since the cassava flour brings a sourness and binding quality that requires fermenting the millet, a step they can now eliminate. And while rice consumption has gone up, the rice being eaten is imported from Asia, even though there is a rice-growing valley in Ghana that grows several local varieties, leaving local producers struggling. I started wondering about other grains; in particular, the indigenous millet, a crop that doesn't require a lot of high-quality soil and needs less water than rice. It seemed like a perfect choice for a changing climate with erratic rainfall.

I went to a grocery store in Accra to get some millet but was told they don't carry it and that I had to go to a local market to find it. When

I did eventually track some down, I decided to use it as a whole grain in a cold salad with some diced mangoes and fresh herbs and spices. I handed over the game plan to one of my cooks and came back a few hours later to a beautifully plated salad. I found a fork and dug in. First bite, *ccraaa*. Second bite, *crrrrrra*. I had a mouthful of fresh herbs, mango, millet, and STONES. My cook assured me she had washed and cleaned the millet and taken out all the stones by hand herself. My next thought was to call my cousin who had grown up in the northern part of Ghana to get some tips on processing the grain. She invited me over and showed me how to clean millet the traditional way, using two calabash, dried hollowed-out gourds used as bowls, and water. This technique utilizes density and water displacement to separate the light grains from the heavier stones. We filled the larger calabash with water, then filled the smaller calabash with millet, and then slowly and methodically dipped the bowl of millet into the bowl of water as the tiny waves of water transferred the light grains into the larger bowl of water and the heavier stones remained in the small calabash. We did it together, and it worked beautifully; that's the same technique we use to this day in my kitchen.

This simple salad spoke volumes about a broken food system, the loss of knowledge from rural to urban life and from the older generation to the younger one. There is limited distribution for indigenous crops that were the mainstay of subsistence farming, and as a result, recipes and uses for these crops are dwindling. But in this salad, I also see solutions. Among the countless tragedies of enslavement and colonialism are the undeniable breakdowns of Black food systems and value chains—the people and processes that bring a crop from the field to the consumer. Modern agricultural systems in many parts of Africa continue to perpetuate colonial financial structures, where a dependence on imported food means a loss of local food cultures and diminished income for those local producers.

Millet offers some promise for mending this broken system. The solutions are straightforward but require many hands to come together. The mild nutty flavor of the grain enables it to work well with flavors in various dishes. It can be used in much the same way as other whole grains and accompaniments. On the supply side, we need to understand the challenges in production, from the incentive structures in place for farmers, to seed quality; from harvesting methods, to post-harvest processing; from pricing and packaging, to distribution. On the demand side, we need to collect recipes, generate buzz from influencers and with the media, and engage with government for procurement and institutional partners to form marketing strategies that both honor culture while highlighting the aspirational desires of consumers.

I am excited to see the tide changing, as we forge a new path where Black food is dictated by us. In my kitchen, I call my cooking New African Cuisine. I draw on culture, community, and cuisine to support the environment, promote sustainability, and create new economies. As consumers and producers, we can thoughtfully create supply and demand around our traditional crops such as millet. It's a simple, easy, and delicious three-step plan to return this important crop to its rightful place in our cuisine. Step 1 is to understand the bottlenecks around production and the use of millet. Step 2 is to encourage the consumption of millet while working with producers to grow higher-quality millet. Step 3 is about promotion and finding new outlets to sell millet, including institutional partners.

As we're eating salads, breakfast cereals, cakes, breads, dumplings, and yet-to-be-created dishes filled with millet, we will be creating the future of Black food. We will be creating better soil, fighting against climate change, improving our nutrition, respecting our culture, and supporting local farmers and producers. Won't you join me in creating a new story with millet?

# HOW BLACK INTELLECT INFORMS THE FUTURE OF COOKING SHOWS

## by Rahanna Bisseret Martinez

The appetite for learning new cooking techniques, the craving to find out the winning dish, the desire to taste and smell what we see on screen are some of what viewers love about cooking shows. We are not responsible for what appears on our screens, but we *are* supporting corporations when we put our time and attention at their disposal.

In 1949—in the same decade that both James Beard and Julia Child appeared on televised cooking shows—the *Lena Richard's New Orleans Cook Book* cooking show debuted. It featured Chef Richard with her daughter, Mattie, demonstrating their culinary prowess on camera. Yet, Lena Richard's wisdom was not limited to a show; it was expressed in her restaurant, catering business, a line of frozen food products, a private cooking school, and a cookbook. Imagine how impactful a cooking show with these two Black women demonstrating their authority and techniques would be to the viewing public during the Jim Crow South.

Unfortunately, there is zero footage of this powerful cooking show. The true power of Lena Richard's legacy lies in the impact it *would* have had all those years ago on young Black girls realizing that there was a cooking show by someone who looked like them. On those Black children, who saw Black chefs and foodways present at the origin of cooking shows.

Cooking shows wield significant power. When new cooks become proficient with culinary techniques learned from a cooking show, the program has imbued them with a certain authority and confidence to imagine their own recipes. For some, watching television chefs inspires them to write their own cookbooks and produce their own programs. But for all cooking show viewers, Lena Richard's story is inspirational: the blockbuster cooking show platform was originally fueled by a Black woman's brilliance.

Therefore, when reflecting on the possible future of cooking shows, I seek the intellect of Black writers to navigate the historic anti-Blackness in this space.

From the same tumultuous time period as Lena Richard, Ralph Ellison and Zora Neal Hurston wrote authoritatively about Black foodways, namely the humble sweet potato. The sweet potato originated with and belongs to the indigenous people of the Americas. It has been adopted as both a staple of Black culinary heritage and of its child, southern cuisine.

Imagine the sweet potato as a metaphor of the Black American existence. In Ralph Ellison's *Invisible Man*, the main character (who previously shunned any proximity to Blackness prior to his life in the city) enjoys a sweet potato from a street cart. Consuming it with fervor, in public, wearing his business clothes, and on his way to work, he throws away any preoccupation with anti-Black social perceptions. The modern reader may think this is nothing out of the ordinary other than the rarity of sweet potato carts today. But, in that moment in the book, we are reminded that when we reject our traditions, we are only rejecting ourselves and denying our own joy. Ellison shows that embracing Black identity has the power to reignite the love and happiness of Black traditions.

But who controls our joy and in what manner? Zora Neal Hurston's book *Their Eyes Were Watching God* explores the cruel world of the 1930s sharecropper South and a woman's resilience. The main character, Janie, was married off young. Janie cooked for her abusive husband, Logan, but her care and effort were taken as a given, with no compassion in return. Janie grew the courage to leave and marry someone else; there, she was appreciated for her food, and equal effort was given.

Zora Neal Hurston's writings urge us to embrace the notion that we control our happiness and joy. And the parallel is clear: If we as cooking-show viewers and creators are not being treated with respect, we must leave and create new content on new platforms. There is a strength in that unity.

Anti-Black tropes remain prevalent in today's cooking shows. Hurston and Ellison share how we, as either the viewer or creator, can find real joy, not by settling to others' expectations but by embracing what it means to be unapologetic and unashamed. Hurston and Ellison also note that this is not easy. It took the narrator in *Invisible Man* and Janie in *Their Eyes Were Watching God* to have a life-transforming experience to celebrate themselves. We as cooking show viewers must acknowledge that Lena Richard long ago pioneered a cooking show and that anti-Black actions persist to the current day. We can apply the lessons of Hurston and Ellison, not by entirely leaving the world of cooking shows but by acknowledging the suppressed knowledge and acting for change.

# THE CHURCH OF THE FULL MOON COMMUNION

## by Amanda Yee

In the book *Dust Tracks on a Road*, Auntie Zora devoted a whole chapter to exclaiming, "My people! My people" in exasperation. She described "being forced outward for pity, scorn, and hopeless resignation." If Auntie Zora could see us now! Today, we use that exclamation as a call to gather, to expand beyond, and to harvest during the full moon.

When you partake of the biscuit, imagine it as the collective Black body. When you drink the rice milk, do it as testament to the prophetic urgency of our ancestors, who hid rice in their braids during the Middle Passage for our survival. The communion can be consumed gradually through each call and response or be eaten contemplatively, once all is said and done. The communion should be done in a gathering of at least two.

**FOR THIS COMMUNION, YOU WILL NEED:**

2 (4-ounce) glasses rice milk

2 Vegan Sweet Potato Coconut Biscuits (page 16)

A comfortable and quiet place to sit and stare at the full moon

## CALL:

My People, My People—Gather your 2,048 ninth great-grandparents, who labored to bring you here.

My People, My People—Taste the fruits of your sacred work!

My People, My People—What are your fantasies, your prophecies, your imaginings? Reap them.

My People, My People—What are your dreams? No, do not stir. Rest. Tell us when you wake.

## RESPONSE:

This is our body, whole and unbroken for you.

Worthy of shea butter and glistening

This is our fantasy; drink, and as often as you do, do this in proclamation of us.

Because I say to you, whoever shall dream with our body and envision for our flesh

shall have a place as the rested.

## CALL:

My People, My People—Full in love!

My People, My People—Full in joy!

My People, My People—Full in wellness!

My People, My People—Full in peace!

My People, My People—Full in the trust of our own power, despite the darkness!

My People, My People—Full in abundance!

My People, My People—Full in Black bliss!

My People, My People—Full in one another!

My People, My People—In all of time.

## RESPONSE:

This is our body, whole and unbroken for you. Worthy of shea butter and glistening

This is our hour, our minute, our time; drink and as often as you do, do this in proclamation of us.

Because I say to you, whoever shall restore our body and emancipate our flesh

shall have a place in the jubilee.

## CALL:

My People, My People—Our language is for us. We need no interpreter!

My People, My People—Our dance is for us. We need no interpreter!

My People, My People—Your being is for you. You need no interpreter!

## RESPONSE:

This is our body, whole and unbroken for you.

Worthy of shea butter and glistening

This is our song; drink, and as often as you do, do this in proclamation of us.

Because I say to you, whoever shall sing for our body and sway for our flesh

shall have a place in the melody.

## CALL:

My People, My People—Can you see us in the future? Look again.

My People, My People—Where are you in the future? Look again!

My People, My People—I see our children in the future! Found. In their giggles. Safe. Whole.

## RESPONSE:

This is our body, whole and unbroken for you.

Worthy of shea butter and glistening

This is our safety; drink, and as often as you do, do this in proclamation of us.

Because I say to you, whoever shall prophesy for our body and proclaim for our flesh

shall have a place in the future.

# CHARRED RED CABBAGE

## with Spiced Tomato Relish

# by Gregory Gourdet

MAKES 4 TO 6 SERVINGS

*Like all chefs, I am obsessed with super seasonal produce. However, the demands of everyday life sometimes call for the ease and comfort of dishes that can be made year-round with just a few pantry ingredients—that still deliver big flavor. Sun-dried tomatoes have tons of umami, and for this relish, I flavor them with Haitian and Caribbean spices of Scotch bonnet, pepper, ginger, and thyme. Charring them first is a great way to create more taste and texture. Honey is the preferred sweetener, but it can be made vegan by swapping out the honey for brown sugar.*

**TOMATO RELISH**

**2 cups sun-dried tomatoes, finely chopped**

**½ cup extra-virgin olive oil**

**2 teaspoons kosher salt**

**¼ teaspoon ground black pepper**

**15 garlic cloves, thinly sliced**

**1 large Scotch bonnet chile, stemmed and minced with seeds**

**2 large shallots, cut into ⅛ inch dice**

**2 tablespoons peeled and finely chopped ginger**

**2 tablespoons tamari**

**2 tablespoons honey or brown sugar**

**1 tablespoon picked thyme leaves**

**Zest of 1 lime, thinly grated**

**2 pounds red cabbage (about 1 small head), blemished outer leaves removed**

**⅓ cup extra-virgin olive oil**

**2 teaspoons kosher salt**

**Small handful of parsley leaves for garnish**

**TO MAKE THE RELISH:** Combine the tomatoes, oil, salt, black pepper, garlic, chile, shallots, and ginger in a medium heavy skillet. Set the skillet over medium heat and give it a stir. Wait until the oil gets hot and the aromatics start giving off liquid, causing the mixture to bubble rapidly. Stirring frequently now, cook until the ingredients have softened and browned a bit at the edges, 8 to 10 minutes. Stir in the tamari, honey, and thyme and reduce the heat to gently simmer until the liquid is gone and everything is golden brown, shriveled, and a little chewy, about 5 minutes more. Turn off the heat and stir in the lime zest.

**TO MAKE THE DISH:** Adjust the oven rack to the top position and preheat the oven to 450°F. Cut the cabbage through the core into twelve wedges (about 1½ inches thick), so the layers in each wedge remain intact. Evenly drizzle 1 tablespoon of the oil onto a large sheet pan, then arrange the wedges flat on the pan in a single layer. Evenly sprinkle on the salt and drizzle on the remaining oil.

Roast the cabbage on the top rack until the white parts have turned purple, the leaves look soft and supple, and the wedges turn brown at the edges, about 10 minutes. Remove the cabbage, preheat the broiler, then broil the cabbage on the top rack until the edges are black and crispy and the insides are tender with a slight bite, about 5 minutes. Use a spatula to flip each piece, then broil again for 5 minutes more to char the other sides.

**TO SERVE:** Transfer to a serving platter, spoon on the relish, and serve hot or warm. Sprinkle on the parsley just before serving.

# BUTTERMILK CORNBREAD MUFFINS

## by Alexander Smalls

MAKES 12 MUFFINS

"Let Us Break Bread Together..."

The power of a field of wheat . . . rows of corn tilled . . . watered and harvested . . . stone-ground and milled . . . gathered, married in a bowl of kind ingredients . . . baked to perfection into a crusty goodness . . . an offering of pride . . . heritage fulfilled from Mama's kitchen

the art of farm to the table . . . a bedrock of ancestral rituals . . . bread for the soul . . . African Americans have worked the land . . . toiled in the fields, seeding their roots into the landscape of America's bounty . . . the nation's harvest . . .

As we break bread together, we offer abiding grace and blessings . . . Honor our ancestral legacy and cultural expression . . . The centerpiece of our nurturing spirit . . . gifts from African American people who understood and lived by the generosity of shared humble kindness . . . stories and human engagement . . .

Freshly baked cornbread, an offering of love, heart, and spirit . . .

Bread of my fathers . . . the hope of my mothers . . . We give thanks in song to thee . . .

"Let us break bread together on our knees . . . Let us break bread together on our knees . . .

When I fall on my knees with my face to the rising sun . . . Oh, Lord, have mercy on me . . ."

*This is a hearty bread that works with serious proteins: red meat, chicken, duck, and venison. It makes an equally great pairing with vegetables, hot or cold.*

½ cup white cornmeal (I use Dixie Lily or White Lily. Avoid coarse or stone-ground.)

½ cup all-purpose flour

3 tablespoons light brown sugar

1½ teaspoons ground coriander

1 teaspoon baking powder

¼ teaspoon salt

¼ cup whole milk

¼ cup buttermilk

2 tablespoons vegetable oil

2 eggs

¾ cup fresh corn kernels (frozen and thawed will work, too)

Preheat the oven to 400°F. Line a 12-cup muffin pan with paper liners or coat the muffin cups with non-stick spray.

In a large bowl, whisk together the cornmeal, flour, brown sugar, coriander, baking powder, and salt. Whisk in the milk, buttermilk, and oil, then whisk in the eggs until the batter is smooth. Stir in the corn until well combined. Spoon the batter into the prepared muffin cups, dividing it evenly.

Bake until a toothpick inserted into the center of a muffin comes out clean, 15 to 20 minutes.

Serve immediately.

# CHARRED OKRA TAMALES

## with Curried Black-Eyed Peas, Pickled Mustard Seed & Herb Salad

## by Karina Rivera

MAKES 30 TAMALES

*This dish was inspired by my Mexican and Black ancestors. I started working in restaurants at the age of seventeen. Sixteen years later, I am still at it, now as the executive chef for my pop-up Pantera Negra—and still learning and loving every minute of it. When it came time to start my own adventure in the cooking world, I wanted to make food that represented my ancestral bloodline. I think this dish does that perfectly. The labor of love that goes into hand making tamales and cooking a great pot of black-eyed peas is truly healing and, as it turns out, also very delicious together. Aight y'all, let's do this!*

**CURRIED BLACK-EYED PEAS**

6 garlic cloves, thinly sliced

2 small yellow onions, diced

1 habanero, stemmed, seeded, and super-small dice

¼ cup olive oil, plus more as needed

1 tablespoon salt, plus more as needed

3 tablespoons curry powder

3 cups black-eyed peas (soaked overnight)

2 cups water

1 (13.5-ounce) can unsweetened coconut milk

1 teaspoon black pepper

1 bunch cilantro, chopped

Juice of 2 limes

**PICKLED MUSTARD SEEDS**

1 cup white wine vinegar

1 teaspoon salt

3 tablespoons cane sugar

½ cup mustard seeds

1 small bay leaf

1 small shallot, sliced into rings

**TAMALE MASA**

4 cups Bob's Red Mill masa harina

1 teaspoon baking powder

1 teaspoon salt

¼ teaspoon turmeric powder

3½ cups vegetable stock

½ cup olive oil

**TAMALE FILLING**

3 tablespoons olive oil, plus more as needed

30 to 36 okra, sliced in half lengthwise

Pinch of salt

**HERB SALAD**

1 bunch Italian parsley, leaves picked

1 bunch mint, leaves picked

1 bunch cilantro, leaves picked

2 bunches chives, sliced into 1-inch sticks

30 to 40 corn husks, soaked in water for about an hour before using (you'll make 30 tamales, but it's good to have extra in case they tear)

Crème fraîche for topping (optional)

Lime wedges for serving (optional)

**TO MAKE THE BLACK-EYED PEAS:** In a large pot over medium-high heat, sauté the garlic, onion, and habanero with the olive oil and a pinch of salt for 5 to 7 minutes. Stir in the curry powder and cook until the onions are nicely coated, then add in the beans and water. Turn down the burner to medium-low, cover the pot, and cook for about 20 minutes. Stir in the coconut

CONTINUED

## Charred Okra Tamales, continued

milk, turn down the burner to low, and simmer with the pot cover off for 30 minutes or until the beans are tender. Stir in the 1 tablespoon of salt and add the pepper, cilantro, and lime juice. Taste your beans! Add more salt if you like, keep simmering, tasting your beans until they are seasoned and cooked through to your liking.

**TO MAKE THE PICKLED MUSTARD SEEDS:** In a small saucepan, combine the vinegar, salt, and sugar and bring to a boil. Turn down the burner to low, add the mustard seeds and bay leaf, and simmer for about 30 minutes. Throw in the shallot rings, remove from the burner, and set aside to cool.

**TO MAKE THE MASA:** In a medium to large bowl, whisk together the harina, baking powder, salt, and turmeric. In a large saucepan, warm up the stock. Add the warm stock and the oil to the harina bowl and with a rubber spatula, mix until the dough is spreadable and pulls away from the sides of the bowl with ease.

**TO MAKE THE FILLING:** In a cast-iron skillet, heat the olive oil. Just before the oil starts to smoke, throw in enough okra to cover the base of the skillet, then turn down the burner to medium-low. Season with a pinch of salt. Stir every 2 minutes for about 6 minutes, until golden brown. Transfer to a small bowl and cook the remaining okra in the same skillet.

**TO MAKE THE HERB SALAD:** Combine all the herbs in a small bowl and mix with your hands.

**TO ASSEMBLE THE TAMALES:** Place a corn husk so the wider end is facing up and the narrower end is at the bottom. Spread about three healthy dollops of masa onto the center of the husk, leaving a border of husk around the masa of approximately 1 inch from the top, 2 inches from the sides, and 3 inches from the bottom. Place three or four pieces of charred okra in the center of the masa. Fold the sides of the husk up to meet each other, gently pressing the masa together to seal in the okra. Next, fold the sides over together to the right, then fold the bottom of the husk up. Repeat with all of the tamales.

**TO STEAM THE TAMALES:** Fill a steamer stockpot with enough water so that it's just below the steam basket. Bring the water to a boil. Once the water is boiling, turn down the burner to low and place the tamales on the steam basket standing up, so that the part of the tamale that is open is facing up. Cover the pot and steam for an hour. Check the water level in the pot every 20 minutes or so, adding more water if needed. When the hour is up, turn off the burner, uncover the pot, and let the tamales rest for about 10 minutes.

**TO SERVE:** Unfold each tamale from its husk and put it on a plate. Spoon some black-eyed peas over the top of the tamale and add a teaspoon of the pickled mustard seeds over the beans. Sprinkle the herb salad over everything or simply put a big pinch of it on the side of the tamale. Add a dollop of crème fraîche on top if you'd like, as well as a lime wedge to bump up the acidity.

Any leftover tamales can be kept in their wrappers and sealed in a plastic bag. Keep refrigerated if you plan on eating them over the next couple of days or freeze for up to a month.

**NOTES:** *Soak your beans!* I've tried to cook beans without soaking them, but they just don't come out the same. #soakthembeans. You can also cook the beans days before you make the tamales; in my experience, the beans become more flavorful a day or two after they are cooked.

The pickled mustard seeds are delicious additions to salads, sandwiches, roasted vegetables, and cheese plates. They can be stored in a sealed container in the fridge for up to 30 days.

The herb salad will stay good in the fridge for about 3 days if kept in a sealed container with a damp paper towel placed underneath and on top of the herbs. You can also turn the salad into a simple salsa verde by finely chopping them, covering them with good olive oil, a pinch of salt, and stirring in some macerated shallots.

# VEGETARIAN GUMBO

## by Omar Tate

MAKES 6 TO 8 SERVINGS

I have to admit that creating this recipe felt particularly sinful, maybe even blasphemous. Gumbo is a dish that you don't wanna fuck with. It feels like a psalm or its own story in a holy text. It belongs to a city of saints, kings, and Zulu. Its foundation is a Negro Vatican in its trinity of vegetables—celery, onion, and green bell pepper with okra as its West African pope. This dish tested my faith. My wife, Cybille, who is Haitian, prayed for me and called spirits for my protection in Kreyol. Thankfully, I survived.

I wanted to keep the dish's bones intact. When I thought of what makes a gumbo, keeping its integrity was simple. Beyond the holy trinity, there is protein and usually more than one. For this version, I went with three. One is tofu. This is the ingredient that really brought me to my knees for forgiveness. I needed to be vindicated and asked to be guided through this jettison of tradition. It became a body to me. How do I keep the bones, make up its skin, what of its heart, how does it smile?

For bones (the other two proteins), I went with peas and lima beans. The black-eyed peas and limas, in tandem with tofu, made up for any spiritual transgressions to be had. It was like inviting a friend from college to my house for Sunday dinner.

For its soul, I used palm oil in place of vegetable oil to create the roux. This was a challenge. Typically, one needs to be able to see the color of the flour deepen from off-white to dark brown slowly over time, as it is heated, toasted, and caramelized by the fat. The organically processed bright red-orange palm oil that I used did not allow for sight to be my measure this time. It forced me to use my sense of smell and intuition to know when the

time was right. I likened it to my imaginative experience of being in the shoes of our ancestors.

In the dark of an evening stirring a meal, a pot of gumbo for several people after a long day of cultivating American prosperity in the fields of would-be "masters" was guided by smell and intuition. One of the most important things about Black food history is that it is delicious. Even under the weight of oppression, beneath the blindness of night, and the weariness of bones, we found it necessary to enjoy the taste of our food. That is a triumph of immeasurable desire and fortitude, in my opinion. I blinded myself, but I could see. I smelled the flour transform from white dust to a consumed marriage of perfect doneness, caressed in African palm.

It needed spirit to give reverence in faith of our universe of culture. Behind the chatter of life is substance; we are of the earth, moon, and stars. To satisfy this piece, I created a subtly rich and earthy mushroom stock to live within the body of the gumbo. Finally, in the end is the heart—okra, gombo. It is the fruit of West Africa and the survivor of Black America's diet born of its mother. It is still here, and it is everywhere. It is essential and often discarded but still here. It finds itself cradled in the hands of grandmothers like her favorite leather-bound Bible on a Sunday morning. Placed into the soup to become stew and transformed into a nourishment for our souls eternally.

CONTINUED

## Vegetarian Gumbo, continued

**MUSHROOM STOCK**

1 tablespoon dried thyme

1 tablespoon dried parsley

1 pound cremini mushrooms

4 garlic cloves

16 cups water

1 small onion, cut in half

1 leek, light green and white part only, trimmed

⅓ bunch celery, trimmed

**GUMBO**

2 cups baby lima beans

2 cups black-eyed peas

1½ cups palm oil

1 cup all-purpose flour

3 stalks celery, finely diced

2 medium onions, finely diced

1½ green bell peppers, diced

1 tablespoon tomato paste

1 Scotch bonnet chile

3 garlic cloves

1 (14-ounce) package extra-firm tofu, drained and cubed

4 cups okra

Salt and pepper to taste

1 tablespoon filé powder

Wanda's seasoning to taste

Vinegar or hot sauce to taste

Cooked white rice for serving

**TO MAKE THE STOCK:** Place the thyme, parsley, mushrooms, garlic, and water in a large stockpot.

Char the onion, leek, and celery over flames with the cut side down. Char them until they are black and slightly cooked. Once blackened, place them in the pot with the other ingredients. Pour the water over the ingredients in the pot to cover. Turn your stove on to a low flame and allow the stock to slowly come to a simmer. Once simmering, let the ingredients simmer for 1 hour.

Reserve 8 cups for the gumbo. Store the remainder in a sealed container in the fridge for up to a week.

**TO MAKE THE GUMBO:** Soak the lima beans and black-eyed peas separately overnight.

When ready to cook, add the oil to a large stockpot and heat on low until hot. Add the flour to the hot oil and begin to stir to incorporate. Stir until the flour is toasted and caramelized to make the roux, about 15 minutes.

Once the roux is formed, add the holy trinity (celery, onion, and bell pepper) and begin to stir immediately. Stir until the vegetables are soft and completely saturated with the fat, about 12 minutes.

Add the tomato paste, the chile, and garlic and stir into the palm oil–holy trinity marriage.

Drain the limas and black-eyed peas, then add them to the pot and stir into the mixture.

Pour 4 cups of the reserved mushroom stock into the pot, stir, then add the remaining 4 cups stock while continuing to stir.

Bring the gumbo to a boil over medium-high heat. Once it begins to boil, turn down the heat to a simmer, and allow it to simmer for 20 to 25 minutes.

At the 20- to 25-minute mark, add the tofu and okra together and allow to simmer until the beans and peas are tender, about another 20 minutes. At this rate, everything will cook together evenly, so that everything will still have texture and not be overcooked.

Season with salt and pepper, filé, Wanda's seasoning, and vinegar. By the time the stew is finished, it will be thick and aromatic.

Serve with white rice.

# CRAB & COLLARD "RUN DOWN"

## by Isaiah Martinez

MAKES 4 TO 6 SERVINGS

*My great-grandmother Gwendolyn George is from Grenada. There, the national dish is "oil down" also called "run down," to resemble the separation of the coconut oil from the milk. At its heart, this is a dish that would sustain slaves through a hard day of work. Now it's a personal favorite of mine.*

*I prefer fresh coconut milk over canned for two reasons: (1) the flavor is more developed and potent; and (2) the lack of stabilizer makes the texture better. Fried bake are biscuits that can be fried or baked in the oven and each of the Caribbean islands has its own version. But the result is always a fluffy bread with a slightly sweet flavor, perfect with the run down.*

**1 tablespoon peanut oil or vegetable oil**

**12 ounces smoked ham, diced**

**2 yellow onions, minced**

**2 garlic cloves, minced**

**1 Scotch bonnet or 2 habanero chiles, stemmed, seeded, and minced**

**1 bunch green onions, tops included, chopped**

**1 teaspoon minced thyme leaves**

**3 cups fresh coconut milk (see Note at right), or 2 (13.5-ounce) cans unsweetened coconut milk**

**2 small breadfruit, peeled and cut into chunks, or 4 chayote squash, peeled, parboiled, and cut into chunks, or 4 large Yukon gold potatoes, peeled and cut into chunks**

**Salt and pepper to taste**

**1 pound collard greens, stemmed and finely chopped (use the stems if tender but be sure to keep them thinly sliced)**

**1 whole live medium-to-large crab**

**Lime juice or cane vinegar to taste**

**Cooked white rice or fried bake biscuits for serving**

In a large skillet over medium-low heat, heat the oil. Add the ham, onion, garlic, chile, green onion (reserve the tops for garnish), and thyme. Sauté for 5 to 10 minutes, stirring constantly; don't let the vegetables color. Deglaze the pan with the coconut milk and add the breadfruit and salt and pepper. Reduce the heat to low and simmer, covered, until the ingredients have absorbed a majority of the coconut milk, about 25 minutes. Add the collards to the run down and cook for 8 minutes on low simmer.

In a separate pot, cook the crab in seasoned simmering water for 18 minutes. When finished cooking, turn off the heat, and puncture the crab shell with a sharp knife so it can absorb the stew. Add the crab to the pot and let sit for at least 45 minutes.

Garnish with the reserved green onion tops and lime juice or cane vinegar to taste. Serve with rice or fried bake biscuits.

**NOTE:** To make the coconut milk, you will need 1 large or 2 medium coconuts. Puncture the coconut's eyes with a hammer and screwdriver. Use the hammer to split the coconut by hitting and rotating the coconut in a clockwise direction until you reach the starting point.

Remove the meat from the shell using a strong spoon; it doesn't have to be perfect. Put the coconut water, coconut meat, and hot water to cover in a blender. Blend until the meat is roughly grated. Let sit for 1 hour and then strain the coconut milk through a fine-mesh sieve. The yield should be around 3 to 4 cups.

Fermented Millet Porridge (page 292)

# FERMENTED MILLET PORRIDGE

## by Selassie Atadika

MAKES 4 TO 6 SERVINGS

*One of the classic ways of preparing millet in Ghana is a dumpling called* tuo zaafi, *which often goes with a sauce made of* ayoyo, *or jute leaves. It's one of my go-to comfort dishes. Widespread knowledge of making the* tuo zaafi *with millet is disappearing, and I'm always looking for ways and new versions to share with people. This recipe uses a roughly ground millet and brings a new texture to the dish. The fermentation allows for elasticity in the gluten-free grain and brings a light sourness and acidity to the dish. I've kept the dish light by introducing a broth made of greens rather than a heavier sauce or soup. Serve with tomato gravy, waterleaf broth, and edible flowers or microgreens.*

**FERMENTED MILLET PORRIDGE**

1 cup whole-grain millet

¾ cup millet flour

4 cups water, plus more as needed

Salt to taste

**WATERLEAF BROTH**

1½ cups waterleaf (leaves and branches), or spinach

½ Scotch bonnet chile (or to taste), stemmed

1 cup stock or water

Salt to taste

1 tablespoon dawadawa powder (may substitute 1 teaspoon fish sauce), plus more as needed

½ teaspoon okra powder, plus more as needed

1 tablespoon powdered fish (may substitute dried shrimp); optional

**TOMATO GRAVY**

¼ cup vegetable oil

¼ cup fresh grated onion

¼ cup chopped onion

1 tablespoon minced fresh ginger

½ teaspoon minced garlic

1 tablespoon tomato paste

½ tablespoon cayenne pepper

¼ teaspoon ground allspice

1 tablespoon curry powder

1½ teaspoons salt

1 cup pureed Roma tomatoes (about 8 tomatoes)

½ cup vegetable stock

1 teaspoon fresh basil

Edible flowers or microgreens for garnish

**TO PREPARE THE MILLET:** Place the millet in a blender or spice mill and pulse to get a slightly broken grain. Mix the broken millet and ¼ cup of the millet flour with enough water to create a dense paste. Place in a sterilized fermentation crock or glass jar and cover with a coffee filter or piece of cheesecloth and secure with a rubber band. Leave on a counter to ferment for 24 hours.

Add the 4 cups of water to the crock or jar and mix well. Cover securely with the coffee filter or cheese-cloth and leave to settle and ferment for 2 to 4 more days, depending on the room temperature. You will know it is ready when bubbles rise from the millet and a light foam is on top of the water. Place the container in the fridge until ready to use.

**TO MAKE THE PORRIDGE:** Bring 2½ cups of the fermented water from the millet solution, drained first through a fine-mesh sieve, to a boil. Add the fermented millet and the remaining ½ cup millet flour and salt. Stir continuously as it cooks and thickens; it should have the consistency of thick oatmeal.

**TO MAKE THE BROTH:** Combine the waterleaf and chile with the stock or water in a large saucepan and bring to a boil. Season with salt, add the dawadawa powder, and thicken with the okra powder. Add the fish powder, if using. Allow to simmer for about 5 to 10 minutes; the broth will be thick but still fluid. Adjust the seasoning and okra powder as desired.

**TO MAKE THE GRAVY:** Heat the oil in a saucepan over medium heat. Add the grated and chopped onions, ginger, and garlic and sauté until the onions are soft and starting to get golden.

Add the tomato paste and cook for about 10 minutes. Add the cayenne, allspice, curry, and salt and cook for a few minutes until fragrant. Then add the tomatoes and stock. Reduce the heat to low and let simmer for about 10 to 15 minutes. Add the basil a few minutes before cooking is completed.

**TO SERVE:** Place ¼ cup of the porridge in each bowl and top with 2 tablespoons of the broth and 3 tablespoons of the gravy. Garnish with edible flowers or microgreens.

# COCONUT CORNBREAD PUDDING

## by Nyesha Joyce Arrington

MAKES 1 9x9-INCH
CORNBREAD

*This recipe really is a special one. Cornbread is such a staple in my family. My cooking style always carries notes of culture, heritage, and global flare, and so I wanted to take something that is a comfort food and give it a fresh, new, and delicious take. With the addition of the coconut, I definitely think I achieved that here.*

½ cup masa harina

1 cup gluten-free
cake flour

1 tablespoon Himalayan
sea salt

1 teaspoon baking powder

Whisper of ground nutmeg

Pinch of cayenne pepper

⅛ teaspoon ground
turmeric

1 (13.5 ounce) can
unsweetened coconut milk

4 tablespoons agave syrup

¼ cup coconut oil, warmed

2 cups fresh white or
yellow corn kernels

3 eggs, separated

Preheat the oven to 425°F.

Sift together the masa harina, flour, salt, baking powder, nutmeg, cayenne, and turmeric in a large stainless-steel bowl.

In a separate bowl, combine the coconut milk, agave syrup, oil, corn, and egg yolks.

Whip the egg whites until medium peaks form. Set aside.

Add the egg yolk mixture to the flour mixture and whisk to combine. Then gently fold in the egg whites.

Pour into a 9 by 9-inch square pan lined with parchment paper and bake for 15 minutes. Rest for 5 minutes before serving.

Enjoy immediately.

# BLUEBERRY CHEESECAKE

## by Malcolm Livingston II

MAKES 8 TO 10 SERVINGS

*Growing up in the Bronx, New York, one of my favorite early memories was going to Junior's in Brooklyn just to get my favorite cheesecake. The taste and texture of that original New York–style plain cheesecake satisfied me and lifted me up on days I needed it. When I was in high school, my father became a raw vegan and started to make his own vegan cheesecake at home. I was amazed by the process of being able to make raw cheesecake so craveable. Remembering my dad's made me want to try my own version of vegan cheesecake. Since then, I've been striving to make a better and "cleaner" cheesecake that still tastes incredibly desirable. This recipe is where I've landed in that quest. As the saying goes, always leave room for dessert and, equally, make sure to leave room for the future.*

*This recipe can be made with just Violife cream cheese. However, Miyoko's cream cheese contains more fat because it's made with cashews. When Miyoko's is used in combination with Violife, the cheesecake's richness is enhanced, and it reminds me of a slice of Junior's.*

**CRUST**

1¾ cups (7.5 ounces) gluten-free graham crackers

3 tablespoons coconut sugar

¾ teaspoon sea salt

1 tablespoon coconut oil

2 tablespoons unsweetened coconut milk

2 ounces vegan butter

**BLUEBERRY SAUCE**

½ cup coconut sugar

¼ cup water

1 tablespoon cornstarch

½ teaspoon cinnamon

2 cups frozen blueberries

2 tablespoons lemon juice

**CREAM CHEESE FILLING**

3 cups cashews, soaked for at least 4 to 6 hours but no more than 24 hours, drained

6 teaspoons vanilla extract, or 2 vanilla beans, split lengthwise and seeds scraped out

3 tablespoons lemon juice

2 tablespoons tahini

16 ounces Violife vegan cream cheese

2 ounces Miyoko's vegan cream cheese

1½ cups oat milk

2½ teaspoons agar powder

1½ cups organic sugar

¾ cup coconut oil

**TO MAKE THE CRUST:** Line a springform pan with acetate.

In a food processor, combine the graham crackers, sugar, and salt and pulse until fine crumbs form. Set aside.

In a small saucepan, mix together the oil, milk, and butter and melt over low heat. Add the crumbs and mix to combine.

Press the crumb mixture into the prepared pan and place in the freezer to set for about 45 minutes.

**TO MAKE THE SAUCE:** In a medium saucepan, combine the sugar, water, cornstarch, cinnamon, and 1 cup of the blueberries and bring to a boil over medium-high heat. Then add the lemon juice and the remaining 1 cup blueberries and return to a boil, stirring constantly, until the mixture thickens.

CONTINUED

## Blueberry Cheesecake, continued

Transfer the sauce to a bowl and refrigerate to cool.

**TO MAKE THE FILLING:** Combine the cashews, vanilla extract, lemon juice, tahini, and cream cheeses to a blender.

In a large pot, combine the oat milk, agar, sugar, and oil and bring the mixture to a boil over medium-high heat, while whisking continuously.

Transfer the hot mixture to the ingredients already in the blender and blend on low speed. Try not to blend on too

high a speed or it will incorporate too much air into the cheesecake base. Strain the mixture through a fine-mesh sieve over the prepared crust and set aside to cool.

Once the cheesecake has cooled, add the blueberry sauce on top and freeze for 1 to 2 hours.

**TO SERVE:** Remove from the freezer and remove the springform ring and discard the acetate. Place the cheesecake on a serving plate or tray of your choice and slice.

Keep cheesecake refrigerated.

# FRESH PEACH COBBLER

## with Nutmeg Sauce

## by Edna Lewis from *The Taste of Country Cooking*

MAKES 6 TO 8 SERVINGS

*Traditionally in Freetown, we always made a lattice top, rather than a regular top crust for peach cobbler. It was the great hot fruit dessert of the summer season that everyone looked forward to enjoying and I give it here in three parts.*

**PIE CRUST**

2 cups all-purpose unbleached flour

¼ teaspoon salt

½ cup lard, chilled

⅓ cup cold water

1 8 by 8 by 2-inch baking pan

**FILLING**

7 to 8 large peaches, washed and drained

1 cup sugar

4 tablespoons (¼ cup) butter

**NUTMEG SAUCE**

⅔ cup sugar

¼ teaspoon fresh-grated nutmeg

2 teaspoons cornstarch

Pinch of salt

1 cup boiling water

1 3-inch piece of orange peel, dried or fresh

3 tablespoons brandy

Take a mixing bowl, sift in flour and salt. Add chilled lard, and blend with a pastry blender or your fingertips until the mixture becomes the texture of heavy cornmeal. Sprinkle over the cold water and mix together lightly until the dough sticks together. Shape into a ball and leave in the bowl to rest for at least 15 minutes. Divide the dough in half. Roll out one piece of the dough and line a baking pan that has been greased lightly with lard. After pressing the pastry gently over the bottom, sides, and corners, trim the overlapping dough from edges of pan. Cover with wax paper and set into refrigerator until needed. Roll out the second piece of dough and cut it into 8 strips. Place the strips between wax paper and place them in the refrigerator as well.

Peel the peaches and slice each into 6 or 7 pieces. When all the peaches are sliced, remove the pastry and strips from the refrigerator. Sprinkle 2 tablespoons of sugar over the bottom of pastry in pan and fill in with the sliced peaches; sprinkle the rest of the sugar over the peaches. Scatter thin slices of butter, 6 to 8 pieces, over the sugar. Moisten the rim of the pastry and place the strips of dough, weaving them in by placing one across and one lengthwise until they are used up. Press down along the rim and trim the surplus pastry hanging over edges. Decorate rim by pressing marks on pastry with handle of a dinner knife.

Set the cobbler into the center of a preheated 450°F oven, close the door, and turn the over down to 425°F. Bake 45 minutes. Remove from oven and let cool for 15 to 20 minutes before serving with a nutmeg sauce.

Place the sugar, nutmeg, cornstarch, and salt in a quart saucepan, stir well, and pour in the cup of boiling water, stirring as you pour. Add in orange peel and set over a medium burner to boil gently for 10 minutes. Set aside until ready to serve. Reheat without boiling and add in brandy. Serve warm with peach cobbler (omitting the orange peel).

# BRYANT'S BIO

Bryant Terry is a James Beard and NAACP Image Award–Winning chef, educator, and author renowned for his activism to create a healthy, just, and sustainable food system. He is the editor-in-chief of 4 Color Books, an imprint of Ten Speed Press, and he is co-principal and innovation director of Zenmi, a creative studio he runs with his wife and two daughters. Bryant has been chef-in-residence at the Museum of the African Diaspora (MoAD) in San Francisco since 2015. In this role he creates public programming at the intersection of food, farming, health, activism, art, culture, and the African diaspora. Bryant is the author of five critically-acclaimed, award-winning books such as *Vegetable Kingdom*, *Afro-Vegan*, and *Vegan-Soul Kitchen*. He graduated from the Chef's Training Program at the Natural Gourmet Institute for Health and Culinary Arts in New York City. He is a former doctoral student who holds an MA in history with an emphasis on the African diaspora from NYU, where he studied under historian Robin D.G. Kelly. Bryant lives between Oakland and Napa Valley, California, with his family.
Visit www.bryant-terry.com and follow him on social media @BryantTerry.

# ACKNOWLEDGMENTS

It takes a village to create a book in under a year during a pandemic . . .

Jidan, Mila, and Zenzi, I love you!

To all the contributors who offered words, art, and recipes, thank you for seeing my vision and bringing your brilliance to this project.

Danielle Svetcov, thank you for being such a hard-working, brilliant, and caring literary agent who always has my best interest at heart. Much appreciation to Jim Levine and the whole team at Levine Greenberg Rostan for your support over the years.

Amanda Yee, thank you for your loyalty, candor, brilliant ideas, and artistic lens through which you see the world. I appreciate you pushing me past my comfort zone and encouraging me to take risks.

Kelly Snowden, thank you for working hard behind the scenes to make everything that needs to happen happen. I am so lucky to have you as an editor and ally. I'm grateful for your guidance throughout this whole process and beyond. Looking forward to creating big things with you in the coming years.

Porscha Burke, what an honor and privilege it has been working with you. Thank you for enthusiastically jumping onboard this project and working hard to make it great!

Aaron Wehner and Lorena Jones, thank you for your support of this project since we pitched it, and major thanks for enthusiastically supporting 4 Color.

Jenny Wapner, having you as the project manager for this book is a dream come true. Thank you for bringing your A++ game from beginning to end. There is no way *Black Food* could have come together so quickly without your hard work, publishing expertise, and general brilliance. I owe you everything!

Betsy Stromberg, thanks for creating space for a collaborative vision of what this book could be and holding together so many pieces throughout this process.

Kim Keller, Mari Gill, and Serena Sigona, thank you for all the work you put into pulling this book together so quickly. So lucky to have such seasoned pros on my team.

David Hawk and Windy Dorresteyn, I'm so honored to have the best in the business working on my behalf.

Linda Harrison, thank you for believing in my vision and co-creating the chef-in-residence program that inspired this book. Major shout out to Monetta White, Elizabeth Gessel, and all the staff at the Museum of the African Diaspora for your ongoing support. Mark Sabb and Paul Plale, so glad we got to co-create powerful visuals to represent the work of our ground-breaking programming. Those flyers laid the groundwork for the visual language of this book.

Scott Alves Barton, Dara Cooper, and Thérèse Nelson—the kitchen cabinet I assembled to support me in the earliest stages working on this book—thank you for brainstorming contributors, introducing me to people I didn't know, and offering ongoing feedback to ensure that this would be the brilliant, Blackity-Black book that it is.

To all my brilliant friends who swiftly answer my texts and pick up my unplanned calls when I'm having a moment or just need to run an idea by you: Shakirah Simley, Latham Thomas, Hawa Hassan, Nicole Taylor, adrienne maree brown, Joshua Gabriel, William Rosenzweig, Mike Molina, Khamisi Norwood, Shalini Kantayya, Pete Dosanjh, Chris McNeil, and Larry Ossei-Mensah. Apologies to anyone I forgot.

My old-head, West Coast, text thread crew—you know who you are—y'all wild dudes helped keep me sane during shelter-in-place. So blessed to be in community with such good men at this stage in my life.

Adam Mansbach, thank you for always enthusiastically offering advice, giving edits on the fly, and connecting me with the right people.

Gregory Johnson, we both had to make our way from the dirty South to NYC to meet each other, and I'm glad we did. From our days at NYU until now, you are one of the smartest (and most hilarious) people I know. Much appreciation for listening to me vent, making me crack up in an instant, and giving feedback on my projects, in general. Your contribution to this book, however, is invaluable. Thank you for reminding me about important seminars/lectures we attended and encouraging me to revisit books and essays we've read; thank you for helping me shape the opening essay and offering feedback on the manuscript; thank you for being one of the realest dudes in my circle.

Polly Web, at this point, you are on my team! Thank you so much for always eagerly offering feedback, editing, and making suggestions for improvements.

Elle Simone, I thought that securing you as *Black Food*'s recipe tester would be a long shot. When you agreed to take on this project I knew everything was clicking and in its right place. You and your team went above and beyond to ensure that

these recipes work, and that they are fire! 'Nuff thanks to you!

Paige Arnett, Ali Cameron, Lillian Kang, Jillian Knox, Oriana Koren, y'all are the dream team! Thank you for being so committed to this book-making process in a period that was extremely stressful for all of us. I'm so grateful for your willingness to commit so much time preparing for our photoshoots and bringing your brilliance and magic to set. Words can't describe how much I love and appreciate y'all for what you brought to OUR book, so I'll stop there.

Ashara Ekundayo, thank you for calling in the ancestors and ensuring that we had all the supportive unseen forces present at our photoshoots. Honored to have you as my cultural strategist.

George McCalman, after our conversation inside SFMOMA a few years back, I knew we would create magic together. Who knew you would be designing this book while disrupting the way we imagine book creation, though. Thank you for reminding me that process is just as important as outcome. Thank you for modeling how to run a tight team. Thank you for pushing hard to bring life to this book in the midst of all that you've been holding. I cherish our philosophical conversations, silly moments, and brotherhood. Thanks for seeing me. Thanks for supporting me. Thanks for reintroducing me to the magic of Ocean Beach!

# INDEX

# CONTRIBUTORS

Jocelyn Delk Adams 111

Eric Adjepong 51

Zoe Adjonyoh 220, 232

Zahra Alabanza 242

Nyesha Joyce Arrington 295

Selassie Atadika 272, 292

Mashama Bailey 196

Suzanne Barr 189

Scott Alves Barton, PhD 96

Leeonney Bentick 164

adrienne maree brown 240

Damon Brown 262

Folayemi Brown 30

Jade Purple Brown 116

Rev. Dr. Heber Brown III 101

Demetri Broxton 92

Charlene Carruthers 245

Jenné Claiborne 88

Nina Compton 186

Howard Conyers, PhD 154

Dara Cooper 144

Erika Council 15, 16

Kia Damon 229

Cheryl Day 199

Monifa Dayo 191

BJ Dennis 151

Ebony Derr 213

Selasie Dotse 48

Emory Douglas 138

Gabrielle Eitienne 147

Omer Eltigani 38

Osayi Endolyn 118

Nicole Erica 134

Derek Fordjour 56

DeVonn Francis 206, 230

Rashad Frazier 121

Reina Gascón-López 66

Leigh Gaymon-Jones 214

Kristina Gill 131

Tao Leigh Goffe, PhD 64, 70

Gregory Gourdet 279

Jerome Grant 163

Lani Halliday 201

Jessica B. Harris, PhD 27

LaLa Harrison 226

Hawa Hassan 37

Jamey Hatley 254

Prentis Hemphill 265

Tricia Hersey 104

John T. Hill 268

Charles Hunter III 159

Kanchan Dawn Hunter 256

Jocelyn Jackson 175

JJ Johnson 77

Njathi Kabui 45

Sarah Kirnon 69

Yewande Komolafe 33

Jessica Moncada Konte 131

Keba Konte 20, 123

Naa Oyo A. Kwate, PhD 62

Edna Lewis 300

Adrian Lipscombe 157

Malcolm Livingston II 296

Glenn Lutz 247

Lazarus Lynch 210, 234

Krystal C. Mack 250

Sarina Mantle 238

Sarah Ladipo Manyika 58

Kalisa Marie Martin 180

Isaiah Martinez 83, 289

Rahanna Bisseret Martinez 73, 274

Tracye McQuirter, MPH 170

Adrian Miller 125

Klancy Miller 128

Daniel Minter 8

Michael Otieno Molina 94

Shannon Mustipher 132

Freda Muyambo 22

Gail Patricia Myers, PhD 140

Thérèse Nelson 12

Dadisi Olutosin 81

Frederick Douglass Opie, PhD 261

Christopher Pearson 264

Leah Penniman 99

Ashanté Reese 270

Karina Rivera 283

Fresh Roberson 225

Deborah Roberts 168

Stephen Satterfield 133

David Schmitz 20, 92

Elle Simone Scott 183

Summer Sewell 123

Savannah Shange, PhD 208

Alexander Smalls 280

Omar Tate 285

Nicole Taylor 195

Pierre Thiam 41

Latham Thomas 258

Duval Timothy 30

Toni Tipton-Martin 179

Jacob Fodio Todd 30

Michael W. Twitty 60

Betty Vandy 34

Paola Velez 87

Adrian O. Walker x

Rev. Marvin K. White 10

Monica M. White, PhD 142

Psyche Williams-Forson, PhD 172

Renée Wilson 127

Amanda Yee 107, 276

Sithandiwe Yeni 25

Front cover art by George McCalman
page x: photograph of Bryant Terry by Adrian O. Walker
pages 20–21 and 92–93: photographs of art by David Schmitz
page 30: Green Plantain Chips recipe adapted from *Food From Across Africa*, copyright © 2016 by Duval Timothy,
    Folayemi Brown, and Jacob Fodio Todd. Courtesy of Ecco, an imprint of HarperCollins
page 33: Crispy Casava Skillet Cakes copyright © 2021 by Yewande Komolafe
page 37: Somali Lamb Stew recipe copyright © 2021 by Hawa Hassan
page 78: Dirty South Hot Tamales recipe by Bryant Terry was originally published in *Bon Appétit*, a Condé Nast publication
pages 92–93: [Fight] the Power sculpture courtesy of Demetri Broxton & Patricia Sweetow Gallery, San Francisco
page 138–139: copyright © 2021 by Emory Douglas / Artists Rights Society (ARS), New York
pages 172–175: "My House" (29l.) from *The Collected Poetry of Nikki Giovanni*. Copyright compilation © 2003 by Nikki Giovanni.
    Used by permission of HarperCollins Publishers.
page 179: Whiskey Sour recipe was adapted from the forthcoming *Juke Joints, Jazz Clubs, and Juice: Cocktails from Two Centuries
    of African American Mixology* by Toni Tipton-Martin, to be published in 2022 by Clarkson Potter, an imprint of the Random House
    Publishing group, a division of Penguin Random House LLC. Copyright © 2021 by Toni Tipton-Martin. All rights reserved. Used by
    permission of the Lisa Ekus Group.
pages 220–222, 232–233: "Queer Intelligence" and Baobab Panko Salmon recipe copyright © 2021 by Zoe Adjonyoh
pages 250–252: "A Blessing from My Ancestors" and "Healing Rose Bath Soak & Vibrational Okra Bath" copyright © 2021 by Krystal Mack
pages 268–269: photograph of Edna Lewis used by permission of John T. Hill.
page 300: "Fresh Peach Cobbler with Nutmeg Sauce" from *The Taste of Country Cooking* by Edna Lewis,
    copyright © 1976 by Edna Lewis. Used by permission of Alfred A. Knopf, an imprint of the Knopf Doubleday
    Publishing Group, a division of Penguin Random House LLC. All rights reserved.

Library of Congress Cataloging-in-Publication Data
    Names: Terry, Bryant, 1974– editor. | Koren, Oriana, photographer
    Title: Black food: stories, art, and essays / edited by Bryant Terry; photographs by Oriana Koren.
    Description: First edition. | California; New York: Ten Speed Press, [2021] | Includes index.
    Identifiers: LCCN 2021003655 (print) | LCCN 2021003656 (ebook) | ISBN 9781984859723 (hardcover) | ISBN 9781984859730 (ebook)
    Subjects: LCSH: Food habits—United States. | African Americans—Food. | African American cooking. | Cooking, African. |
        LCGFT: Cookbooks.
    Classification: LCC GT2853.U5 B59 2021 (print) | LCC GT2853.U5 (ebook) |
    DDC 394.1/208996073—dc23
    LC record available at https://lccn.loc.gov/2021003655
    LC ebook record available at https://lccn.loc.gov/2021003656

Hardcover ISBN: 978-1-9848-5972-3
eBook ISBN: 978-1-9848-5973-0

Printed in Italy

Acquiring editor: Kelly Snowden | Project editors: Porscha Burke and Jenny Wapner
Production editor: Kim Keller | Editorial assistant: Zoey Brandt
Art director and designer: George McCalman | Creative director: Amanda Yee
Associate designer: Aliena Cameron | Ten Speed Press art director: Betsy Stromberg | Production designer: Mari Gill
Production manager: Serena Sigona | Prepress color manager: Jane Chinn
Food stylist: Lillian Kang | Prop stylist: Jillian Knox | Copyright director: Deborah Foley
Copyeditor: Dolores York | Proofreader: Adaobi Obi Tulton | Indexer: Ken DellaPenta
Publicist: David Hawk | Marketer: Windy Dorresteyn

10 9 8 7 6 5 4 3 2 1

First Edition

JOCELYN DELK ADAMS ERIC ADJEPON
ZOE ADJONYOH ZAHRA ALABANZA LLAN
ALEXIS NYESHA JOYCE ARRINGTO
SELASSIE ATADIKA MASHAMA BAILE
SUZANNE BARR SCOTT ALVES BARTO
LEEONNEY BENTICK BRADLEY BOWER
ADRIENNE MAREE BROWN DAMON BROW
FOLAYEMI BROWN JADE PURPLE BROW
HEBER BROWN III DEMETRI BROXTO
ALIENA ZOE CAMERON CHARLEN
CARRUTHERS JENNÉ CLAIBORNE NIN
COMPTON HOWARD CONYERS DAR
COOPER ERIKA COUNCIL KIA DAMO
CHERYL DAY MONIFA DAYO BJ DENN
EBONY DERR SELASIE DOTSE EMOF
DOUGLAS GABRIELLE EITIENNE OMB
ELTIGANI OSAYI ENDOLYN NICOLE ERIC
DEREK FORDJOUR DEVONN FRANC
RASHAD FRAZIER REINA GASCÓN-LÓPI
LEIGH GAYMON-JONES KRISTINA GILL TA
LEIGH GOFFE GREGORY GOURDET JERON
GRANT LANI HALLIDAY JESSICA B. HARF
LALA HARRISON HAWA HASSAN JAMI
HATLEY PRENTIS HEMPHILL TRIC
HERSEY CHARLES HUNTER III KANCH
DAWN HUNTER JOCELYN JACKSON JJ JOHNS
NJATHI KABUI LILLIAN KANG MELI
KEMPH SARAH KIRNON JILLIAN KN